NO WAY HOME

A Dancer's Journey
from the Streets of Havana
to the Stages of the World

CARLOS ACOSTA

Scribner
New York   London   Toronto   Sydney

SCRIBNER
A Division of Simon & Schuster, Inc.
1230 Avenue of the Americas
New York, NY 10020

First Scribner hardcover edition May 2008

For information about special discounts for bulk purchases,
please contact Simon & Schuster Special Sales at
1-800-456-6798 or business@simonandschuster.com.

Designed by Kyoko Watanabe
Text set in Stempel Garamond

Manufactured in the United States of America

1   3   5   7   9   10   8   6   4   2

Library of Congress Cataloging-in-Publication Data
Acosta, Carlos.
No way home : a dancer's journey from the streets of Havana
to the stages of the world / by Carlos Acosta.
p.   cm.
1. Acosta, Carlos. 2. Ballet dancers—Cuba—Biography. 3. Ballet dancers—
Great Britain—Biography. I. Title.
GV1785.A326 A3 2008
792.802'8092 B—dc22   2007046023

ISBN-13: 978-1-4165-6629-8
ISBN-10: 1-4165-6629-5

To my sisters, to my sweet mother, and to Pedro Acosta,
one of the greatest men I have ever known

CONTENTS

PART THREE

1993–2003

PART ONE

1973–1988

Chapter 1

MY FAMILY

An enchanted forest bordered Los Pinos, the neighborhood in the suburbs of Havana where I grew up. A combination of city and country, asphalt streets and wooden houses vividly contrasted with the vegetation that filled every available space and lent the landscape infinite varieties of green. Los Pinos was famous for La Finca, a leafy area of fruit trees and red earth covering some five square kilometers, extending as far as the Quinta Canaria Convent to the east, the district of La Guinera to the north, and Vieja Linda to the west. Legend had it that La Finca was inhabited by spirits who turned themselves into owls and hooted not only at nighttime but also during daylight hours.

To reach La Finca you had to climb a hill past the Russian car-repair shop and carry on until you got to Cundo's place. Cundo was the best-known salesman in the neighborhood. His house was essentially a small cooperative that sold sugar cane, coconuts, fresh goat's milk, mangos, and tobacco. A few meters on were the fiberboard caves—half-finished abandoned houses, their floors lined with pieces of cardboard, with grass and weeds growing high around them. This spot was commonly known as the Place of Infidelity. After crossing the first of several streams, where you could fish for prawns, there were natural caves draped with green creepers and huge malanga plants known as elephants' ears. From there you could no longer see the repair shop, nor Cundo's house. The tall royal palms and the avocado and mamey bushes blocked out the sun, making the air dank and humid. The terrain became increasingly irregular. Hills would suddenly loom up that were awkward to climb. You had to part the undergrowth with a *garabato,* a hooked stick usually made from a tree branch, then help yourself along by grabbing on to tree trunks. The atmosphere was full of enchantment as the spirits-turned-owls hooted out their sorrows and songs all around you.

After scaling the biggest hill, you came to a rocky, sandy plateau. This was the only place that was not shaded by trees, and people would dry themselves off there after bathing in the pool, which was an abandoned reservoir about four meters long and three meters deep, filled with filthy, contaminated water. At the bottom there were channels and holes full of broken beer bottles and empty cans. Many people got ill after swimming in that water; one or two drowned. Parents used to forbid their children from going there, warning that they would get worms, or they would threaten us, "If you go into the forest, the owls will eat you." Nevertheless, whenever we were out of the house, we could always be found in those noxious waters, or standing on the sandy plateau, looking out toward the distant streams in the west, the tobacco crops, and the fields of cows.

Most of the inhabitants of the neighborhood were workers, country people, hawkers, and street traders. Carriages pulled by horses took adults and children alike for a ride for a fee of 1 peso, and people used wooden handcarts to carry their food. The noise of those rudimentary vehicles echoed through the streets, mingling with the cries of the scissors sharpener, the mattress stretcher, and the fruit seller.

Each house had a ration book. Foodstuffs that were rationed—such as grain, oil, salt, and sugar—came into the grocery store once a month. It was the same with meat at the butcher's, fish at the fishmonger's, and milk products at the dairy. We would queue from early in the morning, and at nine, when the grocery opened, there would be a giant snaking line of handcarts and people holding sacks, bags, jars, and casserole dishes. Similar queues would form to buy bread, and the three toys that each house was allocated by the government every year. People waited their turn patiently, telling one another their problems and sharing the latest neighborhood gossip. Many would play dominoes, drink rum, and dance salsa together. We lived as part of a community and were grateful for the achievements of the Revolution, even though some of us might secretly listen to rock music, which was synonymous with imperialism.

In the eighties, nearly all the families in my neighborhood received the minimum wage of 130 pesos a month—barely enough to live on—with the exception of a few who earned a little more or a little less. The contrast between families was not really visible. Nobody had washing machines or dishwashers, and the few households with television sets would watch them in black and white. Most people got their information from the radio. Electrical appliances from the 1950s still survived, thanks to people's inventiveness. It was very common to find an American-made refrigerator or cooker functioning with Russian parts. The inside of every house reflected the country's recent history.

Even though it was a poor neighborhood, it was full of proud residents. Every Sunday voluntary work groups were organized—people would cut lawns, paint houses, sweep pavements, and collect litter, competing with the other blocks in the area. A delegation organized by the Committee for the Defense of the Revolution would pass through block by block examining everything, from the lawns to the houses, even the lampposts, and the next day everybody would know which block had won the week's competition. There was also *el Plan de la Calle,* Street Plan competitions, which were big community parties that included singing and dancing contests, sack races, and hundred-meter running races. People sold homemade refreshments like Popsicles, meringues, meat and potato croquettes, and soft drinks. The smell of ripe fruit that was characteristic of our neighborhood was so strong that it impregnated the very fabric of our clothes and canceled out all other odors. The inhabitants of Los Pinos smelled of guava in April, of custard apple in May, and of mango in June. It was the aroma of those people, combined with the humility that poverty brings, that made Los Pinos a magical place.

I spent my childhood in that little town, surrounded by music, dominoes, rum, the smell of fruit, and the hooting of owls. Most of the houses on my block were made of wood. Ours was a strange edifice consisting of six apartments divided by a staircase. Our apartment was in the upper part of this two-story building. When I was a little boy, my home seemed enormous. Really it was a miserable hovel without running water, either because of a problem with the plumbing or by some greater design of God, which meant that we had to carry that precious liquid, bucketful by careful bucketful, up and down the many stairs. It was a narrow house, with rustic furniture and cracks in the walls where families of voracious termites lived. Shining empty beer cans added color to the interior decoration, as did the black doll that represented one of the goddesses of the Yoruba pantheon, a vase of sunflowers, usually wilted, that sat on one side of the shelf among photographs of relatives, faded by time, and a painting of the Sacred Heart of Jesus, a feature commonly seen in humble homes like ours.

In one corner of the living room, my father, Pedro Acosta, hid his shrine, which comprised a pot of long nails; a small bow and arrow; miniature tools made of iron; a stone with shells stuck onto it to represent the eyes and mouth of a face; and a long-stemmed iron cup with a cockerel on top of it, which must never be allowed to fall over, or something terrible would happen. My father was a zealous devotee of Santería, and he lost no opportunity to venerate the African gods with offerings and prayers, even though in those days in Cuba it was a sin against the state to have religious beliefs. Nothing and nobody could come between him and his devotions. Every so often he would leave a buffet at the disposal of the saints: juicy guavas, bananas ripening to yellow perfection, little cakes, and sweets. At times like these, we asked ourselves if he had gone mad. We very rarely had enough to eat; the rice had to be eked out in order to last the month, as did all the other rationed foodstuffs, but the saints were provided with all that luxury despite the shortages. It was terrible profligacy. One day, unable to resist temptation, I shooed away my pet rabbits, Negrito and Canela, who were investigating the shrine, and ate everything: the guavas, the sweets, the piece of cake, even the ants that regularly fed on my father's offerings. When my father found out what I had done, he could only just resist the temptation to crack my head open.

My mother didn't think he should feed food to his saints. She said it was a waste. But it did seem to work: whenever things were getting bad, as if by magic, my father would be sent on a trip to the center of the country and would earn enough money to buy our entire food ration for the month.

My father drove a truck transporting fruit, breaking his back for a monthly salary that was barely enough to feed us. Most of his journeys were interprovincial, which meant that he was often absent for weeks, even months. We got used to living on very little. Every fortnight, my mother would go to the countryside taking our soap and toothpaste rations to exchange for beans and other provisions from the country dwellers. Sometimes she managed to get hold of some clothes for my sisters or a pair of shoes for me. On rare occasions, my father would turn up with some tinned fruit, and we would eat it with such desperation that we woke up with stomachaches. Once, I came home from school and was greeted by the unfamiliar smell of roasting meat. I rushed into the kitchen only to find my rabbits, Negrito and Canela, cooking in a pan. I ran out into the living room and cried and cried until I gave myself a terrible headache. It had been a long time since we had tasted any meat, however, so my mother made me have some. That would be the last time I would ever eat rabbit in my life.

Without being conscious of it, we learned through our parents' example that the only way to achieve something in life was through hard work. We knew that the reason we never celebrated birthdays or other special occasions was because of our lack of money. We accepted without question the peso that each of us received as a birthday present to pay the entrance to the local cinema. We played with wooden pistols, *chivichanas* (rough wooden scooters), and other contraptions that my old man used to dream up in moments of inspiration. When the clothes that we wore could not take any more repairs, we walked around with our butts hanging out.

My father was an impatient man with little time for children's games. At home, he always had to have the last word. I remember his playing with me only once, when he taught me how to ride my sister Berta's old bike. It was an awesome machine with huge wheels like a figure eight, and I was terrified of it, but I was even more terrified of my father, who sat me on the bike, gave me a push, and then let me go. I crashed into the first lamppost I encountered and went home crying with a bump on my head. My mother screamed at my father, telling him that he was an insensitive brute and that I was never going near that damn bicycle again. He calmly retorted that it was the only way to make me overcome my fears. The following morning he seated me on that heap of junk once more, and I promptly smashed into the lamppost again. After numerous bumps on the head, I finally managed to do what my father wanted; though, far from becoming fearless, I developed a genuine terror of the bicycle that I've never overcome.

My father didn't speak much about his past. I learned only recently that my grandfather died when my father, Pedro, was six. His mother was the daughter of slaves who had been born on the sugar mill belonging to the Acostas, a well-known Spanish landowning family from the town of San Juan y Martinez in Pinar del Río. From them came the surname that would be passed on to the rest of my family after my grandfather's death. When he was nine, my father sold newspapers, hawking the latest news around the streets of Pinar del Río. After the death of his father, he had no alternative but to grow up prematurely in order to help his mother and his younger brother. As an adolescent he worked in the docks as a stevedore, loading bags of sugar. By the time his voice broke, his experience was already that of a man twice his age.

My father was born in 1918. His youth was marked by the great inequalities of race and class that existed at that time, when the poor man had to swallow his pride and collect the crumbs that the rich man swept from his table. It was during those days of his youth that my father saw ballet for the first time, in a silent film. The cinema was reserved exclusively for whites, but Pedro managed to sneak in. He did not know what the peculiar dance was, but the ballerinas immediately spoke to his senses as they spun around like Japanese parasols, elegant, delicate, and light. My father lost himself in that unfamiliar world. All too soon the usher arrived to remind him that he was poor and black, and to kick him out onto the street. But from that moment on, ballet had captured him.

In our house, my father slept on mats that he threw down onto the floor of the tiny living room in the space between the wicker armchairs and the ancient sideboard that groaned under the weight of the old American-made, always-broken television, and the Siboney-brand Russian radio. On moonless nights his black skin was camouflaged by the darkness, and you had to follow his cigarette smoke as it floated in the air in order to find him. By the time I was three my parents had divorced, but they shared the house out of convenience. Neither of them had anywhere else to go. Mamá slept with me in the single bed that was jammed up against the wall that divided the bedroom from the living room, while my sisters slept in the double bed on the sagging mattress with sharp springs that poked through the lining. You had to memorize exactly where those springs jutted through in order to avoid getting snagged. Sometimes I had to sleep in the big bed, and the springs would catch my right thigh and ankle and my back. My sisters, Marilín and Berta, knew the position of each and every spring, but I always had trouble remembering where to find them. When, years later, my father brought home a rustic pine bunk bed he had found, it became almost impossible to move in the bedroom, everything was so crammed that you could walk through only in single file. My father moved to the lower bunk bed, Berta to the top, and I moved to the double bed with my sister Marilín, though I never got used to sleeping without my mother's blond hair spreading over my face.

Unlike my father, when my mother started to talk about her childhood, we could not stop her. We knew that her father's family had arrived from Spain in the 1920s and had settled in Almendares, a middle-class district of Havana. My grandfather Carlos Quesada, a tall, fair man with blue eyes, had lent his name to my baptism. Grandfather grew up with few traces of his European roots. He soon identified himself with the cause of the Cuban poor, with those who did not have opportunities, forgetting all about his own status. Not unnaturally this was seen as a great misfortune by his parents, who were horrified that he cared nothing for his social standing. How had they failed? Why had destiny played them such a bad hand? They tried to make Carlos change his opinions, but all in vain. My great-grandparents died in the 1950s within a month of each other, both still relatively young. My mother would never agree with me, but I think they died of grief.

After a long romance, Grandfather Carlos married Grandmother Georgina, an olive-skinned lady with a strong constitution, a broad nose, and legs of steel. They had three daughters to add to the daughter that my grandmother already had from a previous marriage. The oldest of their three children together they named María. This girl, who would one day become my mother, exuded vitality from every pore. She lost her virginity to a local boy at seventeen and was soon obliged to put her childhood games away, for, less than nine months later, on December 25, 1965, she gave birth to my half sister, Berta. This prompted disagreements with my mother's half sister, nicknamed "La Niña," who, being married and with three children of her own, considered herself to be head of the household. There was not room for them all in the house, she said. My mother and her sisters, Aunt Mireya and Aunt Lucia, and baby Berta had to move into the garage at the back of the house. Grandmother Georgina, who was intimidated by La Niña's husband, did little to stop the move. Grandfather Carlos objected, but his words held little weight. He had already been diagnosed with cancer, which would kill him only six months later.

Berta had dark brown hair, a slim nose, and green eyes like Grandfather Carlos. Her father hardly bothered with her when his relationship with my mother was over. When Berta was one and a half and already starting to show signs of a strong character, she carelessly threw a ball into the street and a black man kindly retrieved it for her. My mother thanked him and the man rewarded her with a wide, warm smile that revealed two gold crowns nestling among his upper teeth. It was the start of a new love affair. At first, my mother and the man who would become my father saw each other secretly—after all, he was nearly thirty years older than she, had been married several times, and had eight children already. Soon, though, the romance became public knowledge. The family, the neighbors, the whole world condemned María, railing, "What are you thinking of? Have you gone mad? Honestly! Setting your sights on a black man!" In the late 1960s, the man joined a government fruit-and-coffee-planting initiative called Cordon Round Havana. After a year of work he came back looking for his love, bearing the key to a house in his hand. In that house that same black man would one day give shelter to all those who had opposed the relationship: my grandmother and my aunts, the whole lot of them.

My sister Marilín was born on July 25, 1969. Berta was three and a half years old and had been living in Los Pinos since she was two. Marilín is what is called in Cuba *mulata criolla,* a perfect mixture of black and white. As a child, she had a wide smile with teeth that looked as though they had been carefully chiseled by an artist, slanting eyes like my mother's, dry hair like my father's, and an athletic body with silky skin. Berta wanted to comb her hair and carry her around all the time, as if Marilín were a toy that could talk and laugh.

My grandmother and my aunts occasionally visited our house, especially my aunt Mireya, who often came to take Berta to the beach at Varadero. Marilín could never understand why she could not go, too. Aunt Mireya would tell her that there was not enough room for everyone as she climbed into her boyfriend's car and drove away, leaving Marilín crying. This gave Marilín an inferiority complex that she would never really manage to shake off. My mother always told her that my aunt Mireya loved both her nieces equally and that they were like roses that were beautiful but different.

"Then why is my rose the one that has to stay behind?" my sister would ask tearfully, and my mother would reply that maybe next time it would be her turn to go to the beach at Varadero.

But the next time, Mireya would say, "Let's go, Bertica. Sorry, Marilín, there's not enough room for everyone."

And Marilín would be left behind in tears once again.

I was the last one to arrive, born on June 2, 1973. My father said that I was born at night, while my mother said it was in the daytime, so I have never known the exact hour of my birth. My mother had to have a cesarean because I tried to come out feetfirst. According to my father, the nurse took so long to attend to me that I swallowed some of the amniotic fluid and nearly died. She finally started paying attention only after he threatened her with a pistol, shouting, "If you don't put him on a drip right now, I'll kill you!" The nurse, trembling with fear, inserted the drip via my nostrils.

"And that's why your nose is like it is," my father always told me.

"He got his wide nose from you, not from the damn drip," my mother would reply, rolling her eyes and assuring me that the incident with the gun was just a story my father had made up.

Aunt Lucia, unlike Aunt Mireya, treated us all equally. Perhaps that is why we loved her more, or maybe it was her sweet, retiring nature. She did not visit us frequently, but when she did she would hold us and play with us all without discrimination. Sometimes, when my father was working, they would all visit us at once: Lucia with her tiny baby, Jennie; Mireya with her husband, Frank, and her daughter, Corairis; and Granny. Everyone would sit in the wicker armchairs and on the hard chairs from around the dining room table. Mireya would take Berta onto her knees, and Marilín and I would be left sitting on the floor. Without saying anything, Lucia would pass little Jennie to my mother and would beckon to Marilín and me to come and sit on her lap, which we would do, each taking one of her knees. Apart from my mother, she was the only one who held us.

I was seven years old when they all came to live with us. It was toward the end of 1980, and Cuba had opened its borders to anyone who wanted to leave. My mother kept trying to persuade my father that my grandmother, two aunts, and cousin Corairis (Mireya and Frank had split up, and Lucia's little baby was staying with her father) should come to live with us while they awaited the arrival of their exit permits for Venezuela, where relatives would help them make their way to Miami. But every time my mother mentioned the matter, my father would swallow hard, clench his iron fists inside his pockets, and mutter, "I don't know if I can." Eventually, though, he relaxed his hands, calloused from so much clenching, and managed to stifle his displeasure.

Papá moved back to the living room and I returned to the single bed with my mother so that Aunt Mireya, Granny, and Corairis could have the double bed. Marilín moved into the bottom bunk with Berta so that Aunt Lucia could have her bed, although this arrangement did not last long. Gentle, loving Lucia developed schizophrenia and was admitted to the hospital, where, two weeks later, she took her own life. She was twenty-six years old. Soon after, the paperwork needed to apply for a visa arrived from our Venezuelan relatives, who, in light of the tragedy, had agreed to host everyone, including my mother and my beloved white sister, Berta. Everyone except the blacks. My mother and sister decided to stay with Marilín, my father, and me, but it was very painful for my mother to be separated from the rest of her family.

I understood very little of life and much less of what was happening in the house, but I remember the day that my mother seemed to change into a different person—the moment she said farewell to her mother on the balcony of our apartment in Los Pinos.

My mother had not eaten for days, she was so anxious about the approach of the Friday when they all would part. She knew the day would arrive whatever happened, but she was still hoping for a miracle.

"I don't know what you're going to do, María, but I'm leaving. This is your last opportunity!" Aunt Mireya said to her.

It was unlikely that they would ever see each other again. For all they knew, Granny would die in exile, and my mother would not be at her side to hold her hand and wipe the sweat from her brow when Death arrived to carry off her body and her love forever.

On the other hand, my mother had us, her children, a different kind of love. What could she do? It was an impossible situation, and she lost either way.

"Mireya, why don't you think again?" she pleaded with her sister. "You don't know what's waiting for you there . . . Mami is too old for all these changes, you'll be better off here."

"What? . . . Better off here? No way! You can stay, María. I'm taking Mami."

And she did.

The whole of the neighborhood witnessed the parting. A car was waiting opposite the door of our downstairs neighbor Candida's house. The dogs stood still, watching, as did the families of Cristobál and Delia, along with Milli, Chinchán, and Kenia from over the way, and Diana and El Chino; they were all there. Many sat on the street corners, on the walls, and on the curb. Ramona, the religious neighbor on the right, was sitting in her rocking chair, as were Omar and his family, the neighbors on the left. My mother came out onto the balcony with her arms around my grandmother's neck, resting her head against my grandmother's cheek, trying to show a brave face. She did not manage it. Her fear was so palpable that the dogs could smell it.

We were waiting below next to the car. My father stood next to Marilín, with his arm draped across her shoulders; her arm in turn was draped across mine. I was holding Berta, my white sister, by the hand.

"Berta, come here!" said my aunt Mireya.

Berta let go of me and went over to her. My aunt hugged and kissed her, then whispered something in her ear and Berta began to cry. My cousin Corairis approached and gave me a hug and a kiss, then did the same with my father and with Marilín. Both girls wept. My father and I kept our composure.

My mother had cried out all her tears. She started to come down the stairs, very slowly, leading my grandmother by the arm. When they reached the bottom, they embraced again, my mother's eyes glinting as the full glare of the sun shone onto her damp eyelids. Some of the neighbors had tears in their eyes, even the men. They had probably been through the same thing themselves or were moved by the thought that they might go through it one day.

"Mami, get a move on, we'll be late."

Aunt Mireya shoved the last suitcase into the car and turned to say good-bye to my mother. She hugged her tightly. My mother's face crumpled. My aunt said they would write, and with that went to hug and kiss my sister Berta. She gave Marilín and me a kiss but no hug, and accorded my father a distant handshake; then she bundled my grand-mother and Corairis into the car and slammed the door. The engine revved.

Mamá was left standing in the middle of the street, a shrunken shadow of herself, with swollen eyes and hollow cheeks, watching the car as it drove into the distance. Her gaze did not waver until the car finally disappeared, then she turned to stare at her left hand, in which she was holding a little blue book: her passport.

The promised letters never arrived.

Chapter 2

THE PHOTOGRAPH

I was always called Yuli in the neighborhood, a name my sister Berta had given me. My father, however, had a different explanation for it.

"Yuli is the spirit of an Indian brave from the Sioux tribe in North America. He is with you all the time and I talk to him every day. That's how you got your nickname, and don't let anyone tell you otherwise."

My mother would sigh heavily and roll her eyes up to the ceiling.

By the age of seven I was already known on my block as a fruit thief. My scheme was executed with precision and always worked. Our building stood on a corner where four streets intersected. Directly opposite was Rene's house, diagonally opposite was Zoilita's house, and on the other corner was a wall that was used as a meeting place by the local kids. On Mondays, Wednesdays, and Fridays, I would steal Rene's mangos, and on weekends I would steal Zoilita's. Tuesdays and Thursdays were reserved for Yolanda, the neighbor who lived two doors away from my building. We took our operation very seriously because it was only by selling fruit that we could afford the entrance fee to the local cinema or pay for a ride round the block in the horse-drawn carriage.

Our method was simple: Pedro Julio would ring the doorbell, Tonito would keep lookout to make sure no one was coming from the other direction, and as soon as Rene had gone to open the door, I would squeeze carefully through a hole in the barbed-wire fence that surrounded the backyard and throw all the mangos, plums, and guavas I could lay my hands on into a sack.

The plan worked like a charm until, one day, Rene nearly caught me.

I was happily stuffing fruit into my sack when I heard Pedro Julio and Tonito shout from the street: "Run, Yuli! Rene's coming!"

I quickly threw the sack of fruit into the empty overgrown plot of land on the other side and started to scale the fence, when, to my horror, Rene seized me by one leg.

"I've got you, you little rat. Just you wait and see what I'm going to do with you!"

"Let me go, let me go!" I shouted, kicking my legs.

Rene had never come close to catching me before, and I was terrified. Thank God it had rained the day before, and, as a result, I was completely covered in mud from Rene's waterlogged garden. I slipped from his clutches with one mighty tug of my leg.

"Listen, you little bandit, when I catch you, I'll kill you! I'm going to tell your father."

He never did manage to catch me, though, because nobody knew his garden better than I did.

Having made good our escape, all three of us ambled toward the forest.

"That was a bit close, Yuli. He almost got you. I think we ought to rob some other people and leave Rene alone," said Pedro Julio as we passed the truck-repair shop.

"You always say that, Pedro Julio! Rene's too slow; he couldn't even catch a tortoise," I replied.

Tonito stopped in the middle of the street to count how many mangos were in the bag.

"I think there's enough here to get all three of us into the cinema. Why don't we try to sell them to Cundo?"

"Good idea!" I said, slapping my partner's hand, and we walked toward the salesman's wooden house.

We opened the gate and shooed away the goats that were blocking our path. Cundo hurried out to meet us immediately.

"I don't want to buy anything; go, get out of here!" said the old man grouchily. It was his usual ruse. As soon as anyone tried to sell him anything, he would grumble and say he was not interested so that he could get a lower price for the goods.

"Hey, Cundo, don't start that again; it was the same last time with the avocados. If you don't want the mangos, we'll sell them to Alfredo," said Tonito, throwing the sack over his shoulder.

"Take them to Alfredo then, what do I care? Take them and see what he gives you. You lot aren't the only ones, you know. I've got plenty of other people bringing me stuff."

"This is your last chance!" the three of us answered in chorus, and Cundo's face started to turn red.

"Okay, okay, I'll give you a peso for the sack."

"No way! Anyone'd give you at least five pesos for that sack, so two pesos or nothing," I said, holding the sack up in my hands.

"There's no doing business with you lot," muttered Cundo, as he finally agreed to the price.

We took the money, gave him the sack of fruit, and continued on toward the pool.

"Get me some avocados, or plums, anything, whatever you like, and bring them here; don't let Alfredo have them," we heard him say as he closed the gate.

On the way to the pool, we passed the fiberboard caves.

"Hey, Yuli, listen, sounds like there's someone in there," said Tonito.

We took a few tentative steps toward the caves.

"Tonito, Yuli, keep away! My mother says it's rude to go near the caves when there are people in them."

"What are you talking about, Pedro Julio? Stop bugging us."

Tonito climbed up onto one of the fiberboard sheets and gave me a hand up. Pedro Julio lagged behind. Just as we were at the cave entrance, a woman started to scream.

"Oh, oh, what's this? Oh, oh, I'm dying!"

"They're killing her, we've got to help! Call someone!" shouted Pedro Julio, and he ran off, but Tonito and I peered inside, imagining that we would find the screaming woman with a knife to her throat. What we saw totally confused us. There was a naked man on top of her, thrusting his pelvis backward and forward. She was moaning and sweating and with every thrust she let out a scream.

"I'm dying, I'm dying!"

But there was not any blood.

We whistled to let Pedro Julio know that it was not necessary to call anyone.

"Why was she screaming?" asked my friend.

"I don't know," I replied, scratching my head.

In the end we concluded that the man must have had a knife hidden between his legs, and, shrugging our shoulders in confusion, we continued on our way to the pool.

As soon as we arrived, Tonito and I jumped straight into the water, but Pedro Julio hung back, looking nervously at the trees.

"Pedro Julio, what are you waiting for?" I asked him.

"My mother says I'm not to swim here. Remember what happened to Pichon."

"Pichon said it was the pool, but the thing is he actually already had worms before he swam here," said Tonito, and the three of us laughed.

Pedro Julio could not be convinced, however, so Tonito and I left him standing on the edge while we played "Touched." One of us would dive underwater, and the other one had to stay on the surface and try to tap him on the head. Time and time again we dived down into the dark and filthy channels of the pool, sometimes swallowing the sludgy water. The wind rocked the trees, and their trunks creaked. The owls hooted as always. There were more frogs than ever, and some jumped into the water with us.

"Careful a frog doesn't pee on you, or you'll go blind," said Pedro Julio. Then we heard another voice.

"Blind! I'll leave you blind with the beating I'm going to give you!"

I stuck my head out of the pool and saw the imposing and unmistakable figure of my father.

"You little bastard, how many times have I told you I don't want to see you swimming in that disgusting water?" My father pulled me out of the pool by my ear and threw me onto the rocks.

"Wait, Papito, let me explain!"

He was not in the mood for explanations. "Walk before I crack your head open," he said as he dragged me through the undergrowth and rocks.

"Didn't I tell you to wait in the house? Have you forgotten that today is the day of the photo? I'm going to kill you!"

Shit, I thought as I scrambled along, colliding with the branches and sharp twigs sticking out of the bushes and trees, I had forgotten the photo.

We passed the caves and Cundo's house and started down the hill. The people came out of their houses when they heard my father shouting. My stormy relationship with my father was a source of entertainment in the neighborhood.

"Hey, Peeeedro . . . leeeave the boooy alooone!" said Juanito, the drunk, as my father shook and slapped me about.

"Out of my way, Juanito!" My old man pushed him roughly.

"Heeeey, dooon't you staaart picking on meeee. I'm Juaaaanito the druuuunk!"

We left Juanito with his bottle and continued on down the hill. When we arrived at my building, Zoilita, Rene, Yolanda, Candida, all the neighbors were waiting.

"Finally you're going to make him pay," they all cheered, as if a runaway criminal had just been captured. Rene was looking very satisfied with himself—he had obviously told my parents I had been in his garden. My father walked me straight past them and up the stairs to our apartment. My mother sluiced me down to get the mud off, dressed me in my only pair of trousers, the better of my two pairs of shoes, and my one school shirt. My father insisted that I wear a tie.

"No, Mami, not the tie!"

"You shut your mouth!" said my old man angrily.

"There's no need to yell, Pedro; we'll make it in time," my mother said soothingly.

We went down the stairs once more, and the neighbors started to applaud again.

"Finally they're going to turn you into a respectable human being," said Rene, smiling from his doorway.

No sooner were we inside the big wooden house of the neighborhood photographer than he got out a device as old as Methuselah, set it up on the cool tiled floor, and told me to sit still. Then he put his head under a cloth attached to the back of the antique apparatus and pressed a button with his right hand.

A week later my mother collected the photo, framed it, and placed it in a corner of the sitting room. That was the first photo ever taken of me, and it is the only image that exists of me before ballet entered my life.

Chapter 3

BEGINNING

All I ever thought about was sports. Soccer was my obsession. I had ambitions to become a great player. For a long time, unbeknownst to my parents, I tried to get into a school that trained future soccer players. Sometimes, however, wanting something very badly just is not enough. During the training sessions, I would kill myself doing sit-ups and push-ups and running round the track. The fruit of all my labors was being selected to play in a match. I touched the ball twice during the game and did not make any mistakes. I was proud of how I had done and left the field confident that the coach would give me a scholarship. When the next day the coach treated me with indifference, I did not take it too much to heart. The following day it was the same, however, and gradually over the next few weeks I realized I had no prospects with the team: I just was not good enough. From that moment on, my hopes of winning a soccer scholarship started to evaporate. My dream of becoming the future Pelé crumbled, and though I persevered, every day the coach treated me just a little bit worse, slowly breaking my spirit until eventually he succeeded.

It was around this same time that the break-dancing craze hit Cuba. My sister Marilín was a magnificent dancer, and from time to time she would show me some of her moves and take me with her to street parties. After two months, I had learned how to spin around on my shoulders and even on my head. When Marilín saw me, she was speechless.

"Where did you learn to do that?" she asked, astonished.

"Oh just round about . . ." I replied, unwilling to go into details.

"But when did you practice?" she insisted.

"In my spare time . . ."

The truth is that while Marilín was at school, I would meet up with a gang of friends and practice break dancing all day long. We started to organize a break-dance club in an adjacent neighborhood called Vieja Linda. We would close off the streets with trash bins to stop cars from coming through, turn the music up to full volume, and rehearse new steps so we could compete with dancers from other neighborhoods in Havana. I particularly remember one competition that took place in Parque Lenin, a huge recreation area on the outskirts of the city where, on the weekends, there were salsa contests, singing competitions, and history or science quizzes for children.

When the break-dancing competition was announced, my gang knew that it would be an important contest and that we could not possibly miss it. So there we were, at seven o'clock on a Sunday morning, with all the tools of our trade: dark glasses, gloves (which we wore the way Michael Jackson did), big baggy shirts, and baseball caps. We carried our boom boxes and chomped away on bits of sticking plaster since we didn't have chewing gum.

The first prize was a trophy with a picture of Lenin surrounded by the hammer and sickle, the second prize was a bag of sweets, and the third a diploma. My friend Opito and I were the only members of the gang eligible to compete because the contest was open only to kids under fourteen. Opito and I had won competitions before, dancing as a pair in Cerro and Monaco and other Havana neighborhoods. Two nine-year-old boys—one white with ginger hair and one black—was a combination that never failed.

All the big names from the Havana break-dancing scene were there: Papo el Bucanda; Alexander "the Toaster" el Tostao; that kid from the Embil district they nicknamed Michael Jackson; and Miguelito la Peste, "Mickey the Stink" himself.

Everybody chewed their pieces of sticking plaster and wore their baseball caps back to front as Opito and I got ready to do our thing. As soon as we began to dance, I was filled with an indescribable sensation of release. Growing up poor had taught all of us Los Pinos kids never to ask for anything, not to have any expectations, and because of this I was quite a self-conscious boy. But when I danced, my shyness fell away, and I felt like a different person: confident, attractive, and free. Along with the first drops of sweat came the desire to shout my existence to the world, to become everything I dreamed. I danced my heart out for half an hour.

At the end of the contest, I was baptized El Moro de Los Pinos— the Moor of Los Pinos—by the rest of the boys in the gang, and Mickey the Stink himself held out his hand to me and said, with a challenging smile, "See you around."

I still have that trophy of Lenin with his hammer and sickle. Those gang competitions were my first steps toward the art of dance.

The news that I was running around the streets like a bandit eventually reached my father's ears.

"We have to do something, María; otherwise, we're going to lose the boy," he said to my mother in a fury.

Most of the time their conversations revolved around me: they argued continually over how to sort out my future while I continued break dancing in Vieja Linda and spending my time at street parties. My father swore that he would thrash me to within an inch of my life, but I did not care. I just went on doing what I liked until one day my father happened to bump into our neighbor Candida on the stairs.

She was a good woman with a strident voice who was very much involved with the Revolutionary process. Her nephew was one of the principal dancers with the Cuban National Ballet, and her two oldest sons, Alexis and Alexander, went to the Alejo Carpentier School of Ballet, which was situated on the corner of L and 19 in the downtown district of Vedado. When my father started telling her about my exploits, Candida had a suggestion.

"You say he likes dancing? Why don't you send him to ballet school then?"

My father's eyes lit up. "Ballet!" he said, and for an instant he was transported back to the cinema, where for the first time ever his soul had taken flight. His heart started to beat rapidly as it had on that distant day, and suddenly he had hope. He did not think twice: he thanked Candida, said good-bye almost before she'd finished her sentence, and raced up the twenty or so steps to our apartment to tell my mother about his new idea. They considered each and every possibility, and then they sat together to wait for me.

Returning from one of my usual break-dance practice sessions, I went up the steps to the apartment, where I could see that the door was wide open and a weak light illuminated the interior. My parents were preparing to give me what they promised would be some very good news.

"Sit down, we've got something to tell you!"

There was something unusual about my father's tone, and I sensed that something strange was going on. His voice unsettled me. What could it be about? I sat down nervously.

"So you like to dance, eh? Well, we're going to enroll you in a ballet school," announced the old man.

"Ballet? What's that?" I asked, perplexed.

My father shot a conspiratorial glance toward my mother, who was looking somewhat flustered, and said: "Well, um, it's, um, it's the dance of the parasol ladies."

When she heard this definition, my mother collapsed into giggles, which lifted the tension for a moment.

"What, that boring thing that they put on the telly?"

"Yes, that's it!"

"But, Papi, I've told you loads of times that I want to be an athlete. Anyway, you know that kind of dancing's just for women."

"An athlete? Don't make me laugh! If you go on like you are, the only thing you'll be is a waster! Running around with those gangs, spinning around on your head . . . One of these days you're going to break your neck."

"But what's everyone in the neighborhood going to think? They'll say I'm gay!"

"Listen, you're my son, and the son of the tiger shares his father's stripes. If anyone calls you gay, just smash his face in, then pull down your trousers and show him what you've got between your legs."

"But, Papito—"

"Your mother and I have made up our minds, and that's that. It's your future, my boy!" He interrupted me, grinding his false teeth, his face fixed in that grim expression that told me the conversation was at an end. And so it was. They had decided my career for me. I had to put my dreams of being an athlete to the side and dedicate myself to *the dance of the parasol ladies.*

What now? I asked myself. And what was everyone in the neigh-

borhood going to say when they found out that El Moro had become
a ballet dancer?

A week later, Mamá took me to the audition. We had to catch three different buses to get to the ballet school at L and 19. She was chain-
smoking, puffing away like a chimney; she had a cigarette in her right
hand and was holding on to me with her left. I loathed the smell of
tobacco, but I kept quiet. I was happy and proud to be traveling with
my mother in her dark glasses, which only served to enhance her
beauty. It was certainly more relaxing than going with my old man.
During the journey, I tried to explain to her that it really was sport that
I liked best, and I pulled my saddest, most pitiful face. I knew that playing the victim usually worked with my mother, but on this occasion I
failed.

There were a lot of people and a lot of cars near the school's three-
story building, which was bright and colorful. At the entrance there
was a garden with a well-kept lawn and all sorts of plants: ferns, roses,
and hibiscus. And I was unable to fight anymore against what now
seemed inevitable.

We went in and joined the queue. I looked around. Most of the people there, the men as well as the women, were very well dressed and had
a certain air of refinement about them. The gulf between us seemed
enormous. People looked at my mother and me with curiosity, trying
to work out what the connection was. She was blonde with delicate
features, and I was a sort of cappuccino color. I hated those looks, the
ones that seemed to be saying to me subtly, "Go away, you don't belong
in this place." A haughty-looking man fixed his eyes on me. He did not
say a word, but the message was clear: "You must have made a mistake.
This isn't a center for Afro-Cuban dance. They teach ballet here, understand? It's a ballet school." I smiled ingenuously at him as a harsh,
unmelodious voice shouted out: "Carlos Junior Acosta Quesada!"

I went through to studio number three and was instructed to take
off the shorts I was wearing. As I stood there in my coffee-colored
swimming trunks, the only ones I owned, a tall woman said to me
sweetly, "All right then, son, lift your leg up."

Never in my life have I felt such pain. That woman, who seemed so gentle, yanked my right leg up with such force that I can still feel the sharp, stabbing agony that ripped through the back of my thigh and shot into my tendons and abductor muscles. A large woman and three other judges sat jotting down notes on my torment.

"Okay, son, stretch your foot out."

I did it as well as I could. The four women looked at one another, then wrote something down again.

"Now jump as high as you can," one of them ordered me.

I started to jump up and down like a rabbit until they said, "Fine, that's enough."

My mother remained outside, watching through the glass attentively. I do not know what was going through her head—if she was proud, confused, or simply thought that we had made a mistake in coming.

After the women had manipulated me like I was the subject of a science experiment, they gave me the most difficult test.

"Right, son, now it's time for you to improvise something for us."

"Sorry, to what?"

"We would like you to dance something for us so that we can see your imagination at work."

I knew how to break-dance very well. I was not the famous Moro de Los Pinos for nothing. I started to do some moves with my torso and stomach, which always led to whoops and yells of admiration every time that I performed them at street parties. I saw that the teachers were looking at me with their eyes popping out of their heads, and decided to do something that would really impress them. I was just about to spin around on my head when all four women rushed toward me, shouting, "No! No! Don't do that; you'll kill yourself!"

They returned me to a more human position, both feet planted firmly on the ground, and the largest lady tried to explain.

"Look, we just want you to pretend to be a cook, for example, or a huntsman, or something like that. Understand?" She tried to soften her tone, but her voice was still harsh.

They obviously do not know El Moro de Los Pinos! I thought, but I did not say anything, I just smiled as I always did, showing off the strong white teeth I had inherited from my father. I would not be a huntsman or a cook, I would be a soccer player! I would be Pelé!

The pianist started to play. I ran and leaped and danced. I do not know what I must have looked like. I am still not exactly sure how you imitate a soccer player to the rhythm of classical music.

My mother continued to watch intently through the glass.

When I had finished, they told me to go up to the second floor for a musicality test. I remember counting fourteen steps before we joined another queue at the top of the staircase. Queues, like Santería, are just a way of life in Cuba. I tried to feel optimistic as we stood there waiting our turn, but the truth is, I had never felt so out of my element.

"Next!" said a tall woman with short gray hair, who was smoking with as much enthusiasm as my mother. I went in and sat down.

"Repeat whatever I do, okay?" she said.

"Okay," I replied.

She started with hand claps, and I repeated them. She stared at me and wrote down her assessments in a blue notebook. She made some noises with her mouth, and I repeated them. So there we sat for a while, clapping and making noises like a couple of idiots. It seemed like a big waste of time to me. I was hoping that they would fail me, that they would say to my mother that I was not musical, that I had no flexibility or that my interpretation of a soccer player was not the kind of thing they were looking for. That way my father would admit defeat, and I could happily return to my old routine of break dancing and stealing fruit from the neighbors.

A couple of days later my mother had to return to the school to obtain the results of the audition. When she came home, she found us all on tenterhooks.

"Come on, María, don't keep us in suspense any longer," urged my father.

"Just be patient," she said, and took out her glasses to read the results.

I crossed my fingers.

"It says here that you start on the first of September."

"I knew it!" crowed my old man, bringing to his words all the enthusiasm he could muster—an enthusiasm I failed to share. What a disaster!

My sisters shrieked with delight. They did not know the bitterness that I felt on hearing the news. I looked at my father, and he returned my look with an indulgent smile. The die had been cast. While everyone was celebrating, I drifted away. I went to look for comfort among the pigeons I kept as pets up on the roof. I chose one at random and caressed it to the accompaniment of my choking and stifled sobs. I stayed there and watched the landscape of Los Pinos being swallowed up into the darkness. Happiness reigned in our house, but not for me.

Chapter 4

THE FIRST *GRAND PLIÉ*

The alarm clock sounded at five o'clock in the morning on September 1, 1982. My father turned on the light, but I got the impression he had been wide awake all night, pacing up and down like an unquiet soul. Mamá went to heat up breakfast while my sisters continued sleeping. I washed my face, brushed my teeth, and put on red shorts, a white shirt, and a blue kerchief—the uniform worn by Cuban primary-school children. After drinking my milky coffee, I picked up the knapsack that held my exercise books and the new ballet clothes the school had given me. My father gave me a brief, tight hug. I kissed my mother on the cheek. She smiled at me brightly, her eyes shining with sympathy. Then I went out to meet our neighbor Candida's sons, Alexis and Alexander, to begin the long journey to school.

It was strange and exciting to travel into the city to go to school. I had previously been to the center of Havana on only a couple of occasions when my sister Berta had taken Marilín and me to the ice-cream parlor Coppelia for a special treat. The school was in the very center of Havana, close to all the famous buildings such as the Fosca and the Hotel Capri. Everything was grand and majestic, and the streets were full of traffic and people going to work.

I would be attending two schools. At the first, the Orlando Pantoja, which was three blocks away from L and 19, we would study the usual academic subjects from eight in the morning until noon. The Pantoja consisted of two buildings, one for the pupils from preschool up to fourth grade and the other for fifth- and sixth-grade students. The buildings were elegant old houses. Before the Revolution, they had been the homes of wealthy families, and one could still imagine their former glory, even though they were now an ugly, institutional green and their paintwork was shabby and peeling.

Two hundred schoolchildren studied there. There were about fifty of us dancers, and the rest were kids from the local area. Some were better off than others, and although this should not have mattered, because in Cuba education is free for everyone, I still felt intimidated that first day, believing I did not belong there.

A kid called Ismar and I were the only dancers in the fourth grade. In the other building, there were fifth- and sixth-grade classes just for the dance students. It was much easier for them. I was always getting into fights with my classmates because they called me "Alicia Alonso," "poof," or "fag." I did not mind fights; I liked the chance to work off my anger from time to time, and it did not take much for me to get into a scrap with somebody or other, however big he happened to be. Eventually, after I won enough fights, the kids in my class began to respect me and stopped calling me names, taking it out on Ismar instead. He never answered back; they could call him fag or whatever, and it would not get a rise out of him. More than once, I came to his rescue when the classroom bullies were pinning him down. Finally, after being summoned once too often to the head's office for bad behavior, our classmates decided to leave us in peace.

Our teacher, Nancy, was sweetness itself. She was not like the teacher at my previous school, who had beaten me with a thick, meter-long ruler until I was covered in bruises. Nancy was olive-skinned, with a beautiful smile and a strong, clear voice like a soprano: Maria Callas working as a teacher. Although she attempted to be strict, she could never keep it up for long because she adored children, and she loved each of us unconditionally. Even though I was a rebellious child, a truant, and a troublemaker who often fell asleep during class, I always respected my teachers, and Nancy most of all. Whenever she reprimanded me, I would hang my head in shame, unable to meet her dark eyes because I knew that she wanted me to do well. She used to laugh when I came up with imaginative excuses to justify my truancy. On one occasion I swore that my mother had given me diazepam instead of aspirin for a fever, and that I had slept for two days; on another I claimed that I had been kidnapped by neighborhood bandits. Nancy never shouted at me or threatened me, much less hit me. Instead, she liked my stories. When I had to catch up on schoolwork after my frequent absences, she would stay with me till I was done, helping me through the lessons with kindness and patience beyond the call of duty. I was with Nancy throughout fourth grade, taking classes in tenderness and understanding as well as science and the arts.

In the afternoon we took our ballet classes at the school at L and 19. There were about twenty new students on the day I started. I was very nervous that first day, and kept as quiet as possible. Ramón, the head teacher, a man at least six feet tall, with completely white hair, welcomed us all.

"Dear students, today we see the beginning of the new school year and, with it, a new page in the Cuban Revolution. You are the foot soldiers, the men and women of tomorrow, those who will shape the Revolutionary future. . . ."

After his long speech, the head of the student group, Lorena Feijóo, shouted out the slogan of Cuban primary-school children: "Pioneers for communism!"

And we all had to respond in unison: "We will be like Che!"

I had my own subtle variation: "Pioneers for communism! We will be like Pelé!"

In the hot narrow changing rooms of the school we put on our ballet clothes—leotards, which I hated because they were like girls' clothes, and were uncomfortable to wear because the back bit pulled up between your buttocks. The boys were given trunks to wear over the leotards. I thought I looked ridiculous.

We walked to the studio, where an attractive woman with a lovely smile waited for us.

"My name is Lupe Calzadilla," she said.

She was firm but fair and loved what she did and was amazingly proud of the results she achieved. Lupe was a born teacher. We arranged ourselves at the barre. Some tall, some short, all skinny, except for one pudgy kid called Victor. A boy called Ulises and I were the only blacks in the group.

Lupe showed us the positioning of our arms and legs. She explained to us what a *grand plié* was and a *tendu,* then she showed us an exercise.

So this is ballet? I thought, as she made us all stand with our feet turned out like Charlie Chaplin in something that she called first position.

After that we had to do squats, eight down and eight up; then we had to repeat the same exercise standing like frogs, which was what the teacher called second position. I could not see the point of it.

We continued like this for an hour, repeating things that were strange, ridiculous, obscure, and meaningless. The more I repeated the boring, monotonous exercises, the more I was convinced that this was not for me. We finished by jumping up and down on the same spot. What a joke! I could not face the thought of having to repeat this tedium the next day and the next and the next, until fate decreed otherwise.

I found myself gazing out the window. There were some boys playing soccer on a patch of grass. They were sweaty and shouting and having a great time. I longed to run out and join in the game.

"Now stretch your legs!" said Lupe. She prodded my buttocks to make me clench them. "Correct!"

I looked at myself in the mirror. Oh no! I looked more like Chaplin than ever now, posture, legs, everything—only the mustache, the hat, and the walking stick were missing.

One hour and fifteen minutes later, we were still there, like performing monkeys at the circus. And to think that I would have to do the same tomorrow and every single day afterward. It was too much to bear. Then suddenly I heard the most beautiful sound in the world: the bell.

At the break, we ate our lunch at L and 19. The food was very good, at least compared to what I was used to, but there was always somebody ready to complain that they were tired of eating eggs or sardines, or that there should be more chicken. Eggs and sardines did not bother me. I always ate everything, with one eye on my plate and the other keeping a lookout in case one of the girls was dieting and there were leftovers. Other hungry sharks like me were always circling around, and I liked to get in first.

After the break we had our first French lesson with a teacher called Soraya, a light-skinned woman of mixed race who was always impeccably dressed. Her silk head scarves, expensive perfumes, and immaculate makeup only added to her exotic appeal. She recounted tales of her experiences in Paris, a place of abundance and wonder, where snow fell, trains ran underground, and there were no queues. She told us how once, after using a public lavatory, she had spent twenty minutes trying to flush the toilet. "Then I looked at the floor and saw a gray button; I pressed it, *et voilà!*" We used to laugh at all her stories; we had never heard anything like them before.

For the rest of the afternoon, we had piano lessons with Angela and a class on historical dances with Nuri. We finished at half-past six in the evening.

I emerged exhausted and dazed into the hustle and bustle of central Havana. The streets were full of people and traffic and light and noise. I walked past the emblematic buildings of the capital—the Cuba Pavilion, the Hotel Capri, and the Hotel Nacional, with its tropical groves of coconut palms and its swimming pools, my eyes widening with disbelief and delight at the thought that I was here, alone, at the center of all this life and luxury. But as I approached the bus stop, I saw that it was heaving with people, a seething mass of desperation, suffering, and frustration. I glanced from the hotel to the bus queue and back again. They were two different worlds. With a sigh, I joined the crowd at the bus stop, resigning myself to returning to the real world.

When my last bus finally reached Los Pinos, it was around nine o'clock at night; the odyssey usually took about two and a half hours. A large group of people was gathered outside the shop on the corner and break-dance music was blaring loudly. There was someone dancing in the center of the circle. I approached warily, concealing myself behind walls and trees. I could see Opito in the distance, dancing without his shirt on. He was doing the routines he and I had always danced together as a pair. The onlookers were clapping and whistling in appreciation. I wanted to go up and join him, but instead I got out of there as fast as I could. I was sure that everyone must know by now that my father had made me study ballet, and I did not want to suffer any embarrassment.

My father was in. The green Soviet Zil 59, the truck of the company he worked for, was parked outside.

"How did you get on?" he asked me.

"Fine," I said, not wanting to go to bed smarting from a beating after such a long and arduous day.

"But did you like it?" he demanded.

"I prefer soccer."

"To hell with soccer! Go and get washed; your mother's heating some water for you."

And that was all he had to say.

My mother kissed and hugged me and made a fuss over me, wanting me to tell her every detail.

"Mami, it's really boring, and they make me stand in strange positions."

"What do you mean, strange?"

"Like this, like Charlie Chaplin." And I showed her.

My sisters started giggling.

"It's not funny!" I shouted at them.

"That's enough now, Yuli. Go and get washed, and you girls come and eat. The food's already on the table."

After dinner, I collapsed into bed. That night I dreamed that I was playing in a soccer match and that I had scored the winning goal. The other players carried me on their shoulders and threw me up high, really high, into the air. They were all proud of me, and even the coach, who only a little while before had killed my hopes, was now pleased to have me on his team. I was ecstatically happy for a few seconds.

Then the alarm went off. It was five o'clock. I had slept so deeply that I had forgotten about the bedsprings, and there was a streak of blood on my right thigh. I washed it off quickly and got dressed, still half asleep. My sisters were snoring as always. My father had already left in his truck without saying good-bye.

I remembered my dream, which made me feel happy. I drank my milky coffee, picked up my knapsack, kissed my mother, and went out to meet Alexis and Alexander. We walked to the bus stop, and there we were, ready to start the new day.

To hell with dreams!

Chapter 5

PLAGUED BY UNCERTAINTY

About six months after I started ballet school, I came home one Wednesday evening to hear wailing coming from our apartment. As I hurried up the stairs, the wailing grew louder.

"It's me, Yuli," I called.

My father opened the door. My sisters were sitting in the living room with tears in their eyes that they hurriedly brushed away. I assumed that my father had been telling them off for not doing their homework. It had been a while since I had done mine, so I moved nervously in the direction of the kitchen to look for my mother.

"Yuli, wait," said Papá.

Oh hell, now it is my turn, I thought, breathing deeply and crossing my fingers.

"Your mother's been taken to the hospital."

Then there was total silence in the living room. I did not understand. I looked at the faces of my sisters as they began to cry again, then I looked my father in the eye.

"What do you mean, taken to the hospital?"

"She's had a stroke."

My father's words seemed to be coming from a great distance. I ran to the kitchen in a panic, searching for my mother. I checked the patio and the bathroom, nobody there. I returned to the living room.

"What's a stroke?" I asked, covering my mouth with my hands.

"It's a brain hemorrhage."

"A what?"

"Bleeding inside her brain."

My mother had been doing her housework, washing the floor, dusting. She liked to keep the place spotless. She even cleaned the old man's shrine, getting rid of the flies and other insects attracted by the half-rotting fruit that the stone and iron idols left untouched. She stopped for a moment to go to the bathroom, and a vein exploded in her head. She lost consciousness almost immediately, but not before emitting a few loud screams. My father was working, as always, driving his truck. Marilín and I were at school, but, by some great fortune, Berta was not at class that day. If she had not been at home, my mother would have died there and then, in that tiny bathroom, beside the water tank. As it was, Berta shouted for help, the neighbors came running, and someone called an ambulance, which arrived fifteen minutes later. My mother was carried carefully out of the apartment and driven away.

"What's going to happen?" I cried, terrified, slumping down on one of the wicker armchairs. "Tell me what's going to happen!"

"There's no way of knowing," my father said gravely. His expression was very serious. I could tell he was making a huge effort to appear calm, but he was not quite succeeding.

"We'll have to wait and see how she does after the operation."

"But, Papi, what if she doesn't—"

"We're not going to solve anything by worrying," he said, like an order.

Nobody spoke. I lowered my head and, bewildered and afraid, went to the bedroom. My sisters did the same.

My father brought me some food and put water on the stove to heat for my bath.

"What's going to happen now?" I whispered to my sisters, but their faces only reflected the same question back at me.

I ate and bathed. My father turned out the light. We went to bed.

In the darkness, I stared longingly at the outline of the bed I had shared with my mother for so many years. I had never felt so empty. It was as if my heart had been split in two. I remembered her smile, every detail of her face, how she used to hide herself sometimes in one corner of the patio and ask the moon to keep us healthy and well.

"Papito, I can't sleep," I whispered, sitting up in bed.

His cigarette, which was floating restlessly, remained suspended for a moment in the middle of the living room until, slowly, he came toward me and sat down by my side.

"Do you remember the time we took you to the beach at Santa María?" he asked.

This response confused me.

"What's that got to do with Mamá?" I asked him.

But he took no notice and continued. "It was the hottest summer we'd had in a long time. They used to organize activities like that at my work, once a year, as an incentive. All my workmates were there, the new ones as well as the old: Almides, Guardiminio, Dolly, forty people in all. There were so many casserole dishes filled with rice and black beans, chicken, pork, and fried plantains that we set a new record; we ate enough that day to last us the whole month. You used to like singing that song about the prince and the beggar, remember?

> *"At the end of the road I heard this song*
> *From an old countryman as he ambled along . . .*

"I remember watching you. It was like watching my own self as a boy. I used to like singing, too, but I did not have a father, and we never got the chance to go to the beach with dishes filled with beans and roasted pork. It was good to see all of you enjoying the things that I had never had, and I gave thanks to heaven that day. Do you remember that we lost you? We all started to search, and it was Bertica who found you, sitting under a pine tree, singing that song.

> *"At the end of the road I heard this song*
> *From an old countryman as he ambled along*
> *He was singing of freedom, of friendship and faith*
> *Of the prince and the beggar . . .*

> *"Sleep . . . my little prince . . . sleep . . ."*

And those were the last words that I heard.

I woke up the next morning to find that my father had already left for work. I washed myself and, as my mother was not there, made my own milky coffee. When the time came for my kiss good-bye, I felt horribly sad and sat down for a moment, with thoughts of my mother swirling through my brain. Then I picked up my knapsack and went down the steps. Alexis and Alexander did not talk to me during the journey; they knew what had happened and left me alone with my melancholy. They demonstrated their sympathy with a couple of little pats on the back, and that was that. I did not speak. I felt completely disconnected from the outside world.

At school, as Nancy dictated the lessons with her customary gentleness, everything echoed in my ears. Her voice seemed to come from miles away, and her image was blurred. I was in another dimension. I could not make out what my classmates sitting nearest me were saying either. Maybe they were answering Nancy's questions or maybe they were just chatting; perhaps they were being playful, or perhaps they were laughing at me. I could not decipher the sounds I was hearing.

When class was over Nancy dismissed everyone else and asked me to remain behind.

"What's the matter, Junior? Are you unwell?"

She looked me straight in the eye, and I lowered my head sadly. Then suddenly I could not bear it anymore, and I clung to her. Tears streamed down my face. She did not ask any more questions. She stroked my head and told me that everything would turn out fine. The pain seething inside me kept bubbling up and spilling out onto her blouse. I poured my heart out to Nancy until, exhausted, I stopped babbling and she lifted up my chin, dried the tears from my eyes, and gave me a kiss that was filled with tenderness. She led me outside, explaining, in the way that one does to a child of nine, that sometimes everything turns dark and the sky is covered with gray clouds but that, after the storm, the sun always shines and everything becomes bright again. I smiled and, feeling slightly more positive, caught up with my classmates.

The next day my mother was allowed to have visitors. We arrived very early at the Hospital of Neurology. The cool breeze from the air-conditioning was mixed with the sour smells of all those pharmacological products typical of hospitals, and the air tasted of anxiety and pain. Outside, the weather provided an appropriate backdrop to this dismal scene—thunder, lightning, and fat raindrops falling from leaden skies.

I searched the faces on the ward. None of them looked like Mamá.

The nurse signaled to us, and we moved forward cautiously, not wanting to disturb the silence. There, in cubicle four, stretched out on a solid
iron bedstead, lay my mother. Her fragile body rested on a thick mattress, covered by a cream-colored sheet. We were only a meter from the
bed when Papá stopped us and told us not to come any closer, but it
was too late. We had already seen what was left of our mother.

They had completely shaved her head in order to operate. During
the surgery, the doctors had removed her left temporal bone. The gap
in her temple made her look much older. How is it possible for a
woman of thirty-five to look like a woman of sixty? It was not Mamá.
It was a horrible vision of old age.

My sisters wept inconsolably, gasping with despair, while I stood
silently by, watching. My mind clouded over with questions. Why had
Mamá, out of all the people in the world, been chosen by God for this
fate? Why, I asked Him, did He never explain the reasons behind His
actions? Was there something I did not know? What lesson was to be
learned? I wanted to sob and scream, but I did not cry. I just stood,
motionless, detached, as if I were a stranger observing the scene unfold-
ing before me.

I watched a gray-haired old man approach this unrecognizable
woman—a nurse held him back and told him that the woman was still
very weak and must rest. I saw two adolescent girls weeping in despair,
and I saw the gray-haired man holding them both close to his chest. For
a moment, it seemed to me that they were all crying, but I could not be
sure. I moved a little closer and witnessed something that I shall never
forget—I saw tears rolling down my father's face and dripping onto the
granite floor. I could not believe that my father was crying. He looked
at me like a child lost in the woods, then he turned to look up at the
sky through the big glass window.

After some time, my mother slowly opened her eyes. She looked
all around her, up and down, from side to side, unaware of our presence. Her gaze alighted on something. It seemed that she had noticed
us at last. My sisters waved to her, my old man, too. I remained still.
There was not the slightest trace of an expression on her face: no sign
of recognition, as if nothing that she saw was familiar to her. She lay so
still it looked like she was not even breathing the stale air circulating
around the ward. Horrified, Marilín began to shout incoherently—

loud, manic cries giving vent to her anguish. The nurse led her away quickly to calm her down. Berta continued sobbing, covering her mouth with her hands; her face was swollen, and her green eyes had turned a grayish red. My father hugged her, trying to comfort her, and stroked her head. I shot them a sideways glance, confused, grief surging in my chest.

An hour had gone by, and still God had not spoken. He looked on in silence as He always does. I thought that maybe my father could give me an answer that made sense. I looked into his eyes, but they were quite dry now, and he had adopted his customary expression of unequivocal hardness. He was not lost anymore; there was no sign of that child in his face. He was in control again. He took Berta and me by the hands and led us outside.

I turned for one last glance at my mother, to engrave her image on my mind. She remained unmoving, with her eyes open, expressionless, and pale.

"Everything's going to turn out fine," said Papá.

But I was tormented by uncertainty.

I left the hospital without shedding a single tear.

In the following weeks, our lives became more difficult.

My father tried to cook without having the faintest idea how. He left long, thick hairs on the pork, which made us want to run out and throw it to the dogs; he boiled the rice until it resembled a paste that would have been more useful for building walls; the beans were watery and hard enough to break a tooth. But we dared not complain. We took deep breaths and swallowed his culinary experiments almost with indifference.

Our only preoccupation was the question none of us was allowed to ask out loud: Would Mamá get better?

We could not imagine life without her, and our sadness seemed to permeate the air of the apartment. My sisters cried every day. I always tried to hold out, but the image of her that was etched on my mind would tighten its sinister grip, and then I would dissolve into tears.

We tried to carry on: the old man cooking and working, my sisters going to class, and me getting up at five in the morning to attend ballet school. Even when I made it there on time, however, I found it almost impossible to concentrate—all I could think about was Mamá.

One day, Lupe announced that we were going to learn a new step, and so, with both hands on the barre, she showed us how to execute the *assemblé*. She explained how the step began from fifth position. You did a *plié*, one leg came out, scraping the floor, then you jumped and landed on two legs again. She said that this step could also be performed *en dedans*, which meant that you would start with the front leg and move it backward, but that today we would just do it *en dehors*, which meant starting with the back leg and moving it forward. We spread ourselves out, leaving sufficient space to move without hitting the person next to us. I placed myself just in front of the iron bracket that held the barre up without noticing that the barre was loose. On Lupe's command we jumped. The barre fell to the ground with an enormous crash, and the iron bracket hit me on the neck, leaving a large gash. It happened so quickly that I did not even have time to cry. Within three seconds the flesh was livid and blood was oozing out.

Everybody screamed. My classmates around me all had the expression people wear after there has been an accident with lots of blood—a mixture of ghoulishness and curiosity. They covered their mouths with their hands, but kept their eyes open, not wanting to miss even the slightest detail. The blood kept flowing, completely saturating my T-shirt. Lupe took me to reception, and from there I was taken to a nearby emergency clinic. On the way there, I wished I could be admitted to the same hospital as my mother. We would be able to look after each other. I would visit her every day and make sure that the nurses were tending carefully to the wound in her head so it did not get infected. I would feed her mouthfuls of food and wash her face with a damp cloth. But halfway through my daydream I began to worry that maybe she would not recognize me—she would open her eyes and they would roam around the room without stopping—and then I prayed that my wish would not be granted after all.

At the clinic, they gave me a tetanus shot and disinfected the wound with alcohol. Fortunately it was not too deep and would not need stitches. Stitches terrify me. The smell of medicine terrified me, too. It brought back the image of my mother in her hospital bed, and I was very frightened. Everything in my life seemed to be going wrong. First, my parents force me to do something I hate and stop me from becoming an athlete; then, my mother goes and has a brain hemorrhage; next, I gash open my neck and nearly bleed to death. . . .

The doctor interrupted my morbid thoughts and told me that everything would be fine and that I should rest for two weeks. He repeated the word *rest* several times and explained to me that it meant staying in the house, in bed, and not going outside. He kept on repeating it to me very slowly, as if I had learning difficulties.

"Don't forget, rest means complete rest."

I could see he thought he was being funny.

He finished cleaning the wound and applied a small dressing. I returned to L and 19 to collect my things. I was not at all sorry to have a break from the world of ballet. I was tired of getting up at five o'clock every morning and struggling with the buses. My classmates' parents always collected them, but nobody was ever there to take me home at the end of the day. I wanted to get out of this monotonous existence as soon as possible, which was looking less likely since someone had told my father his son had talent. I did not know how I was ever going to convince him to let me stop now, but I decided to have one last try.

With nothing else to do while I recuperated from my injury, I waited, like a lion watching his prey, for the right moment to speak to him.

One afternoon, the old man arrived home early, in an apparently good mood. He was laughing and humming off-key the tune to a Benny Moré song that he liked.

Now was my chance. I breathed in deeply, hid my fear with determination, and went to meet him.

"Papito, I need to tell you something."

"Go on then, I'm listening."

My father continued humming the song.

"I want to be a normal boy, not a dancer."

The humming ceased. Benny Moré was abandoned as my father adopted the murderous expression that scared me so much.

Everything happened so quickly that I did not have time to take in the peril of my situation. He grabbed me by one ear, dragged me over to the window, and pointed to a group of boys outside in the street.

"Are they what you call normal?" he screamed. "Those layabouts and delinquents? They're not normal, and you're not going to end up like them! I'll kill you first!"

He let go of me abruptly and walked toward the kitchen muttering that I was intolerable. I stayed frozen where I was, in considerable pain. My father had claws instead of nails, and he had stuck them right into me. I was becoming accustomed to a whole lot of new pain. I took a few deep breaths and tried to think about something pleasurable. I needed to forget the pain in my ear. It was just a scratch with red blood seeping from it. Already I was learning that if I thought of myself as a victim, I would suffer more. I wiped the blood away and told myself, "Relax, nothing matters, nothing matters."

Chapter 6

WITH HATE IN MY HEART

After a month had passed, an ambulance pulled up outside our house. Most of the neighbors stopped what they were doing and came out into the street. A few of them stayed inside and watched everything, peeping through their curtains. None of us children had gone to school because we wanted to make the house as nice as possible for our mother's return. Marilín cleaned, Bertica washed the clothes, and I went out to fetch the provisions for the month and to carry some buckets of water upstairs to fill the tanks. The old man had left early for the hospital.

We came out onto the balcony just as the two ambulance men were preparing to carry out the stretcher on which my mother was lying. My father got down from the ambulance to hold the doors open for the stretcher bearers and to warn them repeatedly to take care on the stairs. When they brought my mother out, Ramona, our next-door neighbor, put her hand over her mouth, and many of the other neighbors turned their heads away. Mamá looked like a defenseless dove. Her eyes were closed, and she was as pale as she had been in the hospital. Her body shook as the stretcher bearers made unsteady progress, and her head rolled from side to side, as if she wanted to make sure everyone saw the horrific sunken scar her operation had left her with.

We made way so the ambulance men could get past. My mother was sleeping. She did not seem to be breathing. My father squeezed my shoulders and kissed my sisters. He seemed more animated than he had in weeks. I looked at the faces of the neighbors who had crowded into the street. Some of them gave me the thumbs-up sign. Only Opito was sitting on the wall at the corner making fun of me, flapping his arms like a bird and mincing around, insinuating that I was a prancing swan. It did not matter now. My mother was home. I went into the house and closed the door behind me.

Little by little things improved. My mother recovered some of her color, and the hair on her head started to grow back. When she tried to speak, she mumbled sounds that were mainly incomprehensible, but at least she recognized us. I was just happy to know that she was here, alive.

Our neighbor Marta helped us to care for Mamá in the mornings so my father could go to work and we could attend school. She was a good and generous woman, an affectionate, gentle, warmhearted soul. In fact, everyone in the neighborhood was good and generous: one big happy family, not just when it came to drinking rum, dancing salsa, or playing dominoes, but also in times of hardship and necessity. Delia let us have some eggs, Kenia gave us rice, and Candida donated a little cooking fat. There was always someone on hand with a friendly word of advice or a small act of kindness, things that are very important when you are feeling lost.

Now that things were getting back to normal, I was beginning to get tired of keeping to the straight and narrow and behaving well. Even though I had felt good hearing the applause that greeted my first performance, soccer was still my passion. I had to find a way to play.

One day, I got up as usual at five in the morning to go to ballet school, but instead I took a different bus to a nearby stadium, where I knew the soccer team from the Arturo Montori School trained every day. There was not a soul about, just the early morning sunshine, the soccer pitch, and me. Occasionally buses passed by, making a racket, or a Chevrolet of the kind that abound in Cuba, where the only original parts remaining are the bodywork and the name—ten cars rolled into one. The noise did not bother me. I was totally immersed in myself, thinking about ballet, looking at the soccer pitch, and comparing this glorious morning with my usual school day. Six hours of studying French and piano, the monotony and boredom of standing at the barre . . . versus being here. It was sweet to breathe in the scent of the dew and imagine what my life might have been. There was no hope now of realizing my dreams, but at least I *could* dream—nobody could ever take that away from me. I stretched myself out in a corner, rested my head on my knapsack, and waited for daybreak.

I was so tired that I did not feel the Caribbean sun on my skin as it rose. I was fast asleep on the concrete floor, heavy as an elephant. When I opened my eyes, there were boys out on the pitch, warming up to the rhythm of shouts from the trainer before the start of a game. I leaped to my feet. I counted fourteen boys, all my age. The coach was yelling out questions, and they were responding.

"What is the most important thing in soccer?"

"The warm-up!"

"What does your body need before the game?"

"To warm up!"

They continued shouting as they warmed up their ankles, their knees, and their waists. They did squat thrusts. I copied them. The coach noticed me and called me over to join the group, so I did.

Ten minutes later the game began. We played all morning. For me, it was perfect, and I wished that every day could begin like that.

The match finished at midday, and the coach promised me that I could come back whenever I wanted. I was a sweaty, muddy wreck, but I was so happy, I did not care. I knew I would have to think of some excuse for my appearance, but I could not go home yet anyway because if I got back too early, my parents would realize I had not gone to ballet school.

I decided to catch a bus out to the woods in La Fortuna, where there was a big fishing lake and lots of fruit trees. My plan was to hang out there for a while and then return home about the same time that I usually got back from ballet.

Arriving at La Fortuna, I walked toward the woods and climbed over the barbed-wire fence. The lake was about a mile from the road, between a mental hospital and an abattoir. I needed a good swim to cool myself down a bit. The path was wet from two days' rain, and the air was humid and full of insects. By now I was very hungry, and my gut was making sounds like a cat's mewling. I spotted several white mango trees just a little way off and ran toward them, barging through the undergrowth, pushing branches out of the way as mud splashed up behind me and splattered my shirt. I was too hungry to notice; my only objective was to eat. Under the first tree two juicy mangos were ready and waiting for me. I ate them, skin and all, without even thinking that an insect or two might have gotten there first. I must have eaten at least seven ants and three or four centipedes, but at the time I was not bothered, and my stomach was probably grateful for the minute helping of protein.

Although my hunger was sated, I was starting to feel uncomfortable. I could not avoid thinking about what would happen in a few hours' time. If my father found out what I had been up to, I would get my ears boxed or be whipped with his big buckled belt or the thick cable he kept under the bed to use to defend himself against intruders, or even be hit with the machete he had once threatened me with. I would have to invent a credible story to avoid suspicion. If not, the guillotine.

Despite these rankling worries, however, for the first time in a long while I felt happy and free. It was better to enjoy the little time that was left to me. I collected all the mangos that would fit inside my knapsack and continued on toward the lake. I would keep the biggest mango for my mother, save another for my father, and sell the rest so that I could go to the cinema where *The Girl with the Dimples* was still playing. My father had not given me any money yet to see the film, but with a bit of luck, I would make enough now to see it three times.

At the water's edge, I put my shoes and knapsack beneath a cherimoya tree but kept my uniform on to give it a bit of a wash. Splash! Oh, what delicious water! I got out so that I could dive in again, headfirst this time. A little way to my left, a countryman was collecting a creel full of writhing freshwater fish that glistened in the sunlight. Another man was fishing peacefully from his boat. We were the only three people sharing the birdsong and the damp, softly fragrant breeze; enjoying the beauty of the forest; communing with the fish. It was an idyllic setting for a siesta. I washed my uniform as well as I could and hung it out on a bush to dry, then threw myself down naked onto a pile of dry leaves and fell asleep.

"How come you're home so early?" My father's face loomed in front of me.

"Because I've told you already, I don't want to be a dancer!"

"So you just bunked off because you felt like it?" His face drew closer to mine.

"That's right, and tomorrow I'm going to join a soccer school," I told him defiantly.

"I'll give you soccer, you little son of a bitch!" He reached behind him and swung the blade. A flash of glinting silver . . .

"No, not the machete! No! Papito, no!"

"I'm going to hack your head off for disobeying me!"

I awoke with a start, my heart in my mouth. A bird had shat on my head. I smelled of fresh bird shit. I had no idea how long I had slept. The country folk had gone home. I was alone, and the sun was starting to set. I got up to wash my head, and I picked up my uniform, which was still damp when I put it on.

I got out of the bus in Cisneros Betancourt and headed toward Naranjito, my heart hammering in my chest. At every corner I thought I saw my father, his machete in hand, determined to cut off my head. At Naranjito I was about to check whether my father's truck was parked outside the house, when suddenly—

"Yuli, what are you doing home so soon?"

I flinched with fright and covered my head. "Not the machete, no!" I screamed.

"Calm down, kid, machete indeed!" It was only our neighbor Candida.

My balls dropped back into their proper place.

"Why didn't you go to school?" she asked.

"I did go. What happened was . . . we finished early. . . ." It sounded pretty lame, even to me.

"Look at you, you're soaking wet!"

"It's because I ran all the way from the bus stop. . . ."

"And where are Alexis and Alexander?"

"Don't know . . . haven't seen them."

"Where are you off to?"

"Sorry, got to go now!"

I ran away, not wanting a lecture about how the youth of today did not appreciate the achievements of the Revolution, etc., etc. Once Candida got the bit between her teeth, there was no stopping her, and I really could not get caught up in all that. My father might appear at any moment.

I climbed the stairs to our apartment and found the door wide open, so I went in without making a noise and passed through the living room into the bedroom. Bertica was in the kitchen cooking, and Marilín was in the bathroom. I was creeping toward the bunk bed where Mamá had been sleeping since she came back from the hospital, when she opened her eyes in alarm, as if to ask me, "What the hell are you doing home so early?"

I fished a mango out of my knapsack and kissed Mamá, just before Bertica caught me.

"Yuli, what are you doing here? Papito's going to kill you. Oooh, mangos! Come on, give me one, give me one, my lovely little brother!"

Marilín heard her and came running out of the bathroom. "I want one, too. I want a mango!"

I held on tightly to my knapsack. "You're not getting anything! This one's for Mami, and I'm going to sell the rest."

"Yuli, don't be bad."

"No, Marilín. I want to sell them to go to the cinema."

"Then I'm going to tell Papito that you didn't go to school." Bertica was such a blackmailer.

"I don't give a fuck. Tell him what you like. You're still gonna get a big fat nothing, noth—"

I stopped. Outside we all heard the unmistakable sound of my father's truck as he parked. For about ten seconds you could have heard a pin drop.

"Papito's home, now you're in for it!" said Bertica.

I started to shake, and both my sisters stared hard at me. We heard my father's footsteps on the stairs and then the sound of a key in the lock. I could not hold out any longer. I dived into my knapsack and pulled out four mangos.

"Go on, quick, take them and keep your mouths shut!" I thrust them at the girls.

The door opened.

"Evening, everyone! What are you doing here?" My father zoomed in on me immediately.

"Nothing, we just finished a little bit early today."

"A little bit? You mean about two hours."

"The piano teacher was ill, so we missed the last session."

"And what new things did you learn today?"

My sisters went pale, clearly wondering how I was going to get out of that one.

"Well . . . this . . . we learned how to do *échappé* in fifth position."

"What?"

"It's a ballet exercise; it's a bit weird, it starts . . ."

I pointed my toe to demonstrate.

"What about in your schoolwork?" My father interrupted me.

"I . . . in my schoolwork . . ."

My hesitation finished me. He knew I was lying. I was in for it.

We all held our breaths, but just then my mother beckoned to my father to come over.

He crouched down beside her, and she whispered something in his ear. He listened attentively for a moment, then he got up again and walked toward me.

I was praying for a miracle.

His heavy hand fell onto my shoulder. "Go and get washed," he said.

My sisters' jaws dropped. They looked at me, amazed, as I turned and got out of there as fast as I could. In the kitchen I gave thanks for both Marías—the one up there in heaven, and my blessed savior Mamá, down here on the bed.

But my deliverance would not last long.

Having gotten away with it once, I started to skip class on a regular basis. One Tuesday morning, a couple of months later, the school called my father to inform him that, because I had not shown up for four weeks in a row, I would not be allowed to participate in any of the ballets I was supposed to be dancing in. My old man said there must be some mistake: he himself had been waking me up at five o'clock every morning. Surely they were confusing me with another student also called Carlos? The school told him that this was not the first time that Carlos Junior Acosta had missed extended periods of school, and that he would need to have a serious talk with me if I was to avoid being transferred or expelled.

When my old man heard this, steam started hissing out of his ears, like a coffeepot on the point of percolating. Certainly, he assured the teacher, it would never happen again.

Meanwhile, I had spent a happy day at the lake in La Fortuna, gorging on mangos. When I arrived back in my neighborhood that afternoon, I noticed that my father's truck was not parked outside my house yet, and, as it was still too early to go home, I joined in a game of "Four Corners"—a kind of street baseball—with some friends. Two and a half hours later, I picked up my knapsack and nonchalantly walked home. When I reached our corner, however, I was horrified to see the green truck parked in a different spot from usual. I immediately knew that something was amiss. Why would the old man park his truck around the corner from his usual spot? Was he trying to hide it from me? Had he been home the whole time I was playing? Did he know something? I began to sweat and feel sick.

My father was waiting for me on the balcony. His face was contorted with rage, the veins in his neck were swollen, and his nostrils were flared, like a bull about to charge. He gestured at me to come upstairs, and I knew there was no escape.

As I reached the top step, his great hand grabbed me by the neck and hurled me into the apartment.

My sisters, Bertica and Marilín, looked at me with expectant fear; my mother, in her bed, said nothing. My father slammed the door and walked toward me.

"Sit down!" he commanded.

Marilín's eyes were wide with terror.

Outside, life had stopped. I could not hear the shouts of the neighbors anymore, or the honk of car horns, or Kenia's radio as she listened to her soap operas. I was only aware of my heart pounding crazily in my chest as my father leaned toward me.

"What did you learn today?"

"Um, well . . . I learned . . ."

Crack!

I'm not sure what he hit me with. I only remember that when I came around, I was lying on the floor and my face was stinging badly. I could see blurred figures all around me, and a man with a machete in his hand.

Shit, not that dream again! I thought.

But in the dream, it had been just my father, whereas now there were two figures struggling with him, which ruptured my sense of déjà vu. As they struggled, they looked as though they were contorting themselves in an extraordinary African dance, but there was no sound of drumming, just the machete waving in the air. I blinked, trying to convince myself that it was a dream, but then the figures started to come into focus, and I realized my father really was lurching toward me, machete in hand, and my sisters were hanging on to his arms, trying to hold him back.

"Run, Yuli, run!" they screeched at me.

In her bed, my mother was screaming with her eyes, unable to do anything to save me.

As fast as I could, I jumped over the patio railing, onto the roof of our neighbor Raquel's house. I clambered down the wall and escaped along the alleyway between our buildings, running as fast as I could until I was sure my father could not catch up with me. My father's voice echoed in my ears—"I'm going to kill you, you little son of a bitch!"—and I could still hear my sisters shouting, "Run, Yuli, run!" Panting with panic, I tried to think what to do now.

Where could I go so my father would not find me? Eventually, I thought of Eddie, a pal from my break-dancing days, who lived in Vieja Linda. I ran up the hill, past the car-repair shop, Cundo's house, and the fiberboard caves, then into the forest. My face was still smarting, my mind filled with the image of my powerless mother. What would happen to me? Would I ever see her again? My nine-year-old heart was broken. Still I ran, grabbing on to tree trunks as I climbed up the hill until I got to the pool. I was so hot, it would have felt good to have a dip, but this would be the first place my father would think of looking for me. I continued running, past a tobacco field and cows, and over a stream, until eventually I came to Vieja Linda, in the southeastern part of Havana.

Vieja Linda is not one of the worst districts in Havana, but it certainly is not one of the best. Eddie lived on a hill that we used to close off with trash bins in order to practice our break dancing. He was mixed race, with delicate features and round black eyes. He was much older than me, about twenty-three, and lived alone with his brother Humberto; all the rest of his family were in the United States. I never knew how they got there, but Eddie also dreamed of leaving the country one day, being reunited with his relatives, and following the so-called American dream. That is what got him into break dancing, because it was all the rage in the United States. He used to take every opportunity to pepper his speech with English phrases and swear words.

Eddie was happy to see me because it turned out he had been trying to track me down for ages. There was about to be a break-dancing competition in Almendares Park, and he wanted me to join up with the gang again. I told him what had been happening at home and asked if I could stay with him for a few days. Sure, he said, as long as I competed. I told him it was a deal.

I went to bed and tried to forget about what had happened, but my soul was as bruised as my skin, and as soon as I had fallen asleep, the nightmares started: my father with the machete in his hand, my mother and my sisters crying, my ballet classmates making fun of me. . . .

In no time at all, Eddie was shaking me awake.

We went out to meet up with the rest of the gang. A guy called Lalo had put a piece of linoleum down in the street and was practicing his moves. He was really good at doing "windmills," his legs in a split over his head, moving at great speed and with incredible control.

"How's it goin', bro?" I said, slipping back into the language of the street with ease.

"Hey! Fucking excellent, man! Heard you took up ballet, that true?"

"Yeah, 's'just temporary, though . . . hey, bro . . . Who're we going against for tomorrow?"

"Alta Havana."

"Alta Havana . . . heard they're fucking dynamite!"

"Yeah, and you got picked against Michael from Envi."

"No way! Shit! That's tough!"

"Who you kidding, brother, that's nothing for you."

"I haven't practiced for ages."

"Then whaddya waiting for . . . come on, it's all yours."

He turned the music up even higher, and gave me space to warm up in. I had hardly started to move when I began to sweat. I practiced the moonwalk repeatedly, then I asked Guillermo, another member of the group, to pass me a towel. I put it beneath my knee and started to spin around, gathering momentum, but I soon lost my balance. I tried again. Little by little the old sensations came back, and my confidence grew and grew until I became, once again, El Moro de Los Pinos.

"Hey, brother, you're looking really good!" said Lalo, stretching out his hand to help me to my feet. I grinned, feeling pretty good, until a voice behind him spelled trouble.

"Well, well, if it isn't Alicia Alonso herself, come to grace us with her presence!" Opito had arrived.

"Shut the fuck up, arsehole, or I'll knock you down," I answered him.

"Yeah, yeah. Like you did last time."

"I'm warning you, shitface, I'll punch your head in."

"Hey, hey, hey . . . we're doing some training here, getting this neighborhood a famous name. If you wanna fight, you can both fuck off . . . *unnerstan*?"

On that emphatically American note, Eddie forcibly pulled us apart.

"Opito, get warmed up; it's late, and you gotta practice the moves with El Moro here."

"No, I wanna dance on my own," replied Opito.

"You're gonna dance with who I tell you; if you don't like it, you can *geddafuckout*!"

There was silence. Opito looked at me, then looked at Eddie. There was still tension in the air as we started to rehearse our choreography together. Eddie watched us, chewing on his strip of sticking plaster, his baseball cap on sideways. Slowly, as we practiced, we started to get into it, like in the old days when Opito and I were one. Somebody cracked a joke, and we all laughed. The day ended well.

At eleven o'clock the next morning, Almendares Park was full of break-dancers. It was a lovely place, lush and green, but totally enveloped by the stench that rose from the river. The gang from Alta Havana was already rehearsing some steps, but the dancers broke off when they saw us arrive. The gang leader, Alfredo "the Tire," came over.

"For a moment there, I thought you was getting scared," he said sarcastically to Eddie.

"Scared of who, you? Who you fuckin' kidding, man?"

"You just wait and see, got a li'l surprise in store for you."

"I don't fucking care. You know I can kick your ass anytime."

"Hey, speak Spanish, punk. Up yours!"

Mickey the Stink interrupted them. Black and of medium height, he lived in the Lawton neighborhood and was still considered to be the best break-dancer in the whole of Cuba. He had arrived with a crew of about twenty, including two enormous fat guys.

"Girls, girls," he teased, "we've come here to dance, leave your kisses and hugs for another day!"

One of the fat guys, "Tar Ball," passed him the boom box. The music started. A hundred or so people had gathered in a circle big enough to allow us to dance in its center. Nearly all of them were tough guys who spent hours lifting weights and were anxious to pick a fight and show off their strength.

Eddie's brother Humberto began the contest. His body-popping moves went off to thunderous applause. A guy called "the Coffeepot" did some steps from *Soul Train* and some windmills resting his hands on the ground. Lalo looked at Eddie, waiting for the order to go in. Eddie raised his hand, and Lalo entered the center of the circle to demonstrate his speciality: windmills without using his hands, resting his head on the ground and moving so fast that sparks seemed to fly. There were whoops, whistles, jumps, more applause.

The Tire, looking a little put out, indicated to Michael from Envi—my rival—that he should go in. He started with some steps from "Thriller," grabbing his balls like Michael Jackson, throwing a kick, and moonwalking. Everybody went crazy.

Then Eddie signaled to me. I started with a little bit of "Chardo," a dance that was popular in the 1980s, then I grabbed my balls like Michael Jackson as my rival had done, but I could see Eddie out of the corner of my eye telling me to let Opito have a go. I exited. Opito stood on his head and started to spin: one, two, three, four, five, six, seven . . . By now, the spectators were jumping up and down with excitement, shouting, and rolling around on the ground, unable to contain themselves. Eight turns! Nine! Finally Opito fell over. The whole place exploded. The audience seized Opito and threw him up into the air. The Tire watched, still as a stone, his face eaten up with envy. Eddie, as happy as could be, squeezed my shoulders and shouted, "Well done!"

The competition was over, but suddenly we heard a scream. Everyone froze. Somebody moaned. Everybody started to run in different directions.

"He went that way, catch him, catch him!" shouted Mickey the Stink, holding on to the body of the fat guy Tar Ball, who was bleeding copiously from two stab wounds to his stomach. A group of guys chased after the Tire, who had fled. From my nine-year-old height, all I could see were legs racing frantically and figures scattering. Police sirens were getting nearer and nearer.

"Quick, Lalo, grab everything. Let's go, the cops are here!" cried Eddie, and we fled from the chaos.

Nearly all of those break-dance competitions ended in trouble: in order for someone to win, somebody else had to be defeated, and none of us were good losers.

Eddie said I could stay at his house again, but I knew my family would be worrying about me. I arrived back home at five o'clock in the afternoon. My father was there. He had not gone to work. Marilín opened the door but did not say anything; neither did I. I went through and saw my father. There was no anger in his face now, only pain. He looked completely disillusioned, which made my chest seize up with guilt. Neither of us spoke. I walked into my mother's room. Her face lit up, and she stretched her hands out to me. I fell into her arms, and my sisters rushed over to join us, all four of us in one big relieved embrace. I so wanted to cry and to kneel down in front of my father and beg his forgiveness, but pride would not let me.

I heard the door slam and then the engine start up. I ran over to the balcony just in time to see his green truck driving away, a cloud of dust in its wake. Then I cried inconsolably. I could not get his hurt expression out of my mind. A hand touched me on the shoulder. I turned around and saw my mother standing there. It was the first time that she had walked in six months. We all hugged again, but this time the tears had a different flavor.

The end of the school year was in sight and with it my first stage appearance. We had paraded before, but that was only walking. The moment to show that we really knew how to dance was fast approaching. The girls in my class were dieting. All were skinny and scrawny, but according to them they had to watch their figures. I found this quite convenient since it meant there was more food for me.

At last, the long-anticipated day arrived. Our first performance was at the National Theatre, a modern building that seated more than two thousand people. I was to perform a quick, energetic Polish dance called the mazurka with Grettel, a light-skinned brunette with almond-shaped, honey-colored eyes. Every time those eyes looked at me, a bolero seemed to echo in the air, but I thought she was far too pretty to bother with someone as rough as me. I often saw her chatting with other boys in the class, boys who were well dressed, with neatly combed hair, and who had more class and better style than me. She and I were completely different. I had no refinement, and my hair was never combed. I dropped my consonants and swallowed the ends of words like everyone else in my neighborhood. Most of the children at the ballet school were brought up differently from me. A girl like Grettel was never going to take any notice of a thick-lipped, flat-nosed black kid who lived on the wrong side of town, with a truck driver for a father and an invalid housewife for a mother.

But if she could never be interested in me, at least we could dance together. There were eight of us performing in pairs, making geometrical patterns on the stage as we danced the mazurka. I stretched out my arm to Grettel; she rested hers on mine. She looked at me and smiled slightly. I looked at her and felt as if I had turned to liquid. We both continued to mark time without missing a beat.

The theater was pulsating with music, light, and color. It was like a fantastic vision. I suddenly understood the true meaning of the word *marvelous*. As the dance drew to a close, a great torrent of applause cascaded around us, and for the first time in my life I felt a sense of purpose. All this hard work meant something. I was playing a role in the great circus we like to call life.

"Bravo! Bravo!" the audience cheered.

My heart felt as if it were bursting out of my chest. What a sensation! We beamed as we bowed, and still the applause continued. We bowed again, then retreated upstage. The curtain fell.

I turned to congratulate Grettel, and to my huge surprise she stepped toward me and kissed me softly on the cheek.

"Love me oh so lovingly, treat me oh so sweetly . . ." The bolero played in my head.

I gave a little leap of joy as I went to take off my makeup. I climbed the stairs to the second floor full of that kiss, that gentle kiss, the beginning of my life as a romantic. It was enough for me just to be in the presence of a girl I liked to start making plans as insubstantial as dreams. The same is true today. My lungs fill with oxygen, everything in my life suddenly seems to sparkle, and before I know it I am soaring through the clouds, too high up to see reality. Then I always fall flat on my face and say to myself, "There you are, you stupid idiot, you've gone and done it again!"

I wiped off my makeup, got dressed, and ran down to the lobby to look for the beautiful Grettel, the girl with the almond eyes.

She was not there. I searched the crowd of people, but all I could see were happy parents showering their children with affection, tenderness, and support. One or two of them saw me standing there on my own and smiled at me sympathetically. None of my family had come to watch me. They had to care for my mother. I had never felt so lonely. Leaving the happy crowd behind me, I went outside to the theater steps.

In the distance, the orange rays of twilight were beginning to turn to deep violet. Opposite, Revolution Square loomed imposingly, with its tall buildings and the vast memorial to José Martí in its center. I looked in vain for Grettel. Some of my classmates called good-bye to me, waving their hands out of the windows of their parents' cars, their faces radiating security and jubilation.

There was nothing left for me to do but head for the bus stop.

The tranquillity of the evening encouraged me to think. I asked myself why my life was like this. Why did I have to train myself to live with almost nothing and depend on no one so the pain would not screw me up? Why was no one there to see me dancing, to kiss and congratulate me, to take me off for an ice cream to celebrate my first performance?

I took a deep breath and hung on to one of the rear doors of the 174 bus as it trundled down Santa Catalina and Diez de Octubre. I liked the polluted wind that caressed my face and blew through my hair. I was comfortable, enjoying myself out there, until a woman piped up, "Ladies and gentlemen, move on down, please; there's a boy hanging off the back of the bus!"

They all squeezed up a bit to give me enough space to get on.

"Are you all right, love?" the woman asked me.

"Thanks for destroying my solitude," I felt like replying, but instead I just smiled, breathing in the stench of sweaty armpits made worse by the tremendous heat.

When I finally reached my bus stop, I walked slowly up Cisneros Betancourt toward Naranjito, the street on which we lived. It was a moonless night, and the absence of lightbulbs in the streetlamps meant that Los Pinos was shrouded in darkness.

As I turned the corner, five figures loomed out of the darkness and blocked my way.

"Hey, arsehole!"

I knew what was coming. It would not be the first time that the neighborhood gangs had taunted me.

"Well, look who's here!" sneered my former dancing partner, Opito.

"Get out of my way. I'm not in the mood," I replied.

I already knew the routine. I had been through it all before with other former friends, like Pichón and Tonito.

"Oooh, careful, the swan is touchy!" he baited me.

"Drop it, Opito, I'm not feeling well."

"Oh dear, what's the matter? Is it your mother? I heard they shaved all her hair off. Now you're a fag with a bald mother."

I jumped on him, but I only managed to kick him feebly in the knee before another guy, Milli, grabbed me by one arm while Chinchán caught me by the other. Opito landed me two sharp punches in each eye, saying, "That's so you learn to respect men, you fucking faggot!"

They left me there sprawled on the ground and ran away, laughing and joking. It was a while before I managed to get up: I did so slowly, my vision blurred, and I had to use my hands and a wall to help me. I had become the laughingstock of the neighborhood, the designated clown. I thought of my mother in the hospital, expressionless, withered and wilted like a neglected rose, and I did not have the strength left to hold back the tears that ran down my face from swollen eyes burning with pain.

Somehow I made my way blindly, feeling along the walls, stumbling over every tree and trash bin until at last I collided with my father's truck and knew I had finally arrived home.

I told my father I had fallen over, but he did not believe me and shouted in a fury that he would kill Opito and his gang.

Chapter 7

A PRISONER

The new school term started and, with it, my second year of ballet. I developed a compromise routine: I would play truant for one week out of every month. Unsurprisingly, I was missing a lot of important rehearsals in the process. The school would communicate this to my father and I would suffer the consequences, but I would continue to skip class. I studied ballet, but I thought constantly about soccer. Little by little, I managed to find the balance between what I had dreamed of doing and what had been imposed on me. In spite of my numerous absences, my marks were consistently high, which was a great mystery to me, but I am sure that it was the only reason I was not expelled in my second year. They were giving me some rope and waiting to see what I would do with it.

The summer term would end with the National Festival of the Schools of the Performing Arts, in the city of Camagüey. It was a very important event for the school. Many ballets would be presented, among them *Dreams of Sailors,* by our teacher Lupe Calzadilla, who took me aside and told me that she would include me if I promised to attend all of the rehearsals. I accepted the deal, thinking it would be nice to see another part of the country, and resolved to make a big effort. I abandoned the La Fortuna lake and for the first three months of the year concentrated on ballet. Everyone was so amazed at my transformation that I was given a special mention in front of the whole school.

At home, things were returning to normal. My mother had fully recovered her powers of speech, and she could walk and undertake light activities. It was wonderful to see her up and about again; she illuminated the entire apartment. Marilín and Bertica were growing up.

Marilín was now an adolescent, and Bertica had a boyfriend, a local boy named Joel. The school called my father at work to congratulate him on my improved behavior. When they told him they were thinking of nominating me as a model student, he was so proud he forgot the friction that had existed between us in the past.

There was bad news, too, however. In fifth grade Nancy would not be our teacher anymore. Now we would take classes with María Caridad and María Isabel, who could not stand me. María Isabel constantly told me off and blamed me for everything. Even when it was someone else who farted, she rounded on me and dragged me off to the head's office to be disciplined.

In January, there was to be a performance at García Lorca, the most important theater in Cuba. *The Mazurka, The Cherubs,* and many other ballets were going to be performed there for the first time, and I would be dancing with Grettel again. Unfortunately, she was now the girlfriend of a guy named Idris. I used to see them walking hand in hand near the school and was horribly jealous, but I had also started to flirt with another girl, Ana Margarita. Ever since I had received my special mention, she seemed always to be looking at me and smiling, and soon I began to smile back. Once or twice I even spoke to her. My head swelled to immense proportions. I thought I was a ten-year-old Don Juan, until I discovered that the laughter and the flirting were not for me but for Israel, who sat at the desk behind me. What a fool!

One day, our teacher was ill and could not teach her classes, and so I got to go home early, which I was delighted about because it meant I would be able to play "Eat Mud" with my friend Pedro Julio. On the way home the bus stopped three blocks too early to avoid an enormous crowd of people at the bus stop. Everybody shouted at the driver, but it was no use, he threw us all off. I strolled on contentedly, whistling a popular tune. Just as I approached our apartment, a black cat crossed in front of me to the other side of the street, then it stopped and looked at me. I was not superstitious, but I felt as if the animal was trying to tell me something.

When I arrived home, Marilín was crying.

"What's happened?" I asked.

"Oh, Yuli . . . Papá's had a car accident!"

"Where are Mami and Bertica?"

"Everyone's inside with the doctor. Mamá has to be sedated: her blood pressure went up."

"What's going to happen now?"

"I don't know. Papi's at the police station."

I went to the bedroom with a familiar feeling of dread. A doctor was injecting my mother, who was in a terribly agitated state. There were a few neighbors helping to calm her down, and there was the medicinal smell that I hated. It was like a small hospital. The hairs on the back of my neck stood up. My mother did not notice my presence as I stood observing in the corner, and Bertica acknowledged me surreptitiously so that Mamá would not know that I was there and get even more upset.

My mother fell asleep shortly after the doctor gave her the injection, but my sisters and I waited and waited, awake and anxious. At around three in the morning, my father finally returned home. His exhaustion showed in his face, and we could see from his preoccupied glance that the situation was bad. His eyes darted about constantly, unable to rest on any one thing. He drank a cup of lime-blossom tea that Marilín had made for him and told us all about it.

He had been sitting in his truck at an intersection, waiting for the lights to turn green so he could turn left. The traffic lights changed, and, as he was pulling out, a motorbike crashed into him at great speed. The two men riding it had time to jump clear, but the woman who was traveling with them got her dress caught in the sidecar and was killed on impact. The men suffered a few cuts and bruises, nothing serious. They were both so drunk, said my father, that at first they did not seem to understand that their companion had been killed and her body was lying beneath the truck. When they realized what had happened, they started weeping pathetically, in the way drunks do, and exclaiming: "It can't be true! Help us, God, help us!" On and on they went, lamenting and calling on all the saints, one by one, while my father looked on in shocked silence. In the forty-five years he had been driving, nothing like this had ever happened to him. He thought about the fragility of life, how just one single second can make the difference between life and death, and he thought, above all, about that corpse which just moments before had been a healthy woman. He thought about us, and about how this situation would weigh against us, for after this, nothing would ever be the same for my father again. He stood there, motionless, at the edge of the pavement, until the siren of the police car jolted him out of the paralysis into which he had fallen. The noise of a different siren heralded the arrival of an ambulance a moment later, which transported the corpse to the hospital while my father and the survivors rode to the station in a police car.

My father assured us that the accident had not been his fault and that everything would turn out fine, but the smile flickering about his lips was so thin it filled us with doubt. Papá never smiled like that. When he did smile, which was not often, his smile was full and firm, without the slightest trace of weakness. We knew he was lying.

At last the old man stretched out on the bunk bed and fell into a deep sleep. We made a pillow out of our fears and went to bed with sadness in our souls. I remembered the black cat that had been trying to send me a warning. I pressed my face down hard on the bolster and let exhaustion drag me under.

The trial took place just one month later. The court deprived my father of two years of liberty, even though he had been the least blameworthy party, and the real culprits got off lightly: one was fined 1,000 pesos, and the other went to prison for a year. It did not matter to the judge that they had been drunk and had run the red light; the death had to be paid for in one way or another, and the person who paid most dearly for it was my father.

They sent my father to a prison known as the Combinado del Este, on the east side of Havana, where most of the prisoners were murderers, thieves, and common criminals. In one of the oppressive cells, my father sat and waited.

Although my parents' relationship had been over since I was three, and they were now divorced, this was the first time fate had physically pulled them apart. We did not want my mother to visit the prison—she was not in a state that could bear more suffering—but she insisted on going. All three of us went with her in a bus to Cotorro, carrying a plastic bag full of food, our mouths bitter with injustice, and my mother staring out the window of the bus, silent and confused.

When we arrived at the prison, they made us go through to a room that pulsed with both joy and misery. We saw children playing and running around and desperate men smoking and eating; living people with dead souls.

When my father spotted us, his face lit up and he hurried over to greet us. He had dark circles under his eyes caused by insomnia and malnutrition. He was dressed in clothes so carelessly made they seemed designed to humiliate the wearer. We sat down at a large table in the middle of the hullabaloo so he could eat and talk. He told us that on the same day he arrived, he had witnessed one of the prisoners having his throat slit with a knife during dinner. My father had not been able to sleep ever since.

"God Almighty!" exclaimed my mother, as she squeezed my hand tightly.

My sisters shivered, and I saw their bare arms were covered with goose bumps.

I sat watching all the other prisoners in the room as my father spoke, without missing a word of what he was saying.

The following week they were going to move him to a cadet school, where he could work for a salary. Money was even more of a worry for us now that Papá was in prison. My mother had had to sell our sewing machine to buy groceries for the month. As Papá devoured the meal we had brought him, one of the prisoners said hello to him.

"That's Augusto," he told us. "He's the oldest inmate in the Combinado. He's got life."

"What does 'got life' mean?" I asked him.

"It means he'll stay in prison for the rest of his days."

"Have you got life?"

"No, my boy, no, I'll just be here for a few months, then we'll all be together again."

Papá's big, strong hands stroked my head as he gave my mother instructions on how to feed the saints in his shrine. By then they had gone far too long without food.

My eyes followed Augusto as he wandered out into the courtyard. I stared at the withered face and the white head balanced on top of the slight body that paced to the beat of its own silent drum. Sitting on a wall, bathed in golden afternoon sunlight, he seemed to drift away. Intrigued, I asked my mother if I could go to the toilet, and I walked outside, toward this man in his desolation. There he was, alone. No plastic bag of food for him, not even a little drop of homemade coffee. The sun seemed to be his only friend. Prison, my father would say later, is a place where you have to get used to saying little or nothing at all, to forget about the passage of time and about life on the outside. The hardness in Augusto's eyes showed me that he had learned not to need anything. He turned toward me, and his stare chilled me to the bone. The poor man looked like he had ceased to exist a long time ago, as though his soul was a place where hope had crumbled to dust and ashes.

"Yuli, what are you doing?"

I was suddenly aware of my mother calling me.

"Coming, Mami, coming."

I went back to her, but I never forgot the look of that man, who had spent four hours sitting on a wall, gazing into the void. When we said good-bye to Papá, I saw that Augusto was still there in the same place. The day had become overcast. Even the sun had abandoned him.

After that visit, my nightmares became unbearable. I dreamed that my father was sitting on the wall with Augusto. I would draw near, and just as I was about to hug him, he would suddenly turn and look at me with that same lifeless gaze. Or I would dream that his truck was falling over a precipice and my two sisters were trapped in the back. I woke up every morning with my eyes swollen from crying, but I continued going to class, as I had promised Lupe I would. I did not want to break my word, especially right now, a few weeks before the performance at the García Lorca Theatre would take place.

Try as I might, though, our teacher María Isabel was constantly scolding me.

"You're dirty and you smell," she often said, in front of everyone, and they laughed as if she had cracked a joke worthy of the finest comedian.

I explained that my mother could not wash all our clothes and I often had to wear the same uniform as the day before. Not satisfied, she would ask me in a loud voice if we did not have any soap or deodorant in our house. Ashamed, I lowered my head and tried to work out what it was I had done to offend her so. However hard I tried to be good, she still thought I was worthless. I endured the humiliation for as long as I could, then one day something snapped in my brain. Fury formed a knot in my throat. I started skipping school again.

Even on the day of the performance at the García Lorca, I could not bear to go into class. My mother, ever sympathetic, did not question the lie I told about there being a day's holiday. She cleaned the house, throwing buckets of water around and sweeping away the dead insects, while I slept all day. "Just stay where I can see you," she said when, at about six o'clock in the evening, I eventually got up, put on a pair of torn shorts, and went outside, barefoot and without a shirt.

My friend Pedro Julio was practicing our game Eat Mud on the corner. This involved taking a small piece of wood with a nail in one end, chucking it at the ground, and making it stick upright in the mud. You could throw it from different heights—from the knee, the head, or the elbow—and even make it spin in the air. The loser had to put a mud ball in his mouth and bite it in two. It was my favorite game, even though I quite often had to bite a mud ball, and inevitably I would end up swallowing some of it. It was a miracle I never got worms.

That evening, we were halfway through a match that was very important for both our reputations as mud eaters when I caught Pedro Julio trying to cheat.

"Stuck!"

"It's not stuck!"

"It is so, Yuli. Look, it's standing up."

"I know your tricks, bro; that stick's lyin' down in the mud. Look, look!"

"Shit, bro, that's cheating, nooo!"

I grabbed the mud stick and, balancing it on the end of each finger in turn, threw it at the mud. Pedro Julio turned green because the stick landed upright every time. I kept on throwing it, from my knee, my elbow, my head, and every time the stick fell right down and stuck perfectly. It seemed it was my lucky day.

"Now you're really gonna see how it's done. Get ready to bite!" I crowed.

Preparing my final throw, I took hold of the mud stick by the nail and walked back a few paces. Pedro Julio was sweating. One, two, three, and splat! Stuck!

"That doesn't count; you cheated. I'm not playing anymore!"

"Look who's talking. Stop being a wimp and eat the mud ball!"

"I'm not going to fucking eat it!"

"Bite it, bite it, you lost!"

"I'm not biting nothing."

"Take that, then!"

I rubbed the mud ball in his face. He got another even bigger one and pressed it against my forehead. I jumped on top of him, and we fell into the mud. I had him pinned down good and proper by the neck when a black car drew up beside us.

I felt someone tugging at my arm.

"Let him go, let him go. Junior, let him go . . . !"

Everybody called me Yuli around the neighborhood, a few people called me El Moro, but nobody *ever* called me Junior.

I turned, and in one quick movement an extremely strong man had thrown me into the car.

"Quick, quick, quick!"

Shit, no! It was my teacher Silvia and a driver.

"Hurry up, hurry up, or we'll be late!" she ordered the driver, and then she turned to me.

"How is it possible, Carlos Junior, that you have failed to turn up for a performance that is so important for your school?"

I only managed to say: "Oh my God, I forgot! Miss, it's just—"

"The show has been suspended for the past half hour because the mazurka is incomplete. Do you think that's right? Look at the state of you. You look like a vagrant."

I was completely covered in mud.

The driver put his foot down on the accelerator. He went over every pothole, the car rattling around, as though he were transporting cattle, not people. In the backseat, I was pinned between Silvia and another teacher, who stared at me and smoked as Silvia fired out questions.

"Why were you fighting with that boy?"

"Because he didn't want to eat mud . . ." I replied, all innocence.

"That's no reason to fight . . . of course he didn't want to eat mud. Who would ever think of such a thing?"

I kept quiet. Obviously I had thought of such a thing, as had all my friends who loved to play Eat Mud and enjoyed it when their opponents lost.

When I arrived at the stage door, there were several teachers waiting to whisk me rapidly inside.

"For God's sake, he's completely covered in mud. . . . Where's he been, a pigsty? What are we going to do with you? You're a disaster!"

They all spoke at once as they scrubbed the mud off my face and legs. One applied a bit of makeup to me while another whipped off my clothes and shoved me into a dance belt and leotard. They moved fast, shaking me and manipulating me as though I were a puppet.

"Up, put your hand in . . . stand . . ."

I did what they told me. They finished putting my jacket on, then bustled me out of the changing room. There were a lot of people in the corridor, most of them students who looked me up and down as though I were a Martian. I was just about to go onstage when I heard the music for the mazurka and, behind me, someone shouting: "Your shoes, your shoes, you've forgotten your shoes!"

My heartbeat accelerated. The music was getting to the part when we had to enter.

"Get a move on, get a move on, or we'll go on late!" cried Grettel in a panic.

Someone handed me a pair of shoes and I fell to the floor, put them on my feet, and ran like lightning.

Aaaand . . . a-one, two, three, one, two, three.

Phew! I had made it. I faked a smile and executed the geometrical formations all around the stage, while Grettel shot me furious glances.

Afterward, I lurked in a corner at the back of the theater wearing only my muddy, torn shorts, skulking along the wall like a rat. The phrases I had so often heard echoed in my ears: "You're dirty, you stink, you're a disaster."

They were right. I was a disaster. My life, my world, was a disaster. Perhaps it was fate. Perhaps the saints knew that on June 2, 1973, a disaster of a boy would be born in Los Pinos, a muddle-headed, mud-eating, break-dancing fool with a sick mother and a jailbird father who determined, against all odds, that the boy should study ballet. Perhaps that was my destiny.

I was replaced by Ulises in the Camagüey Festival because of my continued absences. The school won nearly all the medals that year, and our teacher Lupe's ballet, *Dreams of Sailors,* in which I should have been dancing, won most of the prizes. Lupe had done everything she could not to lose me from the cast, but I kept skipping almost a week's worth of classes each month, and everyone was frightened that I would fail to turn up for performances during the festival.

At home we made a pact not to say anything to my father. We did not want to upset him now that he had been transferred from the Combinado to a cadet school. He was working there, earning 70 pesos a month. The salary was not enough for us to live on, so we had to try to cut back on household expenses. We stopped going to the cinema, and we went to school with the exact money for the bus journey and nothing more. I had to keep wearing the same pair of trousers even though they were already too small for me. My sisters sold our coffee and soap rations to get money for food, and my mother resumed her fortnightly trips to the countryside to exchange our rations with the farmers.

At the beginning of September 1984, I enrolled for what should have been my third year of ballet. In fact, I had to repeat my second year because, having started at the age of nine instead of ten, I was a year younger than my classmates. Repeating the year meant that I would be in the correct group for my age: eleven years old, in my sixth grade of schooling and my second year of ballet.

Now that I did not have my father around to pressure me, my absences became more frequent. Whenever we visited my father and he asked how I was doing, I would reply, "Fine, everyone's really happy with me; we won a lot of medals at the Camagüey Festival. It's a lovely city."

I saw that my news really cheered him up, so I began to invent different stories every time we went to see him, elaborating wildly about my achievements.

The truth was that my mother had already been called to the school on various occasions to attend disciplinary hearings. She tried to excuse me by reiterating that we lived very far away; that it was extremely difficult for a boy of my age to get up so early and struggle with four buses; that she also had two daughters and she could not keep a close watch on all of us all of the time. When she came to the part about my father being in prison, she would break down, and so the teachers would give me another chance. I would do well for a while, then start playing truant again; my mother then would have to come in for another hearing, and so the whole cycle went on.

My name became synonymous with bad behavior. Soon some of my classmates were calling me "Junior el Desastre." I hated it, but the more I skipped school to avoid the name-calling, the worse my reputation became. Things got so bad that María Dolores, the pianist who played for us in our ballet classes, took pity on me and decided to take me home with her on weekends. Her son, Israel, was the tallest in our group, and many of his clothes were too small for him and so she passed them on to me. For the first time in my life I discovered what it was like to wear trousers without holes and to sport a silk shirt with a multicolored vest. Even better, I tasted chewing gum for the first time. My sisters were consumed with curiosity when I told them.

"It's really soft and nothing at all like sticking plaster," I tried to explain, but they could not imagine it until María Dolores gave me another piece of gum and my sisters finally had the chance to find out what I was talking about.

"No, nothing at all like sticking plaster," they both concluded.

The end-of-year exams were approaching, and just at that crucial moment, I came down with mumps. This time my absences were entirely justified, and I would certainly have failed everything if my fourth-grade teacher Nancy had not found out I was ill and come to review with me every weekend at Los Pinos. Thanks to her, I managed to pass the year. In June, I turned twelve, and in September the 1985–1986 academic year began. I was now in my third year of ballet and seventh grade at secondary school, where, increasingly, the waywardness of Carlos Junior was becoming legendary.

Some of my classmates made it obvious they despised me. I remember one day overhearing a girl tell her friends, "Get away from him! Keep away. My mother says that badness is catching!"

People saw me as some sort of poison. The lonelier and more miserable I felt, the more frequent my absences became.

But when I spoke to my father on our visits, I spun the lie that I had been made head of the student group at school.

"That's more like it; that's what I want to hear," he said proudly, rising from his seat and striking the table with the palm of his hand.

"Last night I had a magnificent dream," he went on. "You were dancing in a majestic theater in another country, and suddenly a cricket landed on your shoulder."

My mother's eyes opened as wide as two full moons. The rest of us wondered what he was going on about.

"Don't you realize? The cricket represents hope. It means that you're going to be great one day," he announced.

There was silence. I looked at my sisters and then at my father, realizing I had overstepped the mark with my latest lie. Making up stories and misbehaving were the only things I was good at. If my father were to find out the truth, there would be hell to pay. I spent the rest of the day thinking about just how deep I had dug myself into this latest hole. How was I going to get out of this mess? I suspected it was already too late; I could not undo my absences.

Not long after my thirteenth birthday, my father was released from prison. The very next day, the school called my parents in for a disciplinary hearing. We entered the principal's office and sat down; my father was in a good mood, my mother was worried, and I was shitting myself.

"This meeting is to inform you that Carlos Junior Acosta Quesada has not passed his end-of-year exams and therefore cannot continue in this school."

"What?" My father leaped to his feet, his nostrils flaring.

The teachers enumerated my sins. I was the biggest truant in the school; because of this, they had had to pull me out of the cast of the festival; I had missed not only all of my final ballet exams but all my academic ones, too.

"What's this, María?!"

My mother did not dare to look at him.

My father turned to me. I hung my head in shame.

"How's this possible? He told me he'd been to the festival, that he'd really liked Camagüey!" exclaimed my father.

"Well, he's quite expert at making up stories, aren't you, Carlos Junior?" said one of the teachers.

I could not lift my eyes from the floor.

We left, Papá walking fast, as if he could not wait to get me on my own, dragging me by my left arm; Mamá was scuttling along beside, pleading with him to keep calm.

My father thrashed me to within an inch of my life. My mother could not stop him. My sisters were hysterical as they saw my body bounce against the bed again and again. It was one of the worst nights of my life.

The following morning, my father got up early to buy fruit and sweets for his saints. He put flowers on the shrine and chanted prayers from his extensive repertoire. He spent two full weeks repeating this ritual, going without food and rest, spending all his energy on those religious ceremonies.

"Pedro, leave the saints now and come and eat something; you're looking really weak." My mother tried to lure him away, but he paid her no heed.

Not content with merely repeating his rituals, my father started adding new bits to them during the night. The neighbors complained because of the row he made with the maracas and conches and coconut shells that exploded against the floor, but nobody dared stop him.

One day, several weeks after the beating, he called me to him and asked: "Why did you do it?"

What did I have to lose?

"I'm not happy doing ballet," I told him.

"Happiness! You know nothing about happiness!" he scoffed. "Shall I explain it to you? Okay? Happiness is something that you can never count on, understand? It's a feeling that's difficult to define. Many people have moments when they are contented, but anyone who tells you they're truly happy is lying. I have been happy once, just once in my life. Do you want me to tell you when it was?"

He held my eyes for a long time, then averted his gaze.

"Well, no . . . perhaps this isn't the moment to tell you. But what I want you to realize is that happiness is a trip you take, not a destination."

I began to weep, but my old man was not moved. His eyes hardened again, like a bull's.

"Never forget that," he added, and returned to praising his saints, leaving me sitting alone on the balcony.

Two days later the school called him at work to inform him that, owing to the unusually high number of pupils who had failed that year, the Ministry of Education had decided to approve some resits. This meant that I would have to retake my exams, but it was an opportunity to try to pass into the next year at school. My father arrived home and gave us the news, almost jumping for joy. He immediately went to the nearby neighborhood of La Palma and bought two roosters. He killed the birds and sprinkled their blood over the iron objects in his shrine, then sprayed the saints with rum, broke a dried coconut over them, and blew cigar smoke over our faces. He celebrated long into the night, beating upon the saucepans with spoons. Nobody slept in our apartment that night. How could we? A miracle had occurred.

Chapter 8

PINAR DEL RÍO

I made a huge effort to study for my second set of end-of-year exams and managed to pass them all and move up into the next grade. My teachers, however, fed up with my bad behavior, decided I could not remain where I was. It was concluded that the best thing would be to transfer me to an interprovincial boarding school.

"We've already spoken to the Vocational Arts School in Santa Clara, and they've approved Junior's transfer," they told my parents and me when they called us in to give us the news.

My old man apologized once more for all the trouble I had caused, before dragging me grimly home by the arm. He decided to accompany me to the city of Santa Clara.

On the day I was due to start at the new school, we set out together on the six- or seven-hour bus ride, arriving on a Sunday at one o'clock in the morning. A helpful gentleman at the bus station explained to us that the school was about five kilometers away, near La Minerva dam. His information was incorrect: the school we found was the Arts Teacher Training College, not the Vocational Arts School, but by the time we made it there, it was far too late to continue our search, so we asked to pass the night in one of the hostels.

When we finally managed to find the Vocational Arts School the next day, we were received by the principal, an imperious woman of medium height.

"Good day," said my father.

"Good day. How may I help you?"

"I am the father of Carlos Acosta, the new transfer from Havana . . . here is the documentation and his grade-pass certificate."

"Transfer, what transfer?"

"The transfer from the Alejo Carpentier School."

"No one has informed me of any transfer."

"But they said you were expecting us."

"What did you say the boy was called?"

"Carlos Junior Acosta Quesada."

"It's the first time I've heard that name."

"He's starting his fourth year of ballet."

"Well, I'm sorry to tell you that in this school there is no fourth year for boys. We have boys in the third year and the fifth year, but the fourth year is just for girls, so you see, a transfer would be out of the question. The only school that accepts fourth-year boys is the Vocational Arts School in Pinar del Río. They must know that in Havana."

"But they told us to come—"

"I'm sorry."

As we walked back to the bus station, I was secretly triumphant. No more buses at five in the morning, no more jokes, no more black eyes! *Ritorno vincitore!* I would return to Los Pinos with a cape and golden sword, ready to be admired by all the gang members in the neighborhood.

"See that boy, the one who looks so confident? He is El Moro, one of us!" they would say, without sarcasm or innuendo.

But my happiness was short-lived. I could not bear to see my father looking defeated. Where had all his strength gone? What hopes would sustain him now?

There were no more buses back to Havana that day, and we had to spend the night on the uncomfortable benches in the bus station. My father did not say a word. He sat thinking, well into the early hours, his head leaning against a stain on the wall. At last he drifted off, and I looked at his face as he slept. His eyes moved constantly and trembled as though he was having a nightmare. Eventually I also slept, until the hordes of street traders awoke me as they flooded into the tumultuous and shining city. We returned to Havana on a worn-out milk train.

"L and 19 must have been lying about the transfer," my mother concluded, after she recovered from the surprise of seeing us both back.

"We'll have to try another province," said my father.

"But first we have to get things straight with L and 19; they can't go treating people like that. . . ."

"María, we've no time to lose, it's better to leave things as they are."

"So you have to spend a night at a hostel and another in a bus terminal, like a couple of gypsies, let alone blowing a whole month's salary on tickets. . . . If they wanted to expel him, then they should have said so to our faces instead of making us waste our time like this." My mother was outraged.

"Calm down, María, calm down. It doesn't do you any good to upset yourself. Anyway, we won't sort anything out by getting angry. The damage is already done. Tomorrow's another day." This time it was my father who was the practical one.

The next morning, my father kicked me out of bed at four o'clock and dragged me, half asleep, to the bus terminal. Four hours later we found ourselves in the Vocational Arts School of Pinar del Río, and my father was pleading with the headmistress.

"Look, ma'am, his ballet marks are very high and so are his ones for repertoire. All I'm asking is that you at least have a look at the documentation. He's a good boy at heart. He just needs to grow up a little."

I had never seen my father beg for anything before, and I found it horribly embarrassing. The principal tried to calm him down, but she was unequipped to resist his brand of persistence. We left the school that day without a definite answer, but a week later they called my father and said they would put me on probation for a month.

The old man grabbed me by the hand and looked at me in such a threatening way that I understood I had better get into the damn school if I wanted to stay alive.

I never really got used to living in Pinar del Río. It was a long way from home, and so on weekends I had to stay with my half brother Pedro, my father's son from a previous relationship, who lived with his mother, María, and his girlfriend, Nena. At Pedro's I slept on the hard living room floor, which swarmed with cockroaches and mosquitoes. The river was just twenty meters away from the house, its waters petering out among the high malangas. It meandered and turned in on itself, ebbing and flowing silently. It would have been beautiful to sleep there beside it, looking at the full moon, if not for the evil stench that rose off the water. The roof of Pedro's house leaked when it rained, dripping onto the area where I slept. In these fairly miserable conditions, I was also going through the changes of adolescence without my parents or my close family to support me. The only way I had of communicating with them was when Pavel, the school's trumpet teacher, gave me money to travel to Los Pinos for a weekend, but this did not happen very often. During the week the students all boarded at the school, so at least I had the company of my classmates, who shared with me the snacks their parents brought them during the Wednesday visiting hour. But on weekends I felt very lonely, and I would sit on a wall outside Pedro's house, staring at the sky, trying to construct human faces out of the patterns of the stars, and I would think about home.

The Vocational Arts School in Pinar del Río was a huge concrete block on the edge of the city. Its three buildings bordered an enormous interconnecting courtyard and were surrounded by stairs leading up and down to the classrooms for music, the visual arts, and ballet. It was here I discovered love and friendship, as well as other qualities that helped the boy I was become the man I am.

It was here that I found my passion for ballet.

One evening the school organized a visit to the Saidén Theatre on Real Street in Pinar del Río to see the Cuban National Ballet perform. I was annoyed because I wanted to stay in and watch the baseball game between my Havana team, the Industrials, and the Pinar del Río team, the Vegueros, which all the other pupils in the school supported. But I was dragged along with the rest of the group and seated next to our teacher Juan Carlos in an uncomfortable seat in the theater's third row.

My friend Rogelio and I were discussing who would lead the batters that year. Lázaro Vargas was his hero, and Rogelio always imitated his batting style whenever we played in the rough concrete sports area of the school.

We were shushed as the curtain went up. It was a slow piece. "Educational," the teachers might have said; "a jewel of the classical repertoire," a fan or critic might say; a load of crap, I thought.

I was calculating that by now the game would have reached the third inning. The Vegueros were leading the championship. If they lost, the Industrials would be only half a game away from first place. It was not just a game of baseball between Havana and Pinar del Río; there was more at stake than that. My honor as a Habanero was on the line, but I also knew I stood to lose either way. If the Industrials won, then some people would vent their spite and frustration on me; if they lost, three hundred people would shout at me, "Ha, ha, ha, Havana lost the game, you're a yellow Habanero, you can't beat us 'cos we're better than you!" They would push me and tug at the neckerchief that we had to wear as part of our school uniform. I was getting flustered just thinking about it.

I made myself watch the ballet. The ballerinas who floated across the stage as delicately as goose down distracted me from the baseball game for a moment, when suddenly a male dancer leaped across the stage and was suspended in the air for what seemed like a full minute before falling back down to his knees.

Shiiiit! I thought. How the hell did he do that? He was just hanging in the air!

Everyone applauded. I was trying to work out where the wire was, thinking the muscular guy must have been held up by something. He jumped again. It looked effortless. He did not even appear to be sweating, just smiling as he kept time with the heavenly music.

My spirits soared. I felt transported. Perhaps if I worked hard, then I could hang in the air like that!

It suddenly dawned on me why my father had been so tough with me all these years. I saw it all with great clarity. All he had ever wanted was for me to be able to jump like that!

I was mortified to have caused him so much trouble, to have run away to Vieja Linda, to have made him waste his time and money on the trip to Santa Clara, and to have been responsible for his sleeping on the benches in the bus terminal. . . . But at the same time I was so happy and grateful that God had given me another chance.

When we returned to the school, there was a crowd of people waiting for me. The game had gone into extra innings, but the Industrials had lost 2 to 1.

"Ha, ha, ha, Havana lost the game! Yellow Habanero, you're yellow, you're yellow, you're a yellow streak of piss!" my classmates shouted at me, tugging at my neckerchief. But instead of reacting, I simply smiled and thought, One day I'm going to be like that dancer I just saw. One day I'm going to be like Alberto Terrero!

I did not give a damn about the Industrials' defeat, or the fact that the championship hung in the balance, or that my classmates were trying to provoke me. I had heard the clarion call of vocation. It was a sanctuary, a refuge that would help me bear the leaks in the roof of Pedro's house, the cockroaches, the mosquitoes, the overpowering stench of the river, and the loneliness. All I had to do was concentrate on my mission, which was to dance like Alberto Terrero, the ballet dancer whom I had seen fly through the air that day at the Saidén.

Up until then, I had applied myself, at best, about 70 percent. I had grown stronger, and for the little effort I put in, I had done all right, but now it was different. During the week I worked furiously, forcing myself through the corrective exercises that my teacher set for me. At the time, I thought that the olive-skinned Juan Carlos, with his wiry body and his Andalusian eyes, was a brutal taskmaster, but I understand now that he was an excellent teacher. He had been a dancer with the Camagüey Ballet, but his knees could not bear the strain they were subjected to over the years, and one day they gave up and never obeyed him again. So he started again as a teacher, a little disillusioned and resentful, but still with the desire to achieve something worthwhile. His work came to be recognized in the highest educational circles in the country.

Normally, after the school lunch, my body demanded a good siesta, but now I forced it to keep working. I had to adapt my muscles to flight.

Around the same time, I also developed another passion.

Olga.

When I had first met her she was sitting on a wall at the school. I was thirteen; I had arrived just a week before and was still trying to talk as little as possible. My place at the school was not secure, and I did not want to be branded a troublemaker again. I sat down beside her casually, as if it was not a big deal. She was reading the kind of poems that only adolescents can understand. She asked me where I lived, and I said Havana, disinterestedly, my eyes fixed on the rough shacks of the country dwellers and the light-coffee-colored coconut palms and the orange and hibiscus bushes I could see through the fence. She asked if I liked the school. When I turned to look at her, our eyes met for the first time. Her slanting eyes were brown as mahogany, the lower lids full, almost as if slightly inflamed. The breeze blowing across the yard carried with it a tumult of voices that sounded like a flood of water rushing over stones. I fell in love.

I found myself talking incoherent nonsense, as if those eyes had cast a spell on me.

"What . . . ?" she asked me.

"What about what? Oh, I see, if I like the school? Oooh, yes, yes, fantastic, and the province, the palm trees, the sun, everything is very nice."

She smiled knowingly and asked me other questions, but I could only shrug my shoulders or nod my head. It was as though I had lost my ability to speak, as though my tongue had rolled up into a ball, like a parakeet's, and I could not unfurl it again in order to say anything.

Love. I had heard about it in songs, read about it in books, and once at a party I had even told a girl that I was in love with her, but I really did not know what it was all about. When I met Olga, I understood.

The thought of her body, sculpted by some god, kept me awake at night, even during the occasional blackouts. When the whole world rested, all I could think was how pleasurable it would be to have that body next to mine.

I learned that she liked the singer Roberto Carlos and dancing salsa, and that her legs—round, hard, and alluring—liked to be touched. I found out about her relationship with Eduardo; about how she had kissed William, on the third floor, up in the music department; and about her flings with Rosca and Molina. But even though I knew that our love—or rather my love for her—was not exclusive, the urge to possess her grew ever stronger.

I was driven by an overwhelming desire for my feelings to be reciprocated. I could not stand being second best, just another soft toy to add to her collection, lying forgotten in a lonely corner, waiting for her to bring me out again into the light of day. Love tormented me every second. I was ensnared, unable to wriggle from its clutches.

I wrote her a poem and gave it to her with a rose. She liked it, and I liked that she liked it, imagining I had gone up a few notches in her estimation. We linked hands and went for a stroll as a strong breeze bounced off the walls of the school and the sun sank into the coconut palms over to the west.

We shared one of those kisses that make you sweat.

I was no expert in kissing. I had done it only three times. Olga taught me how to run my tongue over each and every corner of her mouth and her full lips. I kissed her and felt her legs, warm and strong like the earth, as I ran my hands up and down her body. We fell to the floor, two fires together, scorching the ground as the sun does when the sky is cloudless. I was oblivious to everything except the power of orgasm. There was magnificent release and then delicious drowsiness, until gradually the chill wind of evening dampened the fire in our bodies. She whispered she would return, her eyes shining like bright moonlit pools.

When she had not returned half an hour later, I went in search of her. I caught her in the music department kissing Eduardo. He was doing with his filthy tongue what I had just done. Voices in my head clamored for me to throw him from the third-floor window, push him over, smash his face, but I turned on my heel and left, my arms hanging down and my head held low. Love, so recently acquired, had become the enemy.

The next evening there was a huge moon. It was a Saturday night, so I was at Pedro's. My heart still aching from Olga's betrayal, I was sitting in the alleyway that ran along the side of the house, doing my best to hide my broken heart by talking to the next-door neighbor about the new salsa orchestras. Orchestra Revé was at the height of its fame, with its Changüí ringing out on every radio station at every hour of the day and night. From out of the darkness, my half brother Pedro approached, staggering in the direction of the house. His shadow looked like a clumsy headless monster lumbering toward us, and I leaped up to help him in. He could hardly stand, owing to the vast quantities of rum he had consumed. I returned to the passageway, but it was impossible to continue any conversation over the storm of insults and the crash of breaking plates that soon issued from the house.

I was used to scenes of this sort between Pedro and his girlfriend, Nena, and kept my distance so that I did not get involved. After the row had subsided, his mother, María, came out into the yard, a resigned expression on her face.

"Yuli, take the mosquito net and the sheets and go sleep in the other house," she said.

The "other house" was no more than a rickety shack where on rainy days it rained more inside than out. The house was right by the river, and it had the pestilential stink of a toilet. It was made of wood, with a guano roof and a dirt floor, unfinished, like a moment of inspiration that had died halfway through. It was not the first time that I had slept in the place, and I had a very clear idea of what kind of night was in store for me.

Meanwhile, in the other house, the row had started up again. The echo of Nena's insults ricocheted down to where I was. I heard footsteps. I went out and saw Pedro stagger out of the house, clutching at the walls to stay upright.

"Pedro, where are you going?" I called.

"There's no reasoning with that woman," he told me.

"Go on, get lost, you shameless womanizing drunk. Tell her to wash and iron for you. Tell her, see if she does it!" Nena shouted after him. Then she broke down into heavy sobs, crying her eyes out while María comforted her, putting her arm around her shoulders.

I wanted to get some sleep so that I would be in good shape in case I saw Olga at school on Sunday evening. I crept under the mosquito net, covered myself with the sheet, and tried to block out their screaming.

I woke at six. Water was leaking through the roof and soaking the mosquito net, the sheets, and the mattress, turning the earth into a thick and evil-smelling mud. It seemed as if the river itself was pouring in. I went outside. The wind blew strongly, scratching the trees as though it had nails, and the rain pelted down. I stood in the darkness, getting soaked through by water that was as black as the night. If the rain wanted to claim me, soak me, subsume me in mud, I would not fight it. Suddenly, as if satisfied, the sky started to clear. I could see the clouds fast asleep over the town and imagined a warm blanket over the town's inhabitants. In the east the sun started to break through, and the mist slowly lifted, leaving only sheen on the bare rooftops. In the distance, the trees remained in shadow, and most people continued to snore, although yellow lights appeared in a few houses. A little bird flitted across the streets, sounding the first note of dawn. Soaked through, I watched and marveled, standing in the alleyway next to Pedro's house with my arms crossed, watching the approach of a beautiful day.

The fever that followed later that day left me without a voice and with bones that ached so much that I could hardly get out of bed. Despite this, I caught my usual bus back to school on Sunday night. The next morning I was no better, however, so the school called a nurse, who came to look after me and gave me medicine to lower my temperature. There was talk of sending me back to Pedro's, but by Tuesday morning I started to feel better. I could swallow with less difficulty, and my temperature was returning to normal, although I was still pale.

Tuesday afternoon, Juan Carlos was teaching us. He marked out the first warm-up exercise, and ten seconds later the piano started to play. He watched me warm up my knees, my neck, and my ankles, and marked out the second exercise without taking his eyes off me. He corrected me during the *fondu,* pushing down my shoulders to make the *plié* deeper, until I felt pain in my Achilles tendons. Afterward he corrected me during the *frappé,* emphasizing the *en dehors* of the lower leg.

"Out, leg out!" he ordered.

Now the pain was in my knee.

In the *grand adagio,* he lifted up my leg with such force that I achieved a 180-degree angle, something that I had never managed before in my life. I had never felt such pain in my tendons, my knee, or my hip.

I completed the final *grand battement* and then fell to the floor, wondering why I was being singled out like this. He knew that I had been ill over the weekend, but he was pushing me without mercy. By the end of the class, I was dripping with sweat, and my legs would not support me.

Juan Carlos came over to me.

"How do you feel?" he asked me.

"How do you think I feel, since you've been trying to kill me?" I felt like saying, but I simply replied, "I'm aching a little."

"Good," he said. "You'll need to get on top of things, because I'm thinking of using you in my new ballet *Adolescence.* You're going to dance the principal role with Olga."

No! Please, not with Olga . . . Why not with Katiuska or Marinelvis or any other girl? But not Olga, no . . .

"Perfect!" I said.

"Well, get to work!"

It was my last chance. "I'd prefer it wasn't with Olga. . . ." I wanted to say.

"I'll do my very best," I promised him, hardly able to move without pain.

Juan Carlos's brilliant idea made my life hell. No sooner did my hands come into contact with Olga's skin than I became clumsy and uncoordinated. She would whisper "Relax, relax!" into my ear, but that only made things worse.

Even the teacher started to notice something strange was going on, as it was taking me much longer than usual to pick up the choreography. But the torment did not stop there. She brought all her girlfriends to see me looking like a pathetic idiot, with my hair soaked in brilliantine, stammering and tripping over my own feet. They laughed. Juan Carlos frowned, and Olga teased me, "Relax, relax!" playing with my emotions like a juggler at the circus.

Humiliated, I asked my heart, Do you want them to embarrass you? Is it worth feeling like this for someone who doesn't deserve it? But my imbecile heart replied that it was crazy about her, and I had no other option but to obey it.

One day Olga asked me what the time was, and then said, "Oh, but you don't have a watch!"

"Yes, I do. I do have a watch," I blurted out immediately. "It's just that I'm not wearing it."

She gave me a skeptical look and walked away. I didn't see her again for the rest of the day. That evening I found her with Eduardo in the television area. They were necking. Olga was draped around Eduardo, but she was looking straight at me, as if I were the one she was seducing. I played along, standing there, like a fool, watching it all. Her gaze moved toward Eduardo's wrist. The bastard was wearing a watch.

Suddenly all my hopes were pinned on that watch, as if it alone held the answer to my failure. I spent the night wide awake, obsessed. Whenever I was on the point of nodding off, the image of Eduardo's watch would float into my mind. And so it went on, all night, until early morning broke with a cold wind blowing, and the crickets began to sing outside.

I climbed down from my bunk bed and tiptoed to the other end of the dorm, where Eduardo lay sleeping. The trophy I sought was on his wrist. I hesitated, certain the thump of my heartbeat would betray me, then, breathing deeply, slid my hand carefully over Eduardo's. I had managed to loosen the watch strap when Eduardo snuffled and rolled over. My heart accelerated again. I froze, watching him. The wind pawed at the walls and sneaked in through the windows of the hostel, bringing with it a rush of cold air. Eduardo covered himself with the blanket, but the hand with the watch remained outside.

It was now or never. Sweat trickled down my face, and my hands were damp. I knew I should go back to bed and forget about the whole thing, but, instead, I started to slip the watch slowly off his wrist, until I had it in my hand.

Then, suddenly, Eduardo stirred and, still half asleep, leaped up, yelling, "Stop, stop!"

I fled, and he chased me, shouting, "Luis Alberto! I'll catch you, Luis Alberto!" I had barely had time to register the fact that he had my name wrong—was he still dreaming? Did he not recognize me?—when he cornered me. I faced him, grabbed him around the neck, and hissed, "Look, here's your watch! If anyone finds out about this, you're dead. Understand?"

Eduardo put his watch back on his wrist and walked away without saying a word. He did not get upset or try to force a struggle; he simply went back to bed. I tried to convince myself that he had slept through the whole episode. After all, he had not put up a fight, and he had called me Luis Alberto. Maybe he would not remember anything.

Three hours later the reveille sounded. I rose, feeling very nervous, and went to the bathroom to wash. There seemed to be a certain amount of intrigue on people's faces, and my guilty conscience told me they all already knew what I had done. My face must have looked pale and drawn. My friends Rogelio, Julio, and Ariel came over and asked me if I was ill, worried my fever might have returned. I told them I was fine, flashing a slightly wobbly smile. On the way back to my bed, I bumped into Eduardo. My heart skipped a beat, but I looked him in the eye with defiance, intimidating him as much as I could with my expression. He continued on his way to the bathroom, and Omar followed him. That was not a good sign. Omar and Eduardo studied drumming in the same group. They were one year younger than me, and Eduardo was smaller than me, but Omar was sturdy and almost six feet tall, with shoulders and arms made of steel. We had been in a fight together just after I enrolled at the school. It had been like a boxing match, with everybody gathering around trying to get a better view. Omar, furious, chased me, trying to punch me as I ducked and dived, surrounded by a whooping and whistling audience. Eventually, Omar landed a knockout punch that left me with an unwelcome souvenir: the gray tooth he gave me was the first thing I saw in the mirror every morning.

I hurried down to breakfast. I did not want to run into Eduardo and Omar in the dining room, so I took my milk and bread and butter and silently slipped out through the back door. I sat on the school wall to watch the morning light spread over the horizon. I could not stop thinking about the desperate situation I had landed myself in. How could anyone be so stupid as to steal a wristwatch from a classmate? Only someone who was sick in the head would think of such a thing.

As I stared moodily into the distance, a blackbird landed in front of me. It scratched itself with one of its feet, then it put its black head between its wings and fixed me with an accusatory eye. My head was full of paranoid thoughts: Everybody knows, they're laughing because they know, they're talking because they know, and they're breathing because they know. I'm sure of it. . . . The bird settled it for me: it had come to find me and to confirm my guilt.

When the bell rang, the blackbird flew up to make itself comfortable on a corner of the roof. Reluctantly, I tore my eyes away from it and hurried to morning assembly.

My classmates were acting as though nothing much was going on. Rogelio came over and told me the latest joke.

"Hey, mate, listen to this. A woman was breast-feeding her child, when suddenly a drunk approached her and said, 'Excuse me, madam. You're not going to believe this, but your infant has invited me to dine!'"

I could not help laughing. Rogelio went around the room, repeating the joke to everyone. The auditorium seemed to relax with laughter.

Nothing happened. I told myself that Eduardo must have been

intimidated when I grabbed him around the neck and that he had not told anyone because he was afraid.

Morning assembly ended and we seventh-grade students were all heading toward our classrooms, when one of the teachers stopped us and made us go back. The principal asked for the microphone.

"Attention, attention! Today in the early hours of the morning a very serious incident occurred. . . ."

Oh no!

"One of our students, Carlos Junior, tried to steal his classmate's wristwatch. Carlos Junior, come up here!"

Three hundred students and fifteen teachers all turned to look at the figure walking toward the stairs at the front of the room, his head sunk into his chest, his heavy steps seeming to thud upon the concrete floor. When he reached the final step, the principal said, "I want you to promise your school that you will never steal from your classmates again."

An echoing silence filled my ears. I could not hear the words that came out of my mouth. The only thing I heard was the voice of my heart telling me: "I should have followed your advice. I should have listened to you. Forgive me, forgive me!"

My heart kept weeping and groaning, but my eyes were bone dry. I stood there, alone, humiliated, with no chance to explain why I had done what I had done. Three hundred students, fifteen teachers, a boy called Eduardo, a girl with slanting eyes, even a blackbird up there on the corner of the roof were all laughing at me.

My family never visited me, post was erratic, and we had no telephone at home, so my teachers never found a way of informing my parents about the stolen watch. I obviously was not going to tell them, and so they never found out. They knew I had passed the end-of-year exams only when I turned up at home with the marks in my hand.

"That's more like it. Keep on like that" was all my father said.

My sisters, who were almost women by now, made fun of the hair that had sprouted under my arms.

"That's enough, leave him alone," my mother warned. She alone smothered me with kisses and told me she had missed me.

I spent the holidays frequenting the places where I had grown up: the pool in La Finca, where I had learned to swim; the "Aereo-Cid" sports arena, where I had escaped to play soccer. Occasionally I would play Eat Mud with Pedro Julio, but Opito and his gang would always appear and ruin the day for me. However, even their bullying could not alter the fact that I felt completely settled at home again, with my sisters and my parents by my side. I had missed them all so much, and I dreaded the day when I would have to leave them all once more and head back to the lonely wall outside the Vocational Arts School.

The school year of 1987–1988 began. I was fourteen years old, and my body was starting to experience new sensations. When my hands touched the bodies of my female classmates during our repertoire classes, I would get an erection and would have to ask immediate permission to go to the lavatory and wait until things had subsided. Even more embarrassing, the same thing happened with my female teachers. My body had gone mad. Every time I looked at a girl, I wanted to undress her. I started to fool around with Bedelia, a black student flautist who had a sturdy body and large buttocks that I squeezed tightly on the nights when we secreted ourselves in the dark hallways around the school buildings. Another girl, Ademili, had taken to winking at me. She was a violin student, a beautiful mixed-race girl, who I also took to hiding myself with whenever time allowed. But I still continued thinking about Olga.

I was a teenager, and I wanted more than anything to be admired, to fit in, but I was increasingly aware that all my schoolmates had more money and better clothes than I did. What could I do? Despite my public humiliation after being caught the previous year, I started stealing again, taking money from my classmates to buy myself new clothes. Before I realized it, I had become addicted to stealing. I would get up at four in the morning and move like a sleepwalker down the dorm, emptying lockers. Sometimes Rogelio, my great friend from Mantua, and Jesús, from Guanes, would ask me to rouse them, too, and we would steal as a team: food, money, whatever booty turned up, which we would share afterward.

"Guys, I've lost my blue shorts." "Has anyone seen my trousers?"

I would hear my classmates remark, but I continued to act as though it had nothing to do with me, even though I felt as if the eyes of suspicion were always on me. Half of me wanted to shout, "Here it is; it was me! Forgive me! Forgive me!" but I did not have the courage to do so. I was a coward, caught in the grip of my compulsion.

Ironically, I was seen as a good student. My academic marks were relatively high, and in ballet I was always one of the top three in our class of fourteen boys. When we performed, I nearly always danced the principal roles, and my teachers were pleased and congratulated me after each show. They had no idea I was a dirty, immoral coward. I was filled with self-loathing and became increasingly withdrawn. There was no one for me to confide in, no friend to give me advice, and my beloved mother, the only person in the world I trusted, was far away. Sometimes I was tempted to seek help from my half brother Pedro, but I knew he would be sure to tell my father.

Wednesday evenings were the worst. The other parents would visit their children and bring them treats, and they would all gather together in little groups around the school. I could not bear to see my friends with their families when I felt so alone, and I would escape to the few places that were far enough away to be deserted so that I could wallow in self-pity. Why could not my life be the same as everyone else's?

Then the weekends would come around to remind me even more forcefully just how alone I was. The cockroaches at Pedro's house became my friends; they and I had much in common: everyone detested us and wanted to humiliate us, or so I thought. One day I woke up with Pedro's mother, María, shouting at me in a fury for sleeping too much, and, for one weirdly confused moment, I could not remember if I was a human being or a cockroach.

I continued stealing, taking refuge in vice, living the life worthy of a wretched scurrying insect. On Wednesdays I took to stealing the snacks my classmates' parents brought them, until one day, some boys went through my locker and found a vest belonging to a student of the visual arts. I was taken to the principal's office again. A committee of teachers was convened to study my case and decide what to do with me. Some members of the staff suggested expelling me. They compared me to previous "difficult" students, such as Juan de Marcos, another boy from Havana, who for money would eat lizards or put his head in a toilet full of shit. They also spoke of teachers from Havana who had been discovered having sex with students. Habaneros, according to these staff members, were unruly and undisciplined, and a bad influence on the school and the province. Carlos Junior was no exception.

Juan Carlos and Magda Campos, the head of ballet, spoke in my defense. They pointed out that I was a good dancer and was likely to pass the graduation exams at the end of the year.

I was dragged in to witness the debate, thinking that if my father were ever to find out, he would surely kill me. I did not particularly care. Maybe cockroaches deserved to be exterminated.

It was eventually decided that I would receive a conditional suspension, which meant that one more incident or the slightest hint of misbehavior would be enough to get me expelled from the school. Listening to the teachers decide my fate, I wondered, how could I explain to them that every day was a struggle between ambition and apathy, between my desire to succeed and the terrible loneliness that surrounded me and threatened to overwhelm me?

Nevertheless, I resolved to do my best and had almost made it to the end of the year without incident when the school had a soccer match between the dancers and the musicians. I was having a great time when, toward the end of the game, Ariel Baños passed the ball to me from the extreme right-hand side and ran toward the center of the goal. I kicked it high to another guy in my class, William, who headed it, diving forward like a bolting bull. Ariel hammered the ball home with his right foot to score the winning goal.

The musicians stood there with a bitter taste in their mouths, cursing the Blessed Virgin and all the Saints, while we whooped for joy. A chorus of girls joined us in our celebrations. We took advantage of our fleeting moment of fame to hug them and shower them with kisses. All at once, we heard an angry voice.

"Get over here now!"

Juan Carlos was shouting at us. We all put on our shirts and went over to him immediately.

"What are you all doing playing soccer just two weeks away from your grade-pass exam? Don't you know that it's a decisive moment in your careers, the one that will turn you into professionals? Go on, get out of here before I have to go and talk to the principal!" Juan Carlos scolded us.

We turned on our heels to escape up the stairs.

"Not you, Junior, come back!"

This was it, then. I stood in front of him, fully expecting to be told this was the end of my ballet career.

"Are you crazy, boy? Don't you know what *conditional suspension* means?"

"But we were playing in our free time, sir!"

"Don't you see you can't afford to do anything that attracts attention, because if you put the slightest foot wrong, they'll expel you and you won't be allowed to graduate?"

"I'm sorry, sir." I hung my head.

"Look, Junior, I know it hasn't been easy for you," he said. "But I have to get tough with you because I know that you're going to make the grade, and that you have a promising future ahead of you. I'm certain of it."

I clung to those words of encouragement; though as the day of the grade-pass exam approached, I grew more and more nervous. The exam would be in Havana, at L and 19, the school where I had begun to study ballet, and which had later expelled me. Would they still look at me as if I were poisonous? Would they still call me "the disaster"?

Two very long years had passed since my so-called transfer. My neck, legs, and arms had all stretched out, and my voice was beginning to deepen and resemble that of my father. Maybe they would not recognize me, I thought hopefully, as we arrived for the all-important class that would decide whether we graduated to upper intermediate level and moved up to the National School of the Arts for our final years of study.

The room was filled with teachers from all the provinces, twenty-five at least, as well as one or two personalities from the Cuban National Ballet. My former teachers were there as well: Silvia, Marielena Del Frades, María Dolores the pianist. Nancy had come, too. Only Lupe Calzadilla was missing. The central place was reserved for a dark-haired woman with two long braids that she twisted around and around. I thought she must be someone quite important because everyone was treating her with the utmost respect and attention. Her blue eyes were full of mystery, like those of a gypsy fortune-teller.

At the order from Juan Carlos, we fourteen boys filed into the room to take up our positions at the barre, the same barre at which five years ago I had learned my first ballet steps. I looked around me. There was still that mark on the wall, the half-broken mirror, the rough pine floor. Everything was exactly as I had left it, and I could almost hear Lupe's voice as she prodded my buttocks and told me to clench them. My eyes focused on the teachers, and there she was, sitting in a corner, next to the mirror. Lupe had come to see me! I was suddenly overwhelmed by a great desire to dance, to show them what I had learned in my two years away.

One hour after the class had finished, Juan Carlos arrived with the news. Ten of us had passed, a record never before achieved. We shouted and celebrated, lifting Juan Carlos up high and carrying him out into the corridor on our shoulders, but we plonked him down as soon as the other teachers began to filter out of the room. Extraordinarily, many of them stopped to congratulate me. Nancy and Lupe hugged me tightly, and then María Dolores came over. "Look what I've got for you," she said, and she gave me a little packet with ten pieces of chewing gum.

Then, in the midst of the celebrations, I heard the principal of L and 19, the same woman who had "transferred" me, saying: "That boy, what's he called . . . Carlos Junior, he really shows promise."

My face stretched into a broad smile as I watched the teachers disappearing down the stairs. The woman with the braids momentarily fixed her piercing blue eyes on me and winked, and then, in her place, my mother appeared, coming up the stairs, just as she had on the day I had come here for my first audition.

At the sight of her face, emotion overcame me, and I finally burst into tears in my favorite place, that little piece of my mother's chest she reserved especially for me. I had been dragging those tears around with me like a sack of stones, and now that my mother was there at last, the weight of the stones ripped the sack and they all tumbled out. I cried inconsolably, my sobbing heavier and louder with each caress, with each breath, with each memory—the benches in the bus station at Santa Clara, Pedro's leaky house with its cracks and cockroaches, my love for Olga, my loneliness, my stealing—and tears soaked my face.

Trying to comfort me, my mother repeated what Lupe had said to her on the stairs as they passed each other. I had obtained the highest possible score in the exam, something only a few people in the history of ballet in Cuba had ever achieved. I wept even louder. My weeping was contagious: it infected my mother as well as my sisters, who were waiting for us by the exit. Together we all cried, as if by doing so we might wring out the cloth of our suffering.

My father did not cry. He stood to one side, his face unmoving. After all, he probably thought you cannot go crying just anywhere—and while I had my mother's chest to cry on, my father had nowhere to lay his head. His expression gave no indication of whether he was proud of me or indifferent, or whether he merely thought that there is a time and a place for these things, as there is for birth and death and all the other elements that make up life.

PART TWO

1989−1993

Chapter 9

TAKE OFF

It is amazing just how much can happen in one day. One Friday morning in 1989 dawned with a thick, murky enveloping fog, which lifted as the smell of dew began to filter through the bars of the window and the first ray of sunlight touched our sleeping faces in the dormitory at the National School of the Arts (NSA), where I was now studying after graduating from the school in Pinar del Río.

Cuca, the caretaker, opened the dormitory door and announced that everything was ready. My friend Ariel Serrano and I had been chosen by one of the teachers, Ramona de Sáa, whom we called "Chery," to take part in a yearlong cultural exchange with the company Teatro Nuovo di Torino, in Italy. We were flying out that evening. The only things missing were our visas, but Cuca had been assured there was a 95 percent chance that we would have them before noon. The other boys in our group tipped us out of bed to congratulate us. They thumped us with pillows, jostled us, and carried us around on their shoulders, their faces beaming with joy as if they themselves were the ones who would be traveling. In high spirits, we all went down to breakfast together.

The NSA was in Miramar, the most luxurious of the residential districts of Havana, where all the embassies are located, in houses that once belonged to the wealthy. We went to classes in a two-story building that must have been the home of a millionaire in the 1940s. The ceilings and floors were in perfect condition, and I sensed that its former owners had been happy there. I could envisage them drinking their coffee in those vast sunlit rooms, never imagining that one day the space would be turned into classrooms containing rows of desks and books, chalk and erasers, and with green blackboards fixed to the walls.

The house was four blocks from the sea and was surrounded by mango and star-apple trees, hibiscus bushes, malangas, and tropical ferns, whose lush dark foliage contrasted sharply with the bright white granite floor of the entrance. I had chosen to board at the NSA because my home was far from the school, and I did not want to have to go through the daily struggle with the buses. I studied and lived for three years in that house.

The school's ballet headquarters were in the grand García Lorca Theatre of Havana, a magnificent, Renaissance-style building about a twenty-kilometer bus ride from the boarding school. We practiced on the second floor, in rooms with slippery, rough floors that destroyed our dance shoes in seconds. We used to have to mend them with sticking plaster so that they would last a month. When we performed, the school would give us a pair of shoes in good condition, which we then had to return as soon as the show was over.

We shared the space with the Spanish Dance Company and other artistic associations. The rooms were divided by thin walls, which did not completely block out the sounds from the adjoining studios. It was like a madhouse. In one studio, the incessant stamping of heels with guitar and hand claps; in another, the tinkling of a piano, accompanied by the tapping of *pointe* shoes and the thud of jumps landing, which shook the fragile partitions; a little farther down the hall, there might be a tape recorder playing Minkus and Drigo at full volume, and a teacher shouting "Stretch those legs, stretch those legs!" You had to force yourself to distinguish which sound out of so many was the one that corresponded to your work.

We also had to battle with a lackluster, inconsistent diet and insufficient drinking water—the ballet school at that time did not receive much support—but in spite of this, morale was high, and most of the dancers who trained in that school went on to enjoy international prestige. There was no gymnasium, no linoleum, no air-conditioning, and a dance belt was a medical device designed for those with prostate problems. We took cold showers and often had no toilet paper. These days, the National Ballet School has what it deserves: its own headquarters in a magnificent colonial building situated in the heart of Havana, with conditions as good as those in developed countries. I hope the present-day dancers appreciate what they have. On the other hand, maybe those shortages gave us earlier students the impetus we needed.

That particular Friday, we were in the middle of the Cuballet Season—a rare opportunity for foreign and Cuban dancers to mingle in classes and perform together—and some of the stars of the Cuban National Ballet could sometimes be spotted about the place. I had finished my morning class and was on my way to the changing rooms when I bumped into none other than Alberto Terrero, the dancer who had first inspired me as a student at Pinar del Río. He passed me by in the vast marble corridor without noticing that I had become rooted to the spot like a statue. I stared after him as he disappeared into one of the studios. I had been waiting for this moment for such a long time, I could not let him vanish. I breathed deeply to calm myself down and approached the studio door. Terrero was lying on the floor, stretching before beginning his rehearsals.

"Hi, I'm called Junior," I introduced myself nervously.

"Hi," he answered back, with little interest.

"You don't know me but . . . I am . . . well, the thing is, I want to be like you," I stuttered.

Terrero stopped what he was doing and stared at me. "What?" he said.

"It's just that, since the first time I saw you dance, I've thought of nothing else but getting to be like you," I said.

He stared at me for a few seconds longer, apparently thinking about what he had just heard, then he let out a laugh. "Hey, Domingo, get over here, listen to what this kid's saying," he called to another dancer. "Go on, repeat it!" he told me.

I said the same thing again, and they laughed even more. Terrero got up, came over, and gave me a couple of friendly slaps on the back, then went back to his stretching exercises. Slightly confused by the exchange, I turned and went out into the corridor.

That afternoon, as the sky became overcast with gray and threatening clouds, one of my classmates, Lusito, had the idea of breaking into the garden of the house on the corner to steal mangos from the foreigner who lived there. The other boys in the group followed him, clambering over the barbed wire on top of the wall. I stayed on the other side of the fence—those days even the thought of stealing gave me goose bumps.

"Hey, Junior, Junior, climb over, don't be an idiot!" Julio and Ariel shouted to me from over the wall. I had a terrible feeling that something bad was about to happen. The dark clouds above me were looking more and more ominous.

"Get out of there, you lot; they're going to catch us. Ariel, remember we're going to Italy today!" I called.

"Nothing's going to happen!" he called back, shaking the upper branches of a mango tree as hard as he could.

I watched from as far away as possible.

"Junior, man, come and help us collect the fruit and stop being so stupid. Nobody's coming!"

I walked toward the wall, trembling as I remembered that day on the steps in Pinar del Río when I was exposed as a thief. In the muggy air, I could almost smell the scent of those early mornings when I used to get out of bed and try my luck with my classmates' cash boxes. I was swamped with a familiar feeling of guilt, and my heart began to beat like galloping horses, until I could no longer hear the voices of my companions floating to me on the humid breeze.

All at once, two boys shot over the barbed wire at lightning speed, like ninjas.

"Hey, where are you going?" I shouted, as two more boys almost knocked me over.

"Shit, what's happening?"

Nobody answered. They kept on throwing themselves over that three-meter-high wall, grabbing hold of the barbed wire as though it were made of plasticine.

"Run, Junior, run!" someone shouted, but it was already too late.

The policeman seized hold of me and Ariel, who had also fallen behind and was hanging from the mango tree. Clearly relishing the chance to exercise his power over two students from the National School of the Arts, the officer interrogated us, yanking our arms and shaking us as though we were criminals. Ariel and I answered respectfully, partly because the police officer was taking everything very seriously, but also because we did not want anything to stop our flying to Italy that night. He kept on twisting our arms with his enormous hands as he led us toward the school.

"Look at the bruises you're giving me, sir!" I shouted in pain, but the policeman showed no mercy, as if he wanted to prove to us that we were no different from any other thieving scum.

Despite his efforts, we got off lightly, with only a severe reprimand from the school's principal, Marta Ulloa. Much worse, however, was the news that our Italian visas still had not arrived and that, as a result, the trip would have to be postponed. Ariel and I looked at each other in frustration. We had nearly everything we needed to travel—passports, exit permits, tickets—and we had been dreaming about the trip for months, wishing this day would come, but it had arrived *without* our visas.

It seemed it was going to be just another ordinary day.

Little did I suspect then that it would be one of the luckiest days of my life.

"If something bad happens, it's always for a good reason!" my father said. Our eyes were glued to the television set, my heart almost leaping out of my chest. The newsreel showed policemen stopping traffic, firefighters clambering through burned-out houses and pulling out incinerated corpses. They were doing a good job, given that there were television cameras all around broadcasting the accident live.

"I told you so, I told you so!" my father crowed. It was later that Friday night, I was home for the weekend and watching in horror as the newscaster reported the accident. Behind me, my father was leaping excitedly around the room, repeating his favorite saying: "If something bad happens, it's always for a good reason. Never forget that!" I barely noticed as he performed a cleansing ritual around me, waving an egg over my head and whacking my arms and neck with a bunch of basil leaves. He gave the saints offerings of glasses of water, fruit, and sweets, while all the time jumping up and down.

The afternoon's storm had become a cyclone, with winds over a hundred miles an hour, and the airport control tower had ordered the pilot of the plane not to take off. The pilot took no notice of the warning and the airplane had crashed into the houses next to the airport. One hundred and sixty people were dead.

The flight had been bound for Italy.

———

"Ballet: countless hours of trying to adapt your body to all those anti-anatomical movements. Severe injuries, operations; the body can't take it and starts to wear out; a fractured tibia that stops you from jumping; a slipped disc; ankles that won't support you anymore . . . Then, just when you seem to be getting back on track, the company gets a new director who decides your time has passed and your services aren't needed anymore. After all those years of sweating your guts out in the studios, creating ties within the company and with the city, destroying your knees, your ankles, and your back, giving your best . . . And you're already thirty-five years old; it's too late to start somewhere else. . . . Some spend their time remembering better days, when they were the pride of the company; others are filled with vitriol and bile as they keep chasing the ghosts of the past. . . ."

It was a week later. Our visas had come through, and we were in Italy. Our teacher, Chery, stopped her lecture to give instructions to the chauffeur who had collected us from Milan Malpensa Airport. The driver continued down the wet motorway at terrifying speed as our teacher resumed her lecture.

"As you can see, boys, I am only too well aware of the difficulties of this career. But there is another aspect on which you should both concentrate: you are fortunate enough to be among the few who are chosen in this world of fantasy, lights, color, music, and dance. Imagine what rewards await you when you are professionals, how many people will applaud the sacrifice of all those hours of work, the countries you will visit, the hearts you will touch, all the people to whom your art will bring happiness. Only a very few are lucky enough to experience that. Now, however, you have to work."

We listened in silence. Then Ariel said, "But, miss, doing the splits is really difficult; every time I try, I think I'm going to rupture a tendon. And all those steps that Baryshnikov does in the videos, how are you supposed to learn them?"

"Don't you think that he also thought them impossible when he was your age?" Chery said. "But you must persevere. The trouble with you is that you're a bit lazy!"

I began to laugh, and my mirth infected Ariel; then Chery could not help smiling, too. We spent the rest of the two-hour journey to Turin pointing out all the strange things we could see from the car window:

the rolling fields; the peculiar soft green trees, so different from the vegetation in the Cuban countryside; the powerful motorbikes and luxurious cars; the empty buses; the cafés and bars. Everything was new and
exciting.

The chauffeur finally drew up in Corso Moncalieri, in front of an
ice-cream parlor. A heavyset man with a beer belly was waiting for us,
along with a tall, thin woman wearing glasses and an unfashionable
dress, and a teenage girl with chestnut eyes and cheeks as red as apples.

We got out of the car and the man shook our hands.

"Bla, blablibla, bla," he said.

We looked to our teacher for help.

"This is Signor Mesturino, the director of the theater; he is welcoming you," Chery explained.

The woman gave us each a formal hug, while the man kissed Chery
on both cheeks.

The girl had not taken her eyes off me. I noticed that the red of her
cheeks had spread to the rest of her face.

"Hi, I'm Irene," she introduced herself.

"Can you speak Spanish?" I asked.

"Blablabli, bla."

"Ariel, what's she saying? Help me out here, bro!" I looked to my
friend in desperation, but he was as lost as I was.

We took our suitcases and followed the man through a big wooden
doorway and went up three floors to arrive at what would be our apartment for quite some time.

The olive-skinned teacher who opened the door introduced herself
as Nancy. Ariel and I introduced ourselves, each giving her a couple of
kisses on the cheek. She led us across a tiny lounge to a small bedroom
that had only two single beds. Ariel and I exchanged glances. How
were we all going to fit in here? Even Chery seemed perplexed.

"Don't worry, I'll sleep in the kitchen," I volunteered halfheartedly.
I had had plenty of experience with sleeping in strange places, but this
kitchen was barely a couple of meters long, with a refrigerator on one
side that took up half the space and an unappealing lino floor covered
in grease.

"No, no, look! The sofa in the lounge folds out," Nancy explained.
She went into the kitchen and took two little sealed boxes out of the

fridge and gave one each to Ariel and me. We sat down in the living room, trying to work out how to get the cartons open. In Cuba, juice came in bottles.

"How's the company?" Chery asked Nancy.

"Working hard, staging *Carmen.*"

"And Luciana, did she arrive yet?"

"Yes, she got here on Wednesday. I think she's already started rehearsing the *pas de deux* with Marco Pierin."

Those damned boxes would not open. We bit them; we dropped them on the floor, but still nothing happened. Chery and Nancy chatted on, oblivious.

"Are they finally going to hold auditions?" Chery was asking.

"At the end of the month, I think. We need more men. What are the ones from the academy like?"

"These two boys show promise, but they still need work."

Deeply engrossed, they had not noticed us thumping away at the juice boxes until Ariel got up, went to the kitchen, and returned with an enormous knife that he used to hack at the carton.

Nancy looked at him, horrified.

"What do you think you're doing, kid? Use the straw!"

"What straw?"

"The one on the side of the carton!"

Too late. The carton exploded like a cannon and spattered the drink all over the sofa.

"Oh, fuck it!" cried Ariel, desperately trying to suck up the little juice that remained. Sheepishly, I inserted my straw into the small foil-covered opening and took a sip of my juice. I nearly dropped my carton in surprise; I had never tasted pear before. Ariel slurped at his straw, trying to suck up every last drop.

"Don't feel bad; we've all done the same," said Chery, and she told us stories of other dancers during their first trips abroad, which made us feel a little less embarrassed.

The next day, Nancy and Chery got up early to go shopping, promising to cook us the most fantastic rice we had ever tasted when they returned. Ariel and I decided to do our share by giving the house a good cleaning. Since Nancy had given us instructions on how to operate a strange contraption called a vacuum cleaner, we started going over the carpets with it. We washed up all the cutlery and the plates and glasses, and even managed to get the sticky grease off the linoleum. The only task remaining was to clean the bathroom.

"Bro, what are we going to clean it with? There's no scouring brush," I said.

Ariel shrugged his shoulders and looked around. He spotted a tall brush by the side of the toilet.

"This must be an Italian scouring brush," he said doubtfully. I had never seen anything like it, so I shrugged and set to, pleased at the thought that Nancy would return to a sparkling clean apartment.

Toilet brush in hand, we scrubbed the bathtub, the hand basin, even the mirror, happily spreading shit everywhere as we danced salsa to the rhythm of a Los Van Van cassette that Ariel had put in the tape recorder.

When the teachers returned, they stood in the doorway sniffing.

"What's that *smell*? Have you flushed the lavatory?"

Because we had been "cleaning" and were used to the smell, Ariel and I did not understand. The teachers' noses led them to the scene of the crime.

"What were you thinking?" they cried, and we had to clean everything again, this time with strong bleach.

Our first Monday in Italy, we woke up to a gray morning and a cold, strong wind that blew the leaves off the trees. Chery put on a multicolored worsted coat and leather boots. We put on raincoats and the tennis shoes we had bought in the "international" shop in Havana and crossed the street to catch the 67 bus to the Teatro Nuovo. It was freezing cold, so Ariel and I huddled inside the bus shelter while Chery waited on the pavement, pacing up and down impatiently, twiddling the two little locks of hair that fell in front of her ears. When a car crawled along beside her, she thought it was a taxi and signaled to it.

"Come on, boys!" she called, opening the door to get into the front seat. But when the driver saw us emerge from the glass shelter, he revved the car and shot off down the street, leaving us openmouthed on the pavement.

"Oh no! That imbecile mistook me for . . . how dare he!" exclaimed Chery. "Am I wearing too much makeup?" She took a mirror out of her bag and began to rub at the color on her cheeks.

Ariel and I did not have the slightest idea what was going on, but in time we came to realize that we had been standing in a red-light area. From early in the morning, women and transvestites paraded the whole length of the street, touting for business. From then on Chery always asked us to check whether she was wearing too much blush before we left the apartment, and she begged us not to say anything to her husband, Santiago, when he arrived from Cuba.

Everything in Italy was different, and I saw it as though through the eyes of a child. My sixteen years' experience of life was nothing here. It was a new world, immense and overwhelming, and it made me anxious. I had to remind myself constantly that I must represent my school with dignity and not embarrass myself over the course of the yearlong cultural exchange. Out of all the candidates, Ariel and I had been selected, and we must not betray the confidence that had been placed in us. When I was growing up, I had never imagined I would leave my small country village of Los Pinos; I had certainly never dreamed of leaving Cuba. Incredibly, I was now in Italy, and everyone was welcoming and friendly.

I was also getting to work with one of Italy's most respected and well-appointed companies. The Teatro Nuovo had a dance corps of barely fifteen people, but it had at its disposal a modern theater, more than five studios, and even its own dancing school. The repertoire was varied, covering both classical and contemporary pieces, including some of the memorable works of Balanchine. The company toured both nationally and internationally, and its stars were famous in the Italian dance world.

When we finally arrived at the studios on our first day, Chery indicated to us where we should go to get changed before disappearing into her dressing room. On the way to the changing rooms we encountered a group of slender girls about our age, apparently from the school. They all stopped when they saw us. Ariel gave me a mischievous look and strolled over to them.

"Hi, we're lost," he said. "Can you tell us where the changing rooms are?"

One of the girls pointed down the hall.

"Are you sure you don't want to come with me?" Ariel asked, and they all started to laugh, at which point we realized that they understood Spanish.

Ariel's a real danger, I thought admiringly, watching him throw out lines and reel the girls in with his Cuban wiles. The son of a bitch was a master in the art of seduction, and I didn't know how he did it.

"Ariel, hurry up, we'll be late for class," I said.

I noticed that one of the girls had separated from the giggling group. She had dark brown hair, pale skin, and thin lips. Her eyes were accentuated by eyebrows as thick as a man's, and she was looking at me mysteriously.

"Hi, my name's Mela," she said. "You're Carlos, aren't you?"

"How did you know?"

"Chery showed us your photo a while ago."

"Let's go, Junior, the class starts in five minutes," Ariel called.

"It's been a pleasure to meet you," I said to Mela, kissing her on the cheek.

She looked at me, and her eyes seemed to sparkle. "No," she said, "the pleasure has been all mine."

In a rectangular studio with uneven floors and huge, wide mirrors that reflected the depth of the room, ten women, most of them attractive, and five men, most of them short, were preparing for class. When we arrived, they froze and looked at us as if they were scientists in the middle of an experiment, analyzing our anatomy, our clothes, the way we had fixed our hair. We walked toward the barre. A tall, thin gentleman came in with Chery and clapped his hands loudly a couple of times to get the company's attention. Then he uttered a few brief incomprehensible words, and everybody turned toward us and started to applaud. Ariel flashed his white teeth to the whole room. I grinned lopsidedly, unwilling to show the gray tooth that Omar had given me and the wide gap between my two front teeth. They continued applauding.

While Chery positioned herself at the barre to mark out the first exercise of the class, my eyes traveled around the room, then stopped. There was a woman standing in a corner close to the piano, wearing a black skirt and a brown leotard. She had light brown hair with blond bangs that accentuated her features. Her body was curvy, her skin silky, radiant, marvelous. Our eyes met. I felt myself blushing and could no longer resist the temptation to smile. My grin shone out, gleaming like a Cuban sunrise.

Oh hell! My heart was ready to embark on a new adventure!

At sixteen all I knew about love was that it was a constant irritation, like a pebble stuck in your shoe. Olga had left me full of doubt, convinced that dishonesty was something instinctive in women. But it was not to be like that with Narina.

At first she rejected my advances. I tried everything I could think of to seduce her—I offered to show her how to dance salsa and speak Spanish, which were the only things I could teach her, but Narina was twenty-three, seven years older than me, and she thought it might harm her image for us to be seen together. On many occasions, I had to swallow my pride and endure her cool rebuffs and the interminable stretches of silence. Then, one month after my arrival in Italy, during the company's first national tour with the new production of *Carmen,* in the town of Bergamo, I achieved what I desired.

I had been rehearsing with Chery and the choreographer when a break was called and Narina led me out into the corridor, where we could be alone.

"We can see each other, but nobody must know," she whispered.

Overjoyed, I stepped toward her and gave her a passionate kiss, then returned to the stage, euphorically licking away the traces of lipstick her lips had left on mine. The choreographer kept correcting the *relevé* in my pirouettes, but all I could think about was Narina.

The heat of my body melted the snow that covered that small city the night she confessed her love to me.

Sex, once it happens, has its own momentum. Despite our strenuous efforts to keep our relationship hidden, people slowly began to entertain suspicions about us. Ariel was going out with Viviana, Narina's best friend and roommate, so whenever possible I would go and sleep with Narina in their room, and Viviana would stay with Ariel in ours. Inevitably, the next day it would be difficult for us to keep our bodies apart, and they would seek each other out during our ballet work.

When Chery's husband, Santiago, arrived from Cuba, the rest of us let them have the apartment on Corso Moncalieri to themselves. The theater director, Signor Mesturino, housed us in the building opposite, with Nancy on the third floor, and Ariel and me on the first: Ariel with Viviana in one room and Narina with me in the other—all in secret.

After a while, Narina decided that our relationship was becoming too public and that it would be better to finish it. I was just a boy, too young to be able to express to Narina how much she meant to me, but I could not bear the idea of breaking up with her. I spent all my time thinking about what I could do to make her change her mind. I showered her with flowers and presents, and during the nights I stretched my imagination to the limits to keep her satisfied. But it was no use.

"Tu sei un bambino!" she would say to me. "You're a baby!"

She finished with me in the same way that she had started, a clandestine whisper in that same deserted corridor.

Shortly afterward, the company traveled to Venice. Narina was avoiding me. Every time I tried to talk to her, I got the same answer.

"Tu sei un bambino."

I could not believe I was in Venice, the city of lovers, with nobody to kiss on the Bridge of Sighs or in a gondola, as the romantic surroundings demanded. One sunny day, when we had finished class, I went exploring with Ariel and a group of dancers, including Mela, the girl with the sparkling eyes whom I had met on my first day at the Teatro Nuovo. The streets were heaving with tourists, and the charm of the Venetian traders was boundless. It was as if they had been born to sell, and the tourists were powerless to resist all the Murano glass, miniature gondolas, and other knickknacks.

Our group of ten dancers went to the Lido in a vaporetto. Ariel and Viviana kept kissing. I averted my gaze, staring at the famous tower in St. Mark's Square that loomed like a guillotine above the buildings. I remembered Olga and the time we made love in Pinar del Río and how, half an hour later, I had discovered her kissing Eduardo. I had gone on wanting her even when I knew I was just part of her game, and now it was happening again with Narina. Even though she had hurt me, I could not get her out of my head.

"Carlos, what's the matter? Do you feel ill?" asked Mela.

"It's nothing. Don't worry," I said.

"You broke up with Narina, didn't you?" she said.

That took me by surprise. So our relationship *had* become common knowledge. I stared at the water slapping against the side of the boat, feeling angry and bitter.

"I know someone who would love to be your girlfriend," said Mela, with a shy smile.

"Really? Who?" I asked disinterestedly.

"I can't tell you. It's a secret."

We looked at each other for a long time, until suddenly everything became much clearer. I finally understood the reason her eyes sparkled when she looked at me. I was still hooked on Narina, however, and it was too soon to think about anyone else. I quickly broke our gaze, looking away in confusion.

When we arrived at the island, we went for a walk along the beach. There were flowers everywhere and tall palm trees that reminded me of my country. We even found a salsa club, where Ariel and I burst onto the dance floor with such enthusiasm that all the people dancing there stopped to look at us. Relieved to have found somewhere I could forget my woes, I danced all the familiar routines with Ariel, and we sang along to all the songs, as though we were back in the streets of Havana. Ariel gestured to Viviana to come over and learn the steps, and Mela asked if I would teach her. I showed her the basic salsa step, and she was a quick learner. I taught her more and more difficult combinations throughout the evening, until suddenly I realized that everyone else had gone. Mela must have realized the same thing at the same time, because she threw herself at me, almost suffocating me with a kiss.

"Mela . . . I . . ."

"Yes, I already know, but I couldn't care less," she said.

I squeezed her tight, pressing my pelvis against her, and let myself be carried away by the moment. But when we got back to the hotel, Mela went back to her room, and I went to mine. My first steps in love, with Narina and with Olga, had taught me never to let myself go, never to give myself up completely.

Chery, who by this point had become like a second mother to me, knew what was happening and gave me some space during rehearsals, telling me that I would have better luck in the future. She had some good news for me, too.

"The choreographer has suggested that you prepare for the contest in Lausanne."

At first I thought she was talking about something to do with lasagne. But Chery explained that Lausanne was a city in Switzerland where the most important junior ballet competition in the world took place each year. "Though I'll have to talk to Mesturino about it," she said, telling me not to get my hopes up yet.

That night I could not sleep. Huddled in my small bed, myriad thoughts tumbled through my mind: Was my teacher mad? How could I participate in the most important junior ballet competition in the world? I had taken part in some events in Cuba, in the Camagüey contest and in festivals and parades. I had always danced as well as possible, but without any great sense of expectation. The hope of success still seemed remote to me, too high and unattainable for my imagination to reach. If I did compete, I would have to worry about letting down not just my school but my country as well. It was all hypothetical, and I tried to calm myself down. Mesturino was bound to say no, and I would never get a visa to go to Switzerland.

Back in Turin, the prospect of entering the Lausanne competition receded over time and grew ever more hazy, like the fog that shrouded the city on those winter evenings. Even when Signor Mesturino agreed to cover the cost of the trip, the application forms did not arrive for ages. And then, after the forms had been completed and sent off, the registration documents failed to appear.

I started to prepare myself for the competition; as I did so, Chery followed me more and more closely, correcting my technique in every exercise. She emphasized the positioning of my feet, an elegant posture for walking, turns, jumps. In the afternoons, after rehearsing the company's ever-expanding repertoire, Chery and I would go to the stage to rehearse the variation from *Don Quixote* that I would be taking to the competition. The more I practiced, the more determined I became, and I would end up performing almost all the variations in the classical repertoire until Chery would have to stop me and tell me that it was time to go home.

I knew Turin now. What at first was new and fresh was now familiar. I yearned for Narina, and I yearned for home. There was no way of communicating with my family. They did not have a telephone, and letters took months to arrive, but now I finally had something to distract me from my misery and homesickness. In the evenings at the apartment, I continued doing sit-ups and push-ups as well as exercises to improve my flexibility.

"Hey, bro, take it easy. You're going to go crazy if you keep on working like that," Ariel told me, but I had become addicted to dance. It was my refuge.

By New Year's Eve, I still had not received confirmation that I had been registered in the competition, and I could not help feeling disappointed, even though Chery told me she was sure I would be accepted. At Signor Mesturino's New Year's Eve party, I sat in a corner gazing at the great mountains of food, but not even the music and the fabulous fireworks could cheer me up.

Ariel was dancing with Miriam, Signor Mesturino's eldest daughter; Chery was sitting next to her husband, smiling as if in appreciation of the radiance of youth. Irene, the girl who had blushed on our first day, came over and asked me to teach her to dance salsa. With everyone partying and Irene treading on my toes, I tried to think some positive thoughts: Had I not escaped the plane crash? Was I not in Italy, working with one of the most celebrated Cuban teachers?

The dancing was becoming closer now, more romantic, and I imagined that I was dancing with Narina. Her final words to me rang in my head: "You're a baby. . . ." When the countdown to the New Year started, I took a handful of rice from a bowl on a table, threw it over my left shoulder, and made a wish.

A couple of weeks later, we received the official confirmation of my registration, just one week before the competition. However, there was still another hurdle to jump. Obtaining visas with a Cuban passport has always been a problem, and everyone thought that at such a late stage it would be impossible. With only three days left before the event, I continued to follow my exercise routine until late into the night, telling myself, "If I don't go, it will be destiny's fault, not mine."

The day before the competition, I had all but given up hope. We were all in class when Signor Mesturino appeared in the doorway, the pianist suddenly stopped playing, and a deathly hush fell over the room. He uttered three words: *"Domani si parte."*

My Italian was still limited but the applause and hysterical shouting of everyone present told me what I needed to know: "You leave tomorrow."

One hundred and twenty-seven candidates from more than thirty countries were registered for the competition. My number? 127.

Chapter 10

THE GRAND PRIX DE LAUSANNE

We arrived by train on January 25, 1990, at dusk. Chery could not come with me because of the amount of work she had to do staging new productions for the company. In her place, they sent Raul, a tall, bespectacled man in his forties, whom the theater occasionally hired to perform small duties such as making deliveries or acting as a receptionist or a chauffeur. My trip was the most important assignment he had ever been given.

"You do realize that I speak five languages," he told me at least thirty times during the four-hour journey to Lausanne. He constantly checked on my well-being, as though I were a tiny baby, and every so often, he would dip his hand into his yellow bag and bring out all different kinds of chocolate, insisting: "Ramona says that you need to eat chocolate for energy."

I had never been a fan of chocolate, but I did not want to appear rude, so I ate several bars and therefore arrived in Lausanne with a terrible stomachache and at least ten more zits on my face. Raul kept pressing chocolate on me until I had no alternative but to say to him in a fury: "I don't want any more. Look at my face from eating all this chocolate!"

He only laughed. "Don't worry about it. It'll be fine!"

We arrived at a tiny hotel near the railway station, with Raul dragging his heavy suitcase with his left hand and still clutching the bag of chocolates in his right. My luggage was a small bag that Nancy had lent me, and it contained my ballet shoes, shirts, and dance belts; two or three sweaters and pairs of trousers; and a set of dress clothes in case I needed them. I was also carrying the jacket and tights in which I would perform *Don Quixote* and the outfit for *Tocororo*, the contemporary solo that one of my teachers, Carla Perotti, had arranged especially for this competition. The mass of chocolate in my stomach was making me walk very quickly; I urgently needed to find a toilet.

Raul, however, was taking his time. The receptionist was speaking to him in French, and he was replying in a garbled Italian-French-German combination that was clearly confusing her. I jiggled around impatiently. Raul remarked on the receptionist's red hair, and she rewarded him with a coy smile. The compliments continued. He extolled the beauty of her green eyes. I could not wait any longer.

"Pssst, pssst, Raul, Raul . . . get a move on; I need the toilet," I whispered, trying to be discreet.

"What's that?" he replied, without taking his eyes off the receptionist.

"I'm about to fucking shit myself!" I shouted.

That got his attention.

"Arrivo, arrivo!" he yelled, snatching the keys and racing with me to the lift.

The following day we got in touch with the Cuban Embassy in Switzerland to inform them that I was taking part in the competition. We were hoping for some help navigating the unfamiliar Swiss city, but they treated us as though we were a nuisance and even told us it had been a bad idea to enter me in the event without thinking of the consequences for Cuba should I lose. I could not believe what I was hearing. We rang Chery in dismay, and she contacted the Cuban Embassy in Italy, but apparently they said the same thing to her.

"Never mind, Junior, these things happen," she told me. "In any case, you've got other things to worry about!"

The Palais de Beaulieu, a beautiful modern theater, had been the venue for the Prix de Lausanne since its inception in 1973. The competition consisted of four qualifying rounds that led up to the final. First, there would be a ballet class and then a contemporary dance class, at which only the jury, made up of important figures from the international dance scene, would be present. Next would be the first performance onstage of both solos; then the semifinal, this time with makeup and costume; and, eventually, the final and the awards ceremony, which would be filmed for local television. Everybody would compete against everybody else, with no distinction between the sexes, in a great marathon to win an award—especially the Grand Prix de Lausanne Médaille d'Or, the highest honor awarded only on special occasions when the judges decided there was one particularly talented dancer competing.

Waiting for a bus to take me to the theater on the first day of the competition, I could immediately distinguish the dancers from the other people waiting at the bus stop—their long necks and their upright posture made them stand out. Some of them were looking in my direction, uncertain as to whether I was a dancer, too. In those days I wore my hair in an abundant Afro, thick and round like a microphone. I looked more like an adolescent Michael Jackson impersonator than a ballet dancer.

There were 127 contestants, and many of them were accompanied by their families. I was submerged in a huge swell of different languages, an incessant swarm of voices that made it impossible to think. I was very thankful Raul could speak five languages.

Almost immediately, however, it became clear that Raul had exaggerated his abilities. A blond woman spoke in French to Raul, but he did not seem to understand. She tried again, in German, but Raul kept on shaking his head and saying: *"Italiano, italiano, per favore!"* The woman went to find an Italian speaker, which delayed us for half an hour. Finally, they found a man who spoke Italian and told us about a welcome dinner in a nearby hotel and gave us folders containing the timetable for the qualification rounds, as well as some brief information about the teachers who would give the classes and two labels numbered *127,* which I had to wear hanging from my lapel and on my back.

The next day I made my way to the largest studio, where we were to take an informal ballet class that would help to familiarize us with our competition teacher's methods. The studio was filled with the same chattering and babble of languages that I had encountered upon my arrival.

I surveyed the room. There was a boy, perhaps a little bit younger than me, who had his leg raised up so high that it was almost touching his ear.

My God, how's he able to do that? I wondered, but I tried to maintain my composure, knowing it would not be a good idea to show any signs of weakness. I said hello, and the kid looked me up and down

grumpily, his leg still pressed against his ear. In a corner another young-
ster was practicing pirouettes, at least five on each attempt; someone
else was resting in perfectly executed splits, something that I had never
been able to do.

I began to sweat. What could Chery have been thinking when she
decided to send me to this competition? What would everyone in Italy
and Cuba say if I lost? The famous Cuban ballet dancer Lorena Feijóo
had entered the competition previously—she was a model ballerina, the
winner of the gold medal in the Trujillo contest when she was only fifteen and a prizewinner at several national festivals and events; she had
been recognized by the Cuban government as an exemplary dancer—
but even she had not made it past the semifinal. Amid the swarm of
doubts that buzzed around my head, I struggled to recall what Chery
had told me before my departure.

"In a competition, nobody loses. We always win when we know
how to draw worthwhile conclusions from each moment experienced
and when we have the capacity to learn and then to pass that knowledge on. You always win, even when your results don't exceed your
expectations, so long as you compete with yourself and not with the
person next to you. Sixteen years old means that you've got time on
your side and a lot to learn. The very fact of being there, doing your
best, makes you a winner."

The class was not particularly complicated. The teacher seemed to
be one of those relaxed types, who jokes and inspires confidence, and
he was able to ease the tension. The only unusual thing about the lesson was that he repeated each exercise only once. Afterward I found
out that this was intentional, as each dancer's ability to pick up steps
would also be gauged in the class. He seemed so amiable I went away
thinking the next day's class would be a cinch. When it came, however,
the guy nearly finished us off.

I am not sure whether it was nerves on his part or whether he did it
on purpose, but he started to rattle off exercises like a machine gun, and
soon our heads were swiveling like electric fans, turning from side to
side to copy what the person beside us was doing. I was relieved I was
at the far end of the barre so the jury could not see me, but from the
second exercise on we started to rotate position and very soon I found
myself in front of the judges.

The main part of the class was extremely difficult, completely different from the class of the previous day. It was as if our teacher had become another person, somebody we had never seen before, an executioner who was unfamiliar with the word *mercy*. As the class progressed, our physical condition deteriorated. Some people ended up sprawled on the floor, trying to regain their strength and panting like runaway horses. When we performed the variation, in numerical order, to recorded music, our bodies moved purely from habit, any old way, completely disregarding orders from the brain. We were all so exhausted we forgot that this was a prestigious competition and we had a jury watching us. Many people fell to their knees, one person twisted an ankle and had to be taken out to the infirmary, and more than fifteen of us had to repeat the variation at least three times because we could not get beyond the complexity of the first phrase. Only Victor Álvarez, a Spaniard with impeccable technique, managed to perform the variation with no more apparent difficulty than drinking a glass of water.

Then it was my turn. Sometimes it is not so bad to be last. I had enough time to make a promise to God and the saints: "Changó and Jesus, bring me strength, and when I get to Cuba, I'll offer up a pair of roosters to each one of you!"

I did not know if you could offer up roosters to Jesus, but I thought it was better to be safe than sorry.

That evening, we all gathered in a restaurant near the railway station to find out the results of the class. It was Victor, the Spanish boy, who informed us that 20 percent had been disqualified. Raul could not understand what the man who announced the results was saying. In the end, I was the one who told him what was happening and that I had passed through to the second round.

"*Madonna mia!*" he exclaimed, taking a sip of white wine.

We returned to our hotel. Raul was happy, partly because of my success and partly because the receptionist he fancied was working that night. The attraction between them was obvious, even though there were a few problems of communication, and I slipped away to allow them some space after interrupting their courtship so rudely on our first night.

The following day, we all made it through the relatively simple con-temporary dance class to the next round, which would be the perfor-mance onstage of our classical and contemporary variations. This time, being last did me no favors. I had to wait for quite a while, jumping up and down like a grasshopper so that I would not get cold. The announcer told the audience not to applaud, and the parents kept an almost funereal silence, which only served to raise the tension and to increase our powers of concentration.

I had to wait so long I went to the barre in the office to do some stretches and lost track of time. I realized it was my turn only when a woman with mahogany-colored hair interrupted me and led me toward the stage, asking me something I did not understand. The woman shouted for someone to find a Spanish speaker.

"We need to know the tempo of your solo," someone explained, and the pianist started to play the variation of *Don Quixote*.

"That's fine," I said, taking off my leg warmers and heading toward the corner to begin.

I did not have time to think about being nervous, and I felt really good during my solo. My body flew through the air, and I was filled with a genuine sense of happiness, an enormous desire to live as never before. I must have managed to transmit that sense of harmony to the outside world, because when I finished, everybody burst into sponta-neous applause, which continued for a long time after I had left the stage. It was an extraordinary moment, and it made me think of what I had wished for on New Year's Eve in Signor Mesturino's house. Now that I was actually in the competition, with the sound of forbidden applause ringing in my ears, I could not resist the temptation to wish for more. I finished the contemporary solo to a similar ovation.

Until that point all of us had been hidden behind a veil of anonymity, but now people started wanting to know about me. I met Shirley, a girl of Cuban origin who had been born in Miami, and Victor introduced me to his parents. Even the sullen boy with his leg against his ear now wanted to be my friend.

"93 . . . 97 . . . 102 . . . 103 . . . 115 . . . 120 . . . 125 . . ." The man read-ing the results paused.

Raul looked at me nervously. "You danced well, didn't you?" he asked, his mouth twisted into an expression of doubt.

I nodded my head.

". . . and 127."

I had gotten through to the semifinal!

That night, I dreamed that I was in Los Pinos, dancing *Don Quixote* in the middle of the street. My audience was Opito, the break-dancing gang, my family, Olga, Chery . . . and they were all so happy! It was so vivid, so real, that I truly believed it was happening and only realized that I was dreaming when I saw my father crying for joy. *Papito llorando?* No way, I told myself, and woke up. Raul was snoring. I gave him a little shake and told him it was time for us to leave, and he fell out of bed.

Later, at the theater, I did my warm-up with Victor's private tutor, who had very kindly invited me to join him the day before. I was convinced that that evening I would achieve my goal: a diploma, a medal, some sort of award. I was so confident that I was the first one to put on makeup, and then I went down to the stage to find a suitable spot from which to watch the variations as if I were just another spectator. As I was the last to perform in the whole competition, I settled down to observe each and every solo, without realizing the mistake I was making.

As I watched girls barely thirteen years old who already possessed the talent and professional maturity of soloists with big companies, nervousness began to eat away at my confidence. There was one boy with impeccable technique, and another with an impressive physique who managed colossal jumps, then a near-perfect variation performed by Victor Álvarez that finally plunged me into dark despair. I had dared to be confident, and it was too late to learn that with confidence comes danger.

I walked toward the corner of the stage from which I would make my entrance, almost staggering, weighed down by my shame, imagining the ridicule to which I might be exposed in a few moments' time. My hope had completely evaporated. Inside me, numerous Carloses fought for space.

"Are you going to let them brand you a clown, like they did in Los Pinos?" one of the Carloses asked, as I went to place myself in the starting position, a *tendu derrière*. At a vague signal from my right arm, the piano began to play and my legs tried to lift my body, but they managed only the feeblest of elevations in the *double saut de basque.* The second jump, a scissor step, was one of my key jumps, but I executed it so weakly that I almost had to steady myself by putting my hands on the floor. I could not achieve my usual balance during the pirouettes, and when the moment came for the diagonal in the *double tours en l'air,* I already knew there was no way I would be able to remedy all the slips that I had made. There was no point in even trying. I was the clown of not only Los Pinos, but Lausanne, too—a failure, a fool, a mud-eating, thick-lipped disaster. Nothing and no one could save me now.

We made our way back to the hotel in silence. Raul tactfully kept his own counsel. He spoke only when we were heading, as usual, toward the restaurant to hear the results.

"I want you to know that whatever the outcome, I am very proud of you." With that he gave me a tight hug that almost winded me, and we fell back into silence again.

Fear floated on the air; it hung from the lights of the restaurant and coated the assembled faces. The only people smiling were those who had reason to do so, and I was not one of them. Victor, his parents, and his teacher celebrated together at a table. They came over to talk to me about something unrelated to the competition, which only made me feel worse. To cap it all, Raul was looking at me pityingly from a corner. I could do nothing but cross my fingers and lower my head in shame.

"20 . . . 59 . . . 77 . . . 93 . . . 115 . . . 120 . . ."

Time stood still, like that morning in Pinar del Río after I had stolen Eduardo's watch. My ears reverberated with the same deafening echo that had filled them that day, and I saw the same blurred images. I covered my head with my hands, thinking about how badly I had failed my teacher. The disappointed faces of my peers in Italy and Cuba flooded into my head. I knew I had let them all down, my teacher, my school, everyone!

I was so depressed, I did not hear the announcer call out the number 127, nor did I see Raul jump up and run toward me. Suddenly he was shaking me roughly, shouting, "You've done it! You've done it!"

Only then did I understand that a miracle had occurred.

Raul suggested that we go somewhere to celebrate, but I decided to go straight to bed. The following morning, I asked him not to speak to me, instructions he followed to the letter, disobeying only when he plunged his hand into his yellow bag and offered me a bar of chocolate.

There were just eleven of us finalists. I was one of the first to arrive at the theater, and I put on my makeup. Unlike the day before, however, I did not speak to anybody. I barely even responded when Victor said hello. I wrapped my body up well in a red cotton cape that one of my teachers, Marco Pierin, had given me during our tour to the city of Bergamo. I put on two pairs of leg warmers, one nylon, the other wool. I covered my ankles, then I went to warm up alone in the remotest place I could find, where no one and nothing could break my concentration.

Forty minutes later, when I considered myself ready, I went upstairs to dress myself in the black, white, and red jacket of *Don Quixote*. In the corridor, television cameras briefly followed me until I disappeared into the stairwell. The chairman of the competition announced the start of the final round, which prompted a wave of applause that sounded to me as loud as any soccer stadium cheer. I had disappeared into a place so deep inside myself that I could scarcely hear the audience and did not realize that Victor had wished me luck until after we had passed each other on the stairs. I kept on walking as though I had not seen anyone. The only Carlos in my mind now was telling me: "This is your chance to change your future, don't let it get away from you."

At first I repeated this line silently to myself, but after a while I started saying it out loud. Nothing else mattered to me.

The piano was playing the woman's variation from *The Corsair*, and, as soon as the applause died down, the man's variation from *The Nutcracker* started up. Three variations later it would be my turn. I began to sweat, but my hands were like ice, which always happens when I am about to dance. The applause broke out again, and this time it seemed to say, "Strength, Carlos, strength!" as if everybody was on my side.

All my longing to be good, to feel loved, and to make somebody proud of me welled up. I knew the moment had come to achieve my dream of being someone.

"Carlos, Carlos, Carlos, Carlos!" I was sure I heard the audience cheer, even though, in fact, they were clapping because Victor had just finished his variation.

"Carlos Acosta."

My name was announced. I straightened my jacket and placed my left hand on my waist. The reverberation of the microphone, the noise of the audience quieted to a deathly hush. I tensed my buttocks, opened my eyes, lifted my neck, and presented the full force of my smile to the world. I walked out and positioned myself in the *tendu derrière*. This time I cued the music with a confident signal from my right arm, and my body rose up toward the roof of the theater. My legs had turned into eagle's wings. I felt that I was flying and that nobody and nothing could hold me back. My pirouettes were clean, finishing always with a lift of my head to accentuate their perfection. I performed the *double tours en l'air* precisely in time to the music, sustaining the arabesque at the end of each one just as I had been taught to do. All that was needed was one last effort for the final pirouettes. My heart was pounding. For one moment I was assailed by doubt, but as I flexed my thigh muscles I said to myself, "Come on, you bastard, you're nearly there. Don't give in now!"

I prepared myself with a *tendu latéral.* I propelled myself forward, aaaaand . . . Pruuum! The piano fell silent.

I remained kneeling on the floor for some seconds, listening to the thunderous ovation, blinded by the camera flashes that were sparking all over the auditorium. I bowed, my mind running over what I had just done. Those jumps and spins were the howls of the caged animal that I carried inside myself. I had danced myself free.

Twenty minutes later the prize giving began. The chairman of the competition came over to the microphones in the middle of the stage. With a few words in French, he introduced first the chairman of the jury and then the rest of the judges on the panel. Each of them bowed to the audience and then stood to one side of two ballet barres that had been placed on the stage. The television cameras were everywhere, following the competitors as we stood in the wings awaiting the verdict. We were all looking at one another with the same question going through our minds: Have I won? And, in my case, there was also the question, How the hell will I know if I've won?

The chairman said something, and the dancer standing beside me walked out onto the stage. The audience burst into applause. The boy received a diploma, then stepped back so that he could bow. He was followed by a Japanese ballerina. Again the audience applauded, and this time the camera that was trained on us moved in to get a close-up of our reactions. The next one up was an English ballerina, followed by an American dancer. I could not understand a word and so had no idea which prizes were being awarded.

Now there were just six of us left. I glanced toward Victor. He came over and gave me a little slap on my right shoulder.

"Listen, Victor," I whispered, "could you let me know when it's my turn?"

"Don't worry about it, I'm sure you'll realize," he reassured me, smiling.

They called another ballerina, then another, and then the boy who had danced the variation from *The Nutcracker*. And then there were just two of us, Victor and me. When the Spaniard's name was called, the ovation from the audience shook the building. I could see on the monitor that everybody was standing up and applauding wildly. He must have won the Grand Prix, I thought as I waited. The chairman took the microphone again.

"Sbbbbbbywyyd, gggydsjjkss, asdvfgrfb. Carlos Acosta, Cuba."

"Congratulations!" said the chairman of the jury as he shook my hand. He gave me a small box, then stood to one side so that I could bow. Everybody applauded just as they had done with Victor, whistling and shouting and standing up from their seats. I could hardly contain my emotion.

"I told you that you would know which prize was yours," said Victor as I stood by his side after taking my bow. I shook his hand so that he would not realize that I still did not know what I had won. Then I lifted the lid of the box and looked to see what was inside.

The Grand Prix de Lausanne Médaille d'Or.

The most wonderful surprise was that Chery and Nancy had come to share the miracle with me. The four of us—Chery, Nancy, Raul, and I—met up in the area by the offices. We were all crying. Chery kept saying how proud she was of me. In the dressing rooms, I kissed the ground to thank God and the saints for granting me the crazy wish that I had made in Signor Mesturino's house.

If there was a day in my life when I was truly happy, I can say with certainty that was it.

The next day we returned to Italy. When we showed our passports on the train, it turned out that my Italian visa was for a single entry only, which meant I needed to get another visa to get back into the country. After fifteen minutes of pleading, the guard suddenly asked, "Did you say you were a Cuban ballet dancer? You're not by any chance the winner of the Prix de Lausanne, are you?"

Chery showed him my photograph in the newspapers and the guard, instead of locking me up, requested my autograph and let me through illegally.

From then on, I started to dance as a soloist with the company while I was still finishing school. My name was printed on the publicity posters, and I took part in the staging of new works, dancing the principal roles. In the summer, during the Vignale Danza Festival, I was awarded a special prize of merit.

Narina now called me all the time and invited me to go out with her. She constantly asked what it had felt like to have my photograph taken with Princess Caroline of Monaco, but I could not begin to describe how it felt to be that smiling young man in the newspaper, dazed by glory.

When I returned to Cuba several months later at the end of my year in Italy, the whole school was waiting for me at the airport: Julio, Rogelio, Jesús, Rafael, Luis, all my friends. I ran to embrace them, desperate to tell them everything at once, but emotion overcame me, and I started to cry. My friends rubbed my head like I was their younger brother, but soon their hearts softened, and they, too, teared up. The girls also began to weep, and the teachers, too—in short, the day grew long with the outpouring of all our emotions and I had to wait until the following day to recount everything related to my trip to Italy.

The first thing I did upon arriving in Los Pinos, after giving my par-

ents and sisters the presents I had bought them, was to buy four fat
roosters. The two I had promised Jesus Christ I placed by the nearest
cotton tree I could find, as Santería tradition dictated, and the other two
I put on my father's shrine. We had many days of festivities, celebrating and going out as a family to the ice-cream parlor. My parents, full
of pride, held hands as they used to long ago, and my delighted sisters
wore the dresses that my prize money had bought for them and filled
me in on all the latest gossip from home.

Some nights, the clearest ones when there was a full moon, I would
go up onto the roof and sit with my pigeons. I would tell them about
Italy, about Turin, the lovely Valentino Park and its dark, mysterious
river. I described to them the tenacity of the winter and the beautiful
sea of multicolored leaves that would cover the streets in the autumn.
They cooed to me in astonishment as I told them about Lausanne — the
genial Raul, the brilliant Victor, the evil teacher who nearly killed us,
and all about my doubts and fear of failure. My pigeons, of course, said
nothing, but one night, on the murmur of the cooling breeze, I seemed
to hear a sharp voice interrupting my thoughts.

"You have a brilliant future, my friend," said the voice.

"Do you think so?" I answered doubtfully.

"Take care not to lose contact with your family, though." The voice
faded back into the night.

Chapter 11

HISTORY REPEATS ITSELF

During my year in Italy I had been unable to communicate with my family, so I had to wait until I returned to find out what my parents and my sisters had been up to and to glean all the latest gossip from Los Pinos.

I was barely through the door when Berta surprised me: "Hey, little brother, I got married to Eduardo!"

I was happy for her, of course—she had been with Eduardo for a while, and he seemed like a nice guy—but I could not help feeling confused when she added, "It's only temporary. My real husband is God."

I had never heard my sister say anything so peculiar.

"Are you feeling all right, Berta?" I asked her anxiously, glancing at the other bewildered faces in the room.

"I feel better than ever now that I'm married to God," she replied. There was an uneasy silence, then my sister suddenly roared with laughter and everything returned to normal. She went back to being the Berta she had always been. Reassured, I continued handing out the presents I had brought from Italy, without any idea that those were the first symptoms of a change that would be irreversible.

My sister Berta had always been morbidly fascinated by religious matters. During her adolescence, she began to withdraw from daily life and was interested only in studying the Old and New Testaments. Her obsession with the afterlife had also led her to ask for all the details about my aunt Lucia's suicide. I do not know which event was the trigger—if it was my mother's brain hemorrhage, or my aunt's suicide,

127

or something she inherited genetically—but the fact is that at twenty-four years old my sister's gentle character changed completely. She developed a new arrogance that in turn was accompanied by a terrifying physical strength, and she became capable of seriously hurting anyone who stood in her way. She did not believe in Santería and did not mince her words when criticizing our father's religion. She had furious arguments with Papá, and one day, as if possessed by the devil, she threw a glass vase at his head. Luckily, the old man ducked in time.

Soon it was not enough for Berta merely to find refuge in the Bible; she urged us to study, too, so that we would be saved. She believed Armageddon might arrive at any time to end all evil and destroy the sinners and the nonbelievers.

"Marilín, Yuli, my little sister and brother, study the Bible and be saved from the filth of this world," she would extol us, using all her substantial powers of persuasion. And she won. Partly to please her and partly out of genuine fear of divine retribution, we ended up studying the Bible at our next-door neighbor's house whenever I came home for the weekend.

My sister was determined to convert me into a Jehovah's Witness, and, although I tried to please her, I could not seem to learn much about the creation of the world or about Jerusalem. I did manage to pick up the story about a man who built an enormous ark to save the animals from some sort of flood, and about how Eve was made from Adam's rib and they both ended up eating the apple of temptation. Was there not also a serpent? My sister would jab me with her elbow to wake me up in the classes, but my eyelids had lead weights attached to them, and I could not keep them open. Berta started to get angry. I tried to explain to her that I was studying two years in one at school—the year I had lost by being in Italy and the one that I normally would have been studying—so that I could graduate with the rest of my classmates the following year. But no matter how many times I explained it, Berta did not understand, and she eventually stopped talking to me. She said God should never be shoved into the background and I would never attain earthly paradise. I could see from the passion in her green eyes that she really believed it.

At the school boardinghouse, I could not sleep for thinking about my sister's aggressive new personality. I was reminded of my aunt Lucia's similar illness.

My sister's obsession with knowing about the spiritual turned into an intolerable fanaticism, and, not unnaturally, this started to chip away at her happiness with her new husband. Into the midst of this maelstrom, and helping to unleash the chaos, stepped a man called Franz, a young bohemian from the neighborhood. Franz professed to share my sister's religious beliefs, although it was clear to everyone else that his real mission was to put ideas of an amorous nature into Berta's head. Mornings and afternoons, Berta would study the Bible while Franz serenaded her with his guitar—and though at night she would return to Eduardo, she was increasingly unable to sustain the fiction that was their marriage.

"If you don't want to be with Eduardo, then divorce him, but don't do this," my mother told her, but Berta did not pay her any attention and continued seeing Franz. My father kept quiet; the incident with the vase was all too fresh in his memory. One day, out of genuine desperation, I confronted Berta and told her that she should not go to Franz's house, that he did not have good intentions, but she said she would see him whenever she chose to.

Meanwhile, at school, Chery had got it into her head that I should enter the annual Paris International Ballet Competition, but she was having difficulty getting me any sponsorship. She tried every channel, including the National Centre of Arts Schools and the Ministry of Culture, but they all said they had no money. It felt like history repeating itself. We were beseeching, waiting, wondering, desperate, just like we had been before Lausanne. We finally found ourselves at ARTEX, the artists' promotions agency, where the receptionist told us to take a seat and wait. Ten minutes later a tall man appeared and led us through to his office. While he and Chery made polite conversation, exchanging news of mutual acquaintances and reminiscing, I stared out the window and floated off into a vivid daydream in which my sister Berta was in our kitchen, looking the way she had at sixteen. The image was so clear that I even tried to reach out to her, but at that moment she disappeared and all I could see was Franz with his guitar. He was wearing a checked shirt and had a cigarette in his mouth. He was laughing as he spat at a little boy who was quietly playing Eat Mud. It was me. Anger flooded through me, and I clenched my fists as I tried to punch him. Berta intervened and implored me not to. I cried with impotence and rolled in the mud with rage.

Suddenly, I heard Chery making a promise so rash it brought me instantly back to the ARTEX office: "If you can't give me the money, then lend it to me. I'll pay you back out of the prize money."

I couldn't believe what I was hearing. I stared at Chery. Had she gone mad? What if I didn't win? We'd end up in prison.

Chery just kept smiling fixedly at the ARTEX man.

"Very well," he said, with a smile. "In that case, I'll see what I can do. . . ." Then he accompanied us to the exit and asked us to come back the next week.

Outside, Quinta Avenida, normally one of the busiest streets in Havana, was eerily deserted. There was absolutely nobody about: no cars, no people, nothing. Still reeling from my vivid daydream, I took this as a sign that something bad was about to happen and even started to wonder whether God was punishing me for having fallen asleep in Bible class. My teacher appeared completely calm, however, and when I started to protest that her plan was mad, she simply said, "Look, Junior, this is a unique opportunity. I realize you're going to feel pressured, and I'm also aware that you're not in peak physical condition, that you ought to eat better, but you've got to make the effort and leave everything else to one side. Forget about your problems and just concentrate on the competition."

Chery's blue eyes looked deep into mine, and her words gave me pause for thought. I was not going to be able to solve the problems in Berta's love life. After all, these things always happen, and they usually sort themselves out. I told myself it was quite normal for people to have religious preferences. My father was a Santero, my mother believed in a little bit of everything and nothing, and my sister was a Jehovah's Witness. A similar situation prevailed in many homes in Cuba. Anyway, I could not remember a problem that Berta had not managed to handle successfully on her own.

My task was to concentrate exclusively on my career.

Theory and practice, however, are two completely different things. I am sure even Chery would have been worried had she seen my sister's face that afternoon when she met me as I climbed the stairs to our apartment. Berta's eyes were hollow and red; there were gray rings around her eyelids that spoke of insomnia. She was dirty, her hair wild and unbrushed. In her left hand she was holding a Bible, and in her right, a rosary.

"Yuli. Are you ready for the resurrection? Armageddon is approaching," she said, as I stood paralyzed on the steps.

My daydream during the interview at ARTEX had struck me as a presentiment that something bad was going to happen, but I had never imagined this.

"Berta, what's happening, what's wrong, why are you like this?" I asked, my heart twisting with fear inside me.

"Armageddon is coming, and I'm ready," she responded, then started to run.

"Berta, Berta! Where are you going, where? Come back!" I threw my things to the ground to go after her and was nearly knocked over by Marilín and my father, who were sprinting down the stairs at high speed, jumping the steps three at a time.

"Catch her, Yuli, catch her; she's getting away!" yelled Marilín.

I began to run. Berta was almost half a block away when a neighbor stopped her, and even though we arrived quickly, Berta had already bitten and punched him several times in her attempts to escape. She was still struggling like a gladiator when we reached her.

"Quiet, Berta. Quiet, my girl, it's over now. Let's go home," my father tried to soothe her. She did not resist when my old man put his arms around her shoulders. Marilín and I thanked the poor injured neighbor and encircled Berta, forming a sort of protective barrier. My mother was on the balcony with her hands over her mouth to silence her sobs as we brought Berta back inside and laid her tormented head upon my mother's chest, in that sacred spot reserved for the comfort of her children.

The streets were awash with people and dogs, all contemplating the scene. We knew what everyone who had known my aunt was thinking: just like Lucia.

Apparently, my sister had argued with Franz and had not been able to sleep. After a week of insomnia and of preaching the Gospel, knocking on every door, trying to persuade each person that she met to convert to her religion, Berta became delirious. It was something that crept up gradually, until it erupted in the early hours of that morning, when she went out to wander the deserted streets of Los Pinos, to speak to the night, perhaps to the moon and to all those other beings or forces of nature that were capable of understanding her language.

After taking the sedative that my mother gave her and eating some chicken and rice, Berta sat quietly for hours, her gaze wandering everywhere and nowhere in particular. Mamá and Marilín cried rivers of tears, while my father went to look for a doctor. I did not know what to do, so I decided to keep quiet. After a while, Eduardo arrived, as did a nurse. Eduardo was very nervous, as if he, too, was unbalanced. He moved to embrace Berta, but the nurse intervened, saying that Eduardo might make matters worse and that it would be better to keep a distance. The nurse examined Berta, then she administered another sedative and explained that the crisis had been brought about by insomnia, that we should not worry because it could happen to anyone, and that my sister would be back to normal once she had caught up on her sleep.

Berta slept deeply, which put a temporary end to my mother's and Marilín's weeping. Eduardo also calmed down and, following the nurse's advice, went back home. In all this time I had not taken my eyes off my sister. In silence I asked God to let her dream something lovely, something beautiful that would make her forget this nightmare. It was the least He could do for someone who was so good, so devout, and whose faith was so unshakable. I prayed for a return to normality in my house, for all our problems to end.

The next day, the whole neighborhood was awoken by loud, insistent screaming, and we looked out to see my sister standing naked in the middle of the street. Marilín rushed out to cover her with a sheet, and my father went to ask a neighbor if he could borrow his motorbike to take Berta to the hospital. Meanwhile, I tried to comfort my mother. The neighbors came together to help us: Delia held Berta by the arm, and Kenia covered her mouth to dampen her screams. Soon the nurse arrived, and my father returned with the neighbor's motorbike. I fetched a change of clothes, and Berta was dressed and put into the motorbike's sidecar. Marilín stayed behind to comfort my mother, while I climbed on behind my father and we headed in the direction of the Psychiatric Hospital of Havana, also known as Mazorra.

On the way, Berta tried to throw herself from the motorbike. We stopped her just in time. She looked as though she was having a conversation with the sun. She stared at it continuously, burning her retinas in the process. In Mazorra, she was sedated, and we were told to come back the next day.

The following day we returned to find Berta in a hospital ward filled to bursting with the elderly insane. There were loads of them, literally hundreds. We knew we could not leave Berta in that environment for another minute. We took her to the Gali García, the same hospital in which my aunt had committed suicide, but there were no beds available. The only other option was the hospital Aballí. She was put into cubicle eight in the psychiatric department, where she remained for several weeks. After submitting her to various tests, the doctor came to us with the diagnosis. He looked as if the bad news gave his tongue a bitter taste.

"Your daughter has paranoid schizophrenia."

And so I boarded the plane to Paris in silence, with fear and distress burrowing into my heart. I did not care about the long flight—Havana to Gander, Gander to Moscow, Moscow to Paris—nor did I notice that it was thirty degrees below zero in Moscow, nor that we stayed in a seventh-rate hotel, nor that I was hungry, nor that there were hundreds of families waiting in the airport for the chance to escape perestroika.

In Paris, I did not give a damn about winning the competition or what might happen if we could not return the money. I was not bothered by the fact that there were no studios for us to rehearse in so we ended up practicing in the conference room of the embassy. Nothing could touch me; everything became unimportant compared to the terrible weight of rage and helplessness I felt at my sister's condition. Rage at that son of a bitch Franz, who had encouraged the religious fanaticism that had fucked her up, and helplessness because some ills do not have a cure, and my sister's sickness was one of them.

When I held the competition's Grand Prix in my hands, I put on a smile, as any performer does. Nobody realized I was acting—not my teacher, not the other dancers, not the cheering crowd, not even Madame Chirac, France's first lady, who had watched the finals. I looked like the personification of triumph, but it was all pretense. It was not happiness that caused the tears trickling down my face. Perhaps I should have been more grateful—to be otherwise might seem like bad grace on my part—but good luck and misfortune should never be served up on the same plate. I had always thought that success equaled happiness, but I realized in Paris that what we call success is just an ephemeral illusion. I began to understand that to be truly happy you need many things: health, love, friends, money, and family—and for me family is without a doubt the most important. Sometimes, even all this is not enough.

The first thing we did on our return to Cuba was pay back the money we owed to ARTEX. Later on came the articles in the press, the photos, and the Julio Antonio Mella Medal that the government awarded me. My moment of fame was meaningless to me. The prize could not help us at home. Berta was back in her bed, still lost in her faraway world. When I showed her the medals, she did not take any notice. My mother's face crumpled, my father bit down hard on his false teeth, and Marilín came over and put her arm around my shoulders. Then I cried for everybody. I cried for a long time.

For the next year, wherever I was, whether it was in a hotel in a foreign country as part of a cultural exchange or in my bunk bed at the school boardinghouse, I tried to devote the thirty minutes before I went to sleep to thinking about my family. I tried to remember the times when we all slept together in the same room and to conjure up happy, healthy images of my sisters wearing the patched-up dresses my mother used to mend for them. But try as I might, I always kept coming back to the image of Berta, unkempt and wandering around the streets of Los Pinos, preaching the Gospel.

There were days when I blamed it all on ballet. I would seize upon the notion that if I had not been dancing or traveling, I might have been able to do something to stop Berta's illness. Sometimes during rehearsals, my spirits would fail me and I would not have the strength to go on. I would feel as though nothing had any meaning, as if all my work was in vain.

One day, unable to lie awake fretting in the dormitory any longer, I waited until Cuca, the caretaker, had turned off all the lights, then jumped over the terrace wall and headed for home. I arrived at my house at about one in the morning.

When my parents saw me on the doorstep, sweating copiously, they worried that I was bringing more bad news; they calmed down only when I asked how Berta was. They told me she was with Eduardo and was much more peaceful and relaxed.

"I'm going to see her," I said.

"No! Your mother just told you she was fine. Anyway, at this time of night, Pirate's bound to be loose," my father said.

Pirate was Eduardo's Staffordshire bull terrier. We used to call him Cujo, the killer dog.

"All right, I'll stay. But I'm going to see her tomorrow," I told him.

"Tomorrow you have to go to ballet school," my old man said sharply.

"But I want to stay here with you!" I insisted, my voice choking with emotion.

My father turned his back on me angrily and stormed out of the bedroom and into the kitchen. My mother stroked my head.

"Don't worry, everything will be fine. She's much better," she said, leading me over to the bed, when suddenly my father charged back out of the kitchen like a hurricane.

"Listen to what I'm going to say to you, Yuli, and listen well, because I'm only going to say it once," he said, gripping me firmly by the shoulders. "The only way you're going to help your sisters, your mother, and all of us, is by being the best dancer you can be. Don't concern yourself with us anymore. Live your life, the one you've been given, and we'll live ours. Understood?"

"But, Papito, I hardly come home anymore because ballet takes up nearly all my time. I can't help worrying about Berta. . . ."

"Well, you've just got to forget about everything else and concentrate on your career. Thank God you have the chance of a different future. The real crime would be if you threw it all away. It's not only what you owe yourself, it's what you owe us, the ones who didn't have the luck to be born with your talent. Do you understand?"

I felt like punching him.

I did something then that I should not have done. I shouted in his face: "Ballet, ballet, it's the only thing that's ever mattered to you! You put me in that school in Pinar del Río and then you never came to see me. Two long years when nobody gave a damn about me! Two years!

And now I'm not even allowed to miss anyone or to seek a bit of comfort because I have to keep dancing for you and your happiness. You're not the one who's having nightmares every night. You've never shown me even the slightest bit of affection. Even when I was a child, the first time I rode a bicycle and smashed into the lamppost, you were not bothered. You did not even give me a hug. I could go to hell for all you care. Well, fuck ballet. And you know what?" For one split second I hesitated, holding back the words that were on the tip of my tongue, but in my fury I blurted them out. "I hate you. I've always hated you."

My parents did not move. The pigeons on the roof fell silent, and the trees stopped rustling as the wind dropped in order to pay better attention to what would happen when the shouting ended. No one spoke. Papá walked out of the room, his head bowed. Shortly afterward, my mother followed him. I remained on my own in the bedroom, paralyzed. Had I really told my father that I hated him? I could not believe I had done that. But it was already too late.

I left.

At the corner of the street, I turned to look up at the apartment windows. My mother was looking out. The glare from the lightbulb created a shadow that covered one-half of her face. Her right eye stood out from the darkness, staring at me. She continued watching me all the way down the street.

I arrived at the bus stop and threw myself down on the bench, my chest contracting with disbelief. Could I really have told Papito that I hated him? His words kept repeating in my head. "Live your life, the one you've been given, and we'll live ours!"

I realized that it was not my father that I hated, but my life—the terrible, desolate existence that ballet had given me.

I stretched out on the bench and looked up at the starless sky. I felt empty, as though a monstrous worm had burrowed its way inside me and sucked out my happiness and my hope. In the darkness of the night, it seemed to be there beside me on the bench, taunting me with what my old man had said: "Thank God you have the chance of a different future. The real crime would be if you threw it all away." But, later, in the cold light of day, I knew that the real crime was having success and fame and nobody to share it with. I would have given everything up to have my family back.

Chapter 12

CHERY'S DECISION

In March 1991, Chery and I went to Venezuela for two weeks to work with the private company of Nina Nova, a fragile old lady who had, by all accounts, been an excellent dancer in her youth. She wanted to introduce the Cuban technique into her company, so she had organized a seminar, inviting teachers from different parts of the country who were interested in Cuban ballet. We did some demonstration classes with Chery explaining and me dancing. At the end, there were two performances in which I danced with three of the company's ballerinas and also with Mari Fe, who was from Teresa Carreño's company.

While we were in Venezuela, I witnessed the reunion of Chery and her twin sister, Mangui, after more than thirty years of separation. Mangui had followed her husband to the States around the time of the Cuban Revolution, and she had been unable to return after the borders closed, a story familiar among many families in Cuba. She arrived in Venezuela with her daughter early one morning on an airplane from Pennsylvania, and came directly to the Caracas Hilton, where we were waiting for them. The two sisters cried a lot and spoke very little. The similarities between them were still intact, vivid, and marked in their flesh—even after all that time. Chery still wore her hair in the same way she had done when they were young: a long black braid that reached almost to her waist, tied with a multicolored band. Her face was slightly longer than her sister's, and she was clearly wearing makeup. Her clothes were simple, just some gray track pants, a white short-sleeved T-shirt, and some leather Capezio shoes, which dance teachers often wear. Mangui had short hair, squarely cut and dyed a mahogany color. The skin beneath her arms and under her chin was loose. Her makeup was light. She was wearing an expensive dress, conservative in style, with black high-heeled shoes that made her taller until she took them off to measure herself against her sister.

They were both products of the lives they had lived. They had everything, nothing, and too much in common, all at the same time— the same red lips, the same blue eyes, the same large ears and nose. Seeing them standing next to each other, I thought what a powerful force blood is, and it made me think about my mother's separation from her family and how wonderful it would be if they, too, could be reunited one day. I wondered if they would still have anything in common.

Mangui and her daughter could not stay to watch me dance. They were both dancers and were needed back at their private academy in Pennsylvania. We said good-bye in one of Teresa Carreño's studios at the end of a ballet class. The sisters looked each other over one more time, cried, and kissed; then Mangui and her daughter left in a taxi for the airport, each twin going off in a different direction again, as they had done thirty years before.

Three days later, back in Havana once more, we were greeted by the rumor that Ivan Nagy, the director of the English National Ballet, was coming to Cuba to audition and sign up dancers. Gossip spread like wildfire through all the ballet companies. Some said he wanted to hire ten dancers, others that he was just coming to see the Camagüey Ballet and wanted only to engage strong, tall, black male dancers. There was lots of speculation, but nobody really knew anything.

One Tuesday, we discovered that the great man was already in the country and that auditions would be held on Thursday. At eight in the morning on the day in question, there was such a commotion in the corridors of the García Lorca Lyceum, where we had our ballet classes, that it sounded as though the March of the Combatant People had been rerouted from the May 1 celebrations in Revolution Square. As well as the dancers from Prodanza, the National Ballet, and the Camagüey Ballet companies, there were some of my fellow students from the ballet school and a large number of curious onlookers.

I was in my ballet class about to practice some jumps when Laura Alonso burst in to speak to Chery. Laura had been filling Ivan Nagy's head with tales of my prizes and had come to persuade the teacher to let me audition that very instant, despite the fact that I had not even graduated yet. My class was suspended, and, five minutes later, our whole group gathered in the studio on the floor above, an enormous room that is now used to paint sets.

Laura Alonso asked me to improvise the *pas de deux* from *Don Quixote* with Xiomara Reyes, one of the dancers from her company, who was also a graduate of the ballet school. I had last partnered with Xiomara two years previously. She was tiny and easy to manipulate, but because of the time lapse since we had last danced together, the whole exercise proved to be a disaster: we were completely out of step with each other. When Xiomara went to the right, I went to the left. When she jabbed me with her elbow, I tried to mask the pain and keep dancing; but then I also spent the whole time offering her the wrong hand while the music played on, regardless of our clumsiness. Nevertheless, our peers did everything they could to spur us on, cheering and applauding, their faces shining with eagerness for us to succeed. Some of them would leap up suddenly to celebrate a particularly well-executed step, as if a goal had just been scored at a soccer match. It did not matter to them whether we were doing it right or we messed up a lift, the important thing was that we were dancing for our future in that room, and for the dreams of everyone present.

I stole a glance toward the center of the room where Ivan Nagy was sitting, but the sun was shining onto his silver head, casting a shadow over his face and making it impossible to read his expression. When everyone applauded and made a racket, he did not move so much as a finger. At one point he bent down to pick up his water bottle and took a few sips before putting it back on the floor. He tilted his head slightly to one side, like dogs do, and maintained his inscrutable expression. Nobody had any idea what he was thinking.

We found out half an hour later. Ivan Nagy told Chery, in his broken and rusty Spanish, that he wanted me as a principal dancer for his company. Chery, Laura Alonso, and the other teachers were incredulous.

Because his Spanish was so poor, Chery tried to correct him. "Do you mean, sir, that you want him as one of the corps de ballet?"

"No, no! I want him one dancer. One dancer, understand?" the director replied, indicating with his index finger. "One dancer. Only one."

The other teachers were speechless. Chery, however, maintained her serene expression, as though she was totally in agreement with the director's decision. She took down all the pertinent details, explained that I was only seventeen years old and still had to graduate ballet school, but promised Ivan Nagy that they would stay in contact. A little while later, Chery called me over and told me what had happened. At first I thought that my teacher was teasing me, but her eyes held mine, and I knew she was telling the truth. I nearly keeled over in amazement.

June 2 was my eighteenth birthday. One week later, we took our grade-pass exams and graduated as professional dancers. Two days later, our teachers told us where the placements were and which companies we would be joining. Some would go to the Camagüey Ballet; others would be part of a ballet company in Santiago de Cuba that was just starting up. The most fortunate would stay in Havana with the Cuban National Ballet, formerly known as the Alicia Alonso Ballet, after its founder and most distinguished dancer, whose involvement with the company continues to this day, more than fifty years later. Those who were not selected for any of these places would try to get work with Laura Alonso in Prodanza or with Cristie Dominguez in the Television Ballet Company or, perhaps, in a cabaret.

I was one of the five men and two women who were taken on by the Cuban National Ballet, and I was proud to have been chosen, because it was what we all aspired to. Joining the Cuban National Ballet was the accepted route to a successful career in ballet, and it would mean that I would be taking classes with the true stars of our country: with Alberto Terrero, for example, whose jumping had first inspired me. To be part of the Cuban National Ballet was the highest accolade most Cuban dancers dreamed of. Despite this, I could not help feeling a little ambivalent. According to Chery, Ivan Nagy had offered me a contract as principal dancer with the English National Ballet, one of the most prestigious companies in the world. In the Cuban National Ballet, I had a place in the corps de ballet, with a tour of Mexico already scheduled, in which, I was told, I would play the part of the falconer in the ballet *Giselle.* That role consisted of holding a falcon for fifteen minutes. I knew that it would be a long time before I reached the heights of principal dancer with the Cuban National Ballet, if indeed I ever did.

There were dancers in the Cuban National Ballet, such as Julio

Arozarena, Ernesto Kennedith, even Alberto Terrero, who had been with the ballet for years and had never achieved the title of principal dancer, even though any company in the world would have fought to have dancers of such talent. How many years would I have to hold a falcon before getting the chance to show my ability? The awards I had already won would probably mean I would be given some solo roles: the jesters, the peasants, the Mercutios and Benvolios. But many years would pass before I would be allowed to take on the Romeos, the princes.

Another thing that made me anxious was that once I was with the company, I would not have Chery to look after me. With a truck driver for a father and a housewife for a mother, I would definitely need a sponsor, a really powerful one, to overcome the prejudices that might arise when people first saw me. It might be decades before I got my chance to shine, perhaps an eternity. I thought of Andrés Williams, one of the greatest of the greats, who had to be taken out of theaters under bodyguard during a tour to Argentina because the women were raving about his wonderful *blackness,* but even so, he never got to dance the role of Prince Albrecht in the ballet *Giselle.*

I worried that it wouldn't be until some distant, far-off day that someone would give me the opportunity to show the world the royalty that was hidden inside me. Already old and frustrated, I would play the part of a tired prince, evoking the declining years and not the freshness characteristic of Albrecht. The public would criticize me without suspecting that I could have been a star, if I had only had the chance. I feared I would end up being added to the long list of failed Albrechts.

There was always the possibility that one day someone would injure himself and fortune would smile on me, but I did not want to live my life counting on such lucky breaks. I knew I had to create my own future; I had to make my own good fortune and take my chances.

And yet despite these concerns, I was happy that I had been chosen for the Cuban National Ballet, and I was looking forward to the Mexican tour in September. But before that, I was going back to Italy with Chery to dance with the Teatro Nuovo di Torino Company in the Vignale Danza Festival, as well as to tour other cities of Italy as part of a cultural exchange.

Chery, Ariel Serrano, and I left at the beginning of July. Ariel had been dancing with the Camagüey Ballet for a year, but Chery had asked Fernando Alonso, the director, to let him come with us. And so the three of us were together again, just like the old days.

In Turin we were met by three more of our compatriots, among them Osvaldo Beiro, principal dancer with the Camagüey Ballet, who was working as a teacher at the theater school. Together, we made up a Little Cuba in the Corso Moncalieri.

The Italian company was considerably reduced in size since my last visit. Signor Mesturino explained that it had been impossible to maintain so many dancers on the meager subsidy he got from the government. He had had to let ten of them go, my old girlfriend Narina among them. It was now possible to stage the larger productions only by using students from the ballet school. In *Carmen,* I danced the role of Escamillo, the Toreador, alongside Luciana Savignano and George Iancu. We also danced in *The Moon Show,* a kind of collage of poetry and dance, and in the mixed programs I would sometimes dance the solo from *Orfeo,* which Máximo Morricone had staged for me. *Overture Cubana* was always on the bill, as was *Il Giorno della Follia,* both works choreographed by Robert North. We performed in Rossano Veneto, Trieste, Sicily, and Osimo, where I received the Osimo Special Dance Prize, a silver-plated cup that looked very like the trophies presented at international soccer tournaments. We concluded the tour with the Vignale Danza Festival, which was produced annually by Signor Mesturino.

During those two months in Italy, I was also awarded the Positano Dance Prize: a wooden box the size of a medicine chest that contained a piece of sculpture made of clay and a plaque that read "Léonide Massine Prize for Merit." Osvaldo accompanied me to collect it from Positano, a picturesque fishing village surrounded by crystalline waters and immense rocks. The people of Positano were lively and humble, and there were flowers everywhere and stairways that led to the most secret and delightful places that seemed made for romance. From the windows of my hotel room I could see a beautiful island floating on the blue sea.

"That's Nureyev's island!" said Osvaldo.

I shrugged my shoulders. "Who?"

"Do you mean to say you don't know who he is? He's one of the greats, a genius!"

I assured him I had no idea who Nureyev was. I had seen videos of Baryshnikov, Fernando Bujones, and another dancer with big muscles who I thought might have been Danish, but that was all.

Osvaldo was frustrated by my ignorance.

"Nureyev is the reason that you and I are here! And don't you ever forget it!" he proclaimed fervently.

What bullshit! I'm here thanks to my father, to Chery, and to my legs, I thought.

Days later, after the Vignale Danza Festival was over and we were back in the apartments on the Corso Moncalieri, I bumped into Narina, completely by chance, in a nearby café. Her head was bowed, and her loose hair covered her face. It wasn't until she lifted up her chin after taking a sip of her coffee that I recognized her unmistakable beauty.

My heart began to beat rapidly, just as it had when we started seeing each other during the tour to Bergamo, and I recalled all the wonderful things we had shared together—our first kiss, the tortellini she used to make—and all the painful moments, though even those memories had softened with time. I hesitated for a second, but my lips could not resist speaking her name.

"Narina! It's me, Junior," I said as she looked up, bewildered. Then she recognized me and raced over, hooking her arms around my neck with great force.

"They kicked me out," she said.

I hugged her tightly. The tears started and did not stop all afternoon.

I made love to her cautiously, kissing her all over, gradually increasing the little doses of consolation I could offer her, whispering words of affection and encouragement into her ear. I wanted to give her as complete a sense of security as I could. I wanted to show that I was there just for her and I was ready to share her sorrows, but instead I managed only to make her sadder. She clung to me as though she wanted to disappear inside my body. Our hearts became twins again, beating together with the same intensity, until at last she let out a cry of ecstasy and escape, liberty and pain.

The next day I went with her to the Porto Nuovo station, where she was due to catch a train to Milan; she was leaving Turin permanently after living there for five years. The morning was sunny, the air was sweet and heavy with the fragrance of flowers, and the sluggish waters of the Po slipped slowly by like silent tortoises. It was a beautiful day, but not for Narina. Her eyes were still swollen from weeping.

I struggled desperately to think of something to cheer her up.

"Do you know something, Narina?" I began. "For a while now I've been wanting to say three words to you, just three words, and I think this would be the right time to do it. . . . Are you ready? Okay, here goes: a drunk approaches a woman who is breast-feeding her child and says, 'Excuse me, madam, you're not going to believe me, but your child has just invited me to dine. . . .' "

Narina started to roar with laughter. It was good to see her smile again.

"Three words?" she said. "I can see you don't know how to count! You're still a baby. . . ." She tapped me tenderly on the chest and whispered softly, "You're my baby."

That was the last time I saw her. She was smiling when she boarded the 11:15 train to Milan and disappeared from my life forever. As the train pulled away, she got smaller and smaller until she vanished into a black dot on the horizon. I was left there waving at the empty air, with only the memory of her tearful laughter.

With a heavy heart, I caught the bus back to the Corso Moncalieri, where I had an appointment with Chery. She had not told me why she had asked me over, but I expected it was for one of the delicious meals she sometimes cooked. When I got there, however, there was no sign of any kind of food. The table was not laid as it normally was, and neither were there any saucepans on the stove.

In the bedroom, Chery was talking on the telephone in a chaotic mixture of Spanish, Italian, and English, and I wondered who on earth she was speaking to.

"Yes, yes, *va bene.* I need the information for the visa and the air ticket. You can send the contract to . . . Okay? *Nos vemos.*"

She put down the telephone.

"Ah, Junior, you've arrived, come here."

I went to sit on her bed.

"You probably heard my telephone conversation, didn't you? You were asking yourself what the hell I was saying?"

I had been thinking exactly that and collapsed into fits of giggles.

"I know my English is terrible, but I was speaking to Ivan Nagy, the

director of the English National Ballet. He's going to send your contract and your plane ticket to London next week."

"My contract? My ticket?"

We had not mentioned the subject of Ivan Nagy's offer since his
visit, knowing it would be problematic, including the many visa difficulties that would need to be resolved. And I had already decided I
would follow the more traditional route to success in Cuba by agree-
ing to join the Cuban National Ballet. I was dancing the role of the falconer in the forthcoming tour of Mexico; the dates were already
finalized, and I would be letting people down if I left.

Chery took a sip of her Coca-Cola. She put the glass down on the
bedside table and breathed deeply, as if she wanted to get a great weight
off her chest.

"I've been thinking about this for a long time, analyzing all the possible complications and consequences. When I think about your future,
I know that you have to leave. You have something that can take you
far and at the same time might be lost because of a bad decision. It could
be that I will be criticized in Cuba and even punished for deciding what
is good or bad for you, but in this career, time is of the essence and this
is your moment. An opportunity like this doesn't come along very
often. It's your life, your profession, and I am determined that you
should take this step."

She stopped speaking, and we sat for a moment in silence. I started
to feel excited—and nervous.

"But what will they say in Cuba when they find out that I'm not
going back? And what will happen to you?"

"I don't know," Chery answered. "I only know that you have to
accept this contract."

Again there was silence. I did not know what to say, and Chery had
said everything she wanted to. She got up from the bed, went into the
kitchen, and took a little blue pot containing a dessert she had made out
of the fridge. She gave it to me and, with a hug, told me she wanted
some time alone.

My mind was in a whirlwind.

When I arrived at my apartment, the guys I was living with fell upon
the crème caramel as if they were starving. I did not tell them about my
farewell to Narina or the contract with the English National Ballet until

they had finished eating. When, at last, I revealed the news, they were all overjoyed for me, and we celebrated with loud music until the early hours of the morning.

Two weeks later, we all said good-bye in the street. The Mesturino family was there, as well as Ariel, Antonio, Juan Enrique, Osvaldo Beiro, and, of course, Chery. I had written a letter to my family explaining my departure, and those of us there were all rather jolly. The boys were shaking my hand and giving me tips on making love in Nordic countries, and I was cracking up with laughter when I turned to Chery. Her eyes sent a shock through my whole body. They were not her usual sorceress's eyes, powerful, big, and blue; instead, they were sad and intense, and she locked into my own gaze like a mother attempting to transmit a painful message: "You have to start a new adventure now, but I can't come with you this time."

I got into the car, as thrilled by her affection as if my own mother had been there at my side. I was a bit sad and a bit happy, knowing that I was leaving the sweetest years of my adolescence behind in the Corso Moncalieri. When I arrived at the airport, I felt that in the course of the journey I had become a man.

When Chery got back to Havana, she was accused by the directorate of the Cuban National Ballet of acting irresponsibly by exposing me, so young, to the brutalities of capitalism. Her detractors said I would be sure to undergo an irreversible ideological subversion and that foreign influences would undermine my Cuban identity.

It was a difficult battle, but Chery's attitude and her many achievements, which included training generations of Cuban dancers, had always been irreproachable. Because of this, all the accusations designed to tarnish her image and all the energy spent in trying to ruin her reputation gradually dissipated until everything was finally forgotten.

In 2004, Ramona de Sáa, always known as Chery to her students, received the Medal of Merit and was recognized as one of the principal jewels of dance in our country, and today this is how she is referred to. But within the ballet community, people speak of her as the teacher who saved the career of Carlos Acosta.

And I remain as Cuban as I ever was.

Chapter 13

LONDON AT EIGHTEEN

At Heathrow Airport I was met by a man holding a card with my name on it; he drove me to a hotel close to the company base. I could not stop smiling as I looked at London for the first time through the car window. It was September 1991; the sun was shining, and people were out on the streets, shopping, climbing on and off red buses, or drinking coffee in sidewalk cafés. I never imagined that it would be so green. The parks were swarming with people, some playing Frisbee, others soccer, a few even splashing in a fountain. Everyone was clinging to the sun as if it might suddenly disappear: women in bikinis were stretched out on towels sunbathing as if they were on a beach in the Caribbean, while men in brightly colored shirts strolled past, occasionally stopping to stare.

The agreement was that the company would pay for my lodgings for my first week there, and after that I would have to find myself somewhere to live. I had no idea how I was going to manage this with no English, but, before the week was out, my friends and fellow dancers José Manuel Carreño and Lourdes Novoa arrived from Cuba, and we decided to find a place for all three of us. We rented a flat in Olympia, which was conveniently close to the company, but the entire apartment consisted only of one bedroom, a tiny kitchen, a narrow bathroom, and a medium-sized living room with a sofa that would be my bed. The place reminded me very much of my apartment at Corso Moncalieri, both in dimension and design, the only difference being that the sofa here did not convert into a bed. Every night I had to take the cushions off, arrange them on the carpet, and cover them with a sheet. I slept like that for the whole of my ten-month stay in London.

I did not have a problem with sleeping on the floor again. It made sense because José and Lourdes were a couple and needed their privacy, and, in any case, I was so pleased to be living with them that I would have been content to sleep in the bathroom or even on the roof. It also meant that we could save money, which was good because the company salaries were not very high and this was one of the most expensive cities in the world.

José Manuel had been with the company for two years, had a good command of English, and knew his way around. The first thing he told me to do was to open an account at the Gloucester Road branch of Barclays Bank. I did not have a clue how banks worked, so José Manuel explained that our salaries were paid directly into our bank accounts and that this would help me establish some credit in the U.K. After a while I would receive a credit card and checkbook; then I would be able to buy things in advance and pay for them in installments. I thought of my family and imagined my sisters buying things on credit. They were never going to believe me when I told them.

The second thing I had to do, and with much more urgency, was to learn English. Those first few weeks at the ballet, I could not leave José's side. As soon as I did, someone would come up and start speaking English to me, and I would rush off to find him—running up and down the stairs like a lunatic, searching all over the company, dragging him out of a rehearsal—just so that he could tell me someone was simply asking me how old I was.

The first two weeks were a disaster. I had to get my hair cut, so I decided, with José's help, to ask the company receptionist which was the best place to go, because she was a mixed-race woman with hair similar to mine. She recommended a barbershop in Brixton. I did not know London at all and used to get lost trying to find my way back to the flat in Olympia, so I called a taxi to take me to Brixton. When I arrived at the barbershop, I could not help noticing that all the haircuts were a bit odd, like the ones rappers have, shaved really close to the head. Into many of them, barbers had cut words and symbols, using very fine blades. There was a young man, about my age, who had the legend "Mother, there is only one" inscribed onto the back of his head. Clearly all of this made me rather nervous, especially when a female hairdresser chewing gum came up to me holding an electric razor and said a few words that I did not understand. I improvised some instructions about how I wanted my hair cut, using hand signals and a lot of pantomime. The woman stopped chewing and looked at me as though I were an extraterrestrial. She said something else, a longer phrase this time, but I had no idea what she was saying. One of the only words I knew in English was *here*. Touching both sides of my head with my hands, I repeated, "Here and here," then, touching the back of my head, I said, "Not here." Lastly, grabbing the lock of hair that fell over my forehead, I told her "*más o menos* [more or less] here." The woman spat out her chewing gum in order to give me her full attention. I repeated the instructions again: "Here and here, not here, *más o menos* here."

She turned on the electric razor. "I understand," she said, and started to cut the hair on the back of my head, exactly where I had told her not to.

"No, no, stop, stop!"

She turned off the razor as I sprang up to look at myself in the mirror. There was an almost bald strip in the middle of my mass of hair. I almost had a heart attack.

"*Ah carajo!* Shit! I say you *que* not here!" I exclaimed.

She very calmly put another piece of gum in her mouth and said once more, "I understand."

I had no choice but to sit down in the chair again and let her finish the job.

Fifteen minutes later, with my head smoother than a billiard ball, I was up off my seat and out of there like a shot, terrified in case she had written "Mother, there is only one" on the back of my head.

Out on the street, I suddenly fitted in and was greeted with calls of "What's up, man!" and "How you doing, bro?" but when I showed up back at the company, nobody recognized me. When they realized that the billiard ball was me, they all went into shock and fell about with laughter, especially the director, Ivan Nagy. The receptionist, however, kept repeating that she thought I looked really sexy.

A few days later, José informed me that there was to be a gala at Covent Garden to raise money for an organization that protected endangered wildlife. Apparently, Ivan Nagy wanted me to dance a contemporary duet by Robert North with one of the ballerinas from the company. I had scarcely been in London for two weeks, and José told me it was a huge compliment to have been chosen to represent the English National Ballet at the event. World-famous ballet dancers would be participating, like Natalia Makarova, who would present the show, and stars like Alexander Vetrov and Darcey Bussell, who were just beginning to shine. I had never heard of any of them. Needless to say, nobody had ever heard of me either. José added that Diana, Princess of Wales, would be in attendance, and I would likely have the pleasure of meeting her at the end of the performance.

"You're kidding!" I said to my friend, who explained that the princess was the patron of the company, that she regularly attended the ballet—especially performances by the English National—and that this would not be the last time I would meet her at the end of a function.

"When she approaches you, you only have to say, 'Nice to meet you!'" José said. "That's how you say *'Encantado de conocerle'* in English."

The phrase sounded very strange to me, so José said it again, this time more slowly. "Nice to meet you!"

I repeated the phrase until it tripped off my tongue quite easily.

The day of the gala arrived, and while I put on my makeup, I practiced the words again: "Nais tu mit yu, nais tu mit yu!"

I rehearsed the phrase once more during warm-up, and the words slid out fluently. I took off my leg warmers and walked toward the stage to dance. I performed the choreography with all the leaps and turns that the interpretation demanded, and at the end I took my curtain call with a bow. After the performance, all the dancers lined up on the stage to meet Diana.

The princess was tall and elegant. She took her time speaking to the artists, looking attentively into the eyes of each one, as if she wanted to know every detail of their lives: their origins, their hopes, their fears, everything. We all watched in awe, following her every step, her every gesture, as if she were not a woman at all but a goddess. She radiated light and brought a glow to each face present, but as each dancer succumbed in turn to her magic, I was beginning to panic. I had forgotten my words.

"Nais tu michu? Nois tumich?"

Oh hell! What were those damn words again?

"Nais te tomato?"

Diana moved down the line toward me. She was going a little faster now, stretching out her right hand in greeting and continuing on her way.

Shit, dammit, how do you say it? Nais . . . no, no, nois . . . nisee . . . Aha, now I've got it! Nise tu makun!

Suddenly, eyes as blue as the Cuban sea were hovering above mine, putting me into a trance. Gregorian chants echoed in my head. The same thing that had happened with Olga and Narina was happening now with Princess Diana. She offered her hand to me without dropping her eyes. Her skin was as white as pearl and very soft. Her reddish mouth said something. My legs felt weak as she kept her eyes fixed on mine, the royal teeth smiling. I was hypnotized, floating, melting, my ears ringing. As her mouth opened again to say something else, I realized the princess had been asking me questions for quite some time now without receiving any answers. She was probably thinking I was very ill-mannered. I tried to tell her of the immense pleasure I had in meeting her, to tell her that I was called Charles like her husband, that I came from Cuba. I wanted to tell her so many things. My mouth opened wide, my smile still intact, and, gripping her hand, I said the only thing I could.

"Here."

The dancers standing on either side of me let out stifled giggles, covering their mouths with their hands. Diana's countenance hardened, her eyes opened wide, and her eyebrows shot up in astonishment. I understood from the dancers' laughter and from the princess's expression that they thought I was playing the fool. I desperately tried to remember the words that José had taught me.

"Here," I said once more, and again the nearest dancers laughed.

Diana, looking a little taken aback, withdrew her hand and moved on. I buried my head in my hands to cover my embarrassment. Then suddenly, miraculously, just as Diana was offering her hand to the next dancer, I remembered the phrase José Manuel had taught me. Desperate to tell the princess before she abandoned me completely, I yelled at the top of my voice, as if the poor woman were standing a whole block away and not right beside me.

"Nise tu makun!"

There was silence. Everybody's eyes turned to stare at the place where the shout had come from. For the first time in my life I felt my ears burning. The princess looked at me solemnly, then she smiled slightly and proceeded to give her due attention to the next dancer. I just stood there wanting the stage to open up and swallow me.

When I recounted the incident to José Manuel and Lourdes, they did not stop laughing all night.

With so much to learn and so much to do, time passed rapidly, and as winter closed in, the days grew shorter. Suddenly it was night at four in the afternoon. In the studios there was not a single window to show us the outside world. We worked enclosed within walls that were covered with mirrors and wooden barres, breathing old and tainted air. The principal odors were the whiff of rancid cheese that human beings tend to give off, combined with the acrid scent of sweat-soaked warm-up clothes. But after working for five or eight hours daily, the smells seemed less strong, and our revulsion diminished. I had encountered far worse conditions in Cuba, with temperatures in the nineties, struggling with only one pair of ballet shoes, uncomfortable dance belts, and food and water shortages. We never made a fuss there, and I would not do so at the English National Ballet. I had come to learn, not to complain.

Four weeks after my arrival in London, following hours of intensive rehearsal, I was ready to make my debut with the company, dancing the "Polovtsian Dances" from *Prince Igor.* The debut took place in Manchester during the English National Ballet's winter tour around the U.K. The other dancers wished me luck, and some wrote me beautiful words of inspiration on brightly colored cards, which I gathered up and gave to José so he could translate them for me. Before getting into costume, I went to get made up by a woman who painted on elaborately "Chinese" eyes with pointy, sloping eyebrows that made me look as if I were in a bad mood. She drew on an enormous mustache, then shoved a tiny hat on my head.

"Bloody hell!" I exclaimed as I observed myself in the mirror. I looked like a Chinese man, only black.

I put on my costume: a jacket open to the chest, trousers, and boots. Over the PA system in the dressing room, I could hear the sound of the orchestra starting to tune their instruments. My heart was pounding. I took my kit and went to warm up in a small studio. Finally the five-minute call was given, and I walked out onstage. The curtain went up. The music started to play. I leaped out like a lion just freed from its cage, dancing as though this were the final performance of my life instead of my first one with the English National Ballet. At the end of the show, the director and the dancers applauded me to welcome me into their midst, and thus I was baptized as a member of that important ballet company.

In my fifth week with the company, I opened in a three-act ballet, *The Nutcracker*, with choreography by Ben Stevenson. Ivan Nagy himself applied my makeup and again the other dancers gave me cards and applauded me at the end of the show. I realized then that it was part of the company's culture to be happy at the success of others. There was no jealousy, none of that typical bickering and complaining so often found in the dance world. It was like a big happy family.

After two months in the U.K., even the disadvantage of not knowing the language did not bother me anymore. Ivan worked at teaching me how to dance with a partner, correcting the positioning of my hands on the lifts and taking painstaking interest in all the details, allowing me to learn all the subtle skills needed for the art of partnering. Little by little, as I improved and the company became more confident in my abilities, I was given roles in new ballets. *La Bayadère* was next. I danced it in Bristol with my roommate Lourdes Novoa. The *pas des deux* from *Don Quixote* followed, with María Teresa del Real as my partner; we performed in a gala for the company's patrons, on a stage specially constructed in a private house. Meanwhile, I was learning *Our Waltzes* by the Venezuelan choreographer Vicente Nebrada and *Etudes* by Harald Lander, as well as rehearsing the role of Benvolio with Peter Schaufuss for the Frederick Ashton version of *Romeo and Juliet*. I also had the chance to dance with the stars of the time, such as Ludmila Semenyaka and Eva Evdokimova. On several occasions, I paid the price for my inexperience when dancing with such luminaries. Eva Evdokimova was always patient with me as I tried to overcome an eighteen-year-old's terror at dancing with a legend. When I danced with Semenyaka, however, there was never any doubt whose fault it was if any mistakes were made.

One rainy day, when Liz Teuhi and I were rehearsing *The Nut-*

cracker, a stout, blond man appeared, sporting a bright tropical shirt in a vain attempt to conceal his enormous stomach.

"Hi, I'm Ben Stevenson," the choreographer said diffidently. He shook my hand, kissed my partner, and went to sit down beside the ballet coach Woytek Lowski, who indicated to us we should start from the beginning. We danced the adagio, the solos, and the coda. At the end, Ben got up from his seat and spoke to us about the positioning of the arms, how a landing should not detract from the elegance of a jump, and about the conduct of princes and princesses, using his own body to demonstrate what he meant when I struggled to understand his English. He said dance should communicate all sorts of different emotions — beauty, strength, or cruelty — and that the steps, even if they were the same technically, should be imbued with different meaning each time they were performed. He explained what his aims had been in creating the choreography we were dancing, treating us to a lecture of at least half an hour. By the time he had finished talking, our bodies were chilled.

I thought it was odd that he had not paid any attention to the quantity of leaps and pirouettes that I had done during my solos, but instead asked me to use my face and eyes more, and to think about the history of the prince as I performed all the steps. Instead of being impressed, he just kept correcting me. I finished the rehearsal, collected up my things, and started to leave, feeling rather disgruntled, but as I was going out of the room, I heard his voice behind me.

"Hey, Carlos! How's Alicia Alonso?"

"I don't know. Well, I suppose," I replied.

"Is she still dancing?" Ben asked.

"Do you know her?"

"Oh yes. The last time I saw her dance was at that famous gala in Vienna with Margot, Plisetskaya, and Carla Fracci. The bows lasted longer than the whole show, and at the end there was a battle between Alonso and Plisetskaya to see who would get the final bow. Guess who won?"

I started to laugh. Ben continued telling anecdotes, making jokes, and kidding around. He did not seem anything like the person who, just moments before, had been pontificating on the history of our art.

Then he said something I could not believe: "I'd like to invite you to dance with the Houston Ballet."

The words caused a storm of confusion inside my head. Houston is in Texas. Texas is in the United States. . . . The United States! . . . Imperialism! . . . First of May, Committees for the Defense of the Revolution, Blockade! . . . Impossible!

Taking my stunned silence as a refusal, Ben said, "Of course I'd speak to Ivan. I wouldn't want him to think I was poaching you for my company!"

"Please forgive me." I tried to explain my inability to reply. "I would really love to. It's just that it's impossible. You see, the thing is, I'm Cuban, and Cuba and the United States have been enemies for thirty years because of politics. It's impossible for a Cuban to work there without being seen as a defector, and I don't want to do that because I'm terrified of never seeing my family again. . . ."

"Oh, don't worry about that," said Ben casually, mopping his brow. "We can sort it all out with a good lawyer."

He gave me a couple of slaps on the back and started down the stairs, heading toward the exit. On the way he bumped into Ivan Nagy; they whispered something to each other and laughed, then continued together down the stairs.

That night I dreamed that my family was there with me in London. I had just finished dancing, and, at the end of the show, on the way out of my dressing room, there they all were: My mother was wearing an elegant dress and looked like Princess Diana herself. My father, not to be outdone, wore a black suit with a white shirt and a red tie. Marilín was dressed in white, with her hair dyed black; she carried a handbag, also white, which she held with studied disdain; her heels were high, and she wore little makeup. Berta, on the other hand, wore a dark brown dress and low heels, her blond hair loose to the shoulders. They were all dressed up to see me dance. We wept to see one another again, and then went out to eat at an Italian restaurant in Soho. I willed myself not to wake up. Little did I suspect that the next evening, during a meal organized by one of the company patrons, I would meet the Cuban American consul of the U.S. Embassy in London, to whom I poured out my dreams of reuniting with my mother's family in Florida and how, eventually, I hoped for a reconciliation between them and my mother.

Two weeks later, I had a U.S. tourist visa stamped inside my Cuban passport.

After hours of trying, I finally managed to get through to Delia, my only neighbor in Los Pinos who had a telephone. Her house was like a phone booth, with a continuous stream of people going in and out. To actually get through to anyone was nothing short of a miracle. Delia yelled up to my mother, who flew down the stairs to the telephone. Neither my father nor my sisters were at home: Marilín had moved into her boyfriend's apartment about a month before; Berta, whose condition had improved a little, was still living with Eduardo; my father was working. When I told my mother I had an American visa, she ran back up to the house and returned with an old address for my aunt and grandmother.

"Don't worry, Mami, I'll find them," I told her.

"Tell them that I love them and that I haven't forgotten them!"

I promised her that I would tell them and then hung up. I could not bear to hear my mother cry.

The next day I wrote a short letter:

Hallo Aunty,

It's me, Yuli, your nephew. I'm working in London as a ballet dancer. Papi got it into his head to enroll me in a ballet school shortly after you all left. How are Granny and my cousin? We're all fine. We miss you a lot. I'd love to come and see you; let me know if you're still living at this address.

A week later I received her reply, a melancholy letter, as long as a newspaper article, apologizing for her silence of eleven years. I did not recognize my aunt in the letter. She seemed, incredibly, to have softened. She called me "my boy," "my nephew"; she treated me like family. I could not recall a single generous act from her toward my sister Marilín or me, although I could remember all the times she left us at home to bring Berta, our white sister, to the beach.

Well, isn't life full of surprises, I thought, putting my aunt's letter away in my pocket. I still could not shake the memory of her taking my granny away from my mother. "You can stay, María. I'm taking Mami!"

I remembered all those nights when my mother, inexplicably, would curl up in a corner of the patio and, if we discovered her, would claim an onion had been irritating her eyes, then return once more to her cooking. Deep down, we knew her tears were provoked by something much more painful.

"I swear I'm doing this for you, Mamá, only for you!" I muttered to myself.

Two weeks later, I was sitting in a plane, headed for Miami.

I had always thought the nearest I would come to seeing the United States was at the cinema. All Cubans, be it out of curiosity or spite, long to visit the sights they have seen in the movies, like Hollywood, the Big Apple, the Empire State Building. However, finding a Cuban in the United States who has not defected is more difficult than finding a needle in a haystack.

Waiting in line at passport control, I realized that they did not come across Cuban passports with North American tourist visas very often, which made me nervous. There was a neon sign above one of the desks that said RESIDENT ALIENS. I did not know "aliens" was just the way U.S. Immigration refers to foreigners; all I could think about was the film *Alien*, and I felt that was what I was, standing in line—an alien, a terrifying creature, and, even worse, a Cuban alien.

Trembling, I got out my passport and deposited it on the counter. The officer looked as if he, too, was Cuban, and his accent told me he was a native, born on the island, maybe even in Los Pinos itself. Nevertheless, he looked at my passport for a long time, as if he had a precious antiquity in his hands, something from a museum collection. He perused every page, examined each number, each letter, each visa, each stamp. My aunt had said she would meet me at the airport, but the immigration officers kept me waiting for so long, I was sure she would have given up and gone home.

Luckily, she waited for me on the other side, with a beautiful girl I was astonished to discover was my cousin Corairis. Another surprise was waiting in the parking lot.

"This is Roberto, my husband," Mireya said.

Roberto was a black man of mixed race. He was darker than I was. What next? I wondered.

The landscape of Miami was as exotic as a film set. Driving to my aunt's house in Hialeah, we passed hundreds of enormous skyscrapers and amusement parks from which roller coasters loomed high, arriving after about forty minutes in a neighborhood in which each house had its own well-tended patch of green lawn and garage.

My aunt's house was painted beige. Curtained windows framed either side of the front door. It was spacious: three bedrooms, each one with its own bathroom, a huge living room with a tiled floor, a medium-sized carpeted dining room, an open-plan kitchen with a linoleum floor, and a large L-shaped garden that ran down the entire right-hand side of the house before veering off to the left. There was also a tool shed, big enough for someone to live in.

My aunt's situation was better than I had expected. They had electrical appliances we had never even dreamed of having in Los Pinos, luxury ornaments and decorations, many different kinds of lamps, as well as reproductions and lithographs of famous paintings on the walls. As I ran my eyes over the living room, I noticed that among all the various pictures and images there was not a single photograph of my mother or the rest of us.

"Mami, look at this surprise!" said Mireya.

An obese woman got up with enormous effort from the sofa. Her legs were bowed and swollen, covered with dozens of purple varicose veins and red capillaries visible from twenty feet away. Her expression was sweet, and her white hair was flecked with patches of black. My grandmother had become an old woman.

"Hello, Granny, how are you?" I said as I went to hug her.

The black eyes that squinted evasively back at me seemed anxious to hide whatever it was they had been storing up over the years. I would have liked to say to her that I had missed her since she had left, but she would know I was lying. So I said to her, "Granny . . . how time flies!" and with an effort similar to the one that had gotten her up off the sofa, she forced a wan smile across her lips and remained silent. I knew that this woman was my grandmother, that some of her blood coursed through my veins, yet I felt no more for her than I would have for a person I had only just met. All that linked us were some vague memories. It was the same with my aunt and my cousin. I felt as if I were in a house of strangers. However, I told myself, I was there for Mamá. I would take my mother back a detailed description of her mother's features, tell her how she was faring, what kind of splendor she was living in, and all the things that had happened to her over the past eleven years. Mamá would be able to see in my eyes the reflected image of her mother.

The next day they took me on a tour of the city, and I still felt as if I were in the artificial world of the Hollywood movies. It was only when we went shopping and found a ballet shop with a photo of me in one of the magazines that I felt real again.

My Miami family had become devout Christians, and they took me to church for the first time in my life. I was nervous that I would not know what to do, and I wished I had paid more attention in the Bible classes Berta had insisted on taking me to, but when I saw all the people weeping and fainting, some shouting, "Amen, Amen, praise the Lord!" I had to fight the desire to burst into uncontrollable laughter. I had always wanted something to believe in, something that would explain the world to me and fill me with faith, but this certainly was not it.

Amid all these feelings of alienation, I could not stop thinking about the tragic rift between my mother and her family. I relived that terrible farewell: the cold, formal kiss my aunt gave to my sister Marilín and me; the gawking faces of the neighbors; my mother coming down the stairs, embracing my grandmother.

My aunt Mireya seemed to share my distress. One day, she called me into her room so we could talk. She hesitated before speaking the second word, searching for it carefully in her head: "I . . . I'm . . . sorry."

She said that she was repentant about her past, that she knew she had treated my father, Marilín, and me with contempt, and that she was sorry for the suffering she had caused my mother. She promised to write her from now on, though she still had not explained why she had not written for the last eleven years. She wept and told me she had nightmares in which Lucia appeared with the sheet twisted around her neck, and then suddenly her tears poured out like torrential rain.

"Don't cry, Aunt, all those things happened a long time ago." I stroked her head as though she were a child.

"Mamá says that she loves you, that she hasn't forgotten you, and that she doesn't feel any bitterness toward you. It's too late now to do anything about Aunt Lucia, but we can still do something for ourselves, for the whole family."

Little by little her sobs became weaker, like those of a wounded animal, until eventually they ceased. I laid her head back against a large pillow, and there was total silence in her bedroom.

Everyone else in the house was already asleep. I went outside to get some air. The sun had also gone to bed, and the neighborhood was quiet. Occasionally a car would pass by, blaring out salsa music, silence returning as it disappeared into the distance. The neighbors opposite turned out their lights. I breathed deeply, listening to the sound of the insects, the screech of a cat, the barking of a dog, and wondered why my family had to be divided.

On Monday, Corairis and her boyfriend, Ivan, took me out to lunch at Versailles Restaurant on Calle Ocho for an excellent Cuban meal: chicken in sauce, *ropa vieja* (shredded beef), strips of fried pork, fried plantains, cassava root with garlic, *mariquitas,* and the dish of rice and beans famously known as Moors and Christians.

"Cousin, aren't all ballet dancers supposed to be on a diet?" Corairis asked me as I wolfed down the huge helpings.

I replied that nobody was ever going to have to lift me up with one hand.

Ivan coughed awkwardly. "Pardon my ignorance, Yuli," he said. "But somehow I thought all male ballet dancers were gay."

I told them that, of course, this was not true; ballet has nothing to do with a person's sexuality. I went on to say that I knew of masters of karate and Olympic medal winners who were homosexuals. I told them the story of a boy who dreamed of being a ballet dancer but his father forbade it because he said all ballet dancers were faggots, so the boy grew up to be gay but not a ballet dancer. It seemed to give them pause for thought, but I could see that they did not quite believe me.

My aunt's husband, Roberto, obviously had the same problem. He could not understand how it was possible that I did not get a hard-on dancing with all those beautiful ballerinas in their tight-fitting leotards, lifting their legs up into the most erotic positions. I explained to him that the control ballet demands is an art you learn from a very early age, that everything becomes habit, and that you learn to concentrate in order to dance as well as possible. I do not think he was convinced.

It was with Roberto that I had the most alien experience of all, when he invited me to smoke a little marijuana in his toolshed. I had never smoked so much as a cigarette before, and at first I did not think the marijuana had any effect on me. But, a few minutes later, when I tried to help Roberto mow the lawn, I suddenly felt as if my legs were leaving the lawn and carrying me with the mower up to cut grass in the sky. I could still see myself below, also cutting the grass, and I lost all notion of which Carlos I was, the one above or the one below, as if I were actually in two places at the same time. More Carloses appeared in front of me, all of them happily mowing. We waved at each other. Some of the Carloses were break-dancing, others were doing the macarena. It was one big party where happiness, love, and lots of green grass reigned. I was surrounded by happy Carloses, all except one, who appeared not to like me, and would not stop waving his arms around and shouting. As my eyes narrowed to focus on him, I realized that he was not me at all, but a neighbor who was angry because I had ruined his lawn.

I was very sick after that and spent the rest of my holiday in bed, with my aunt tending to me.

When the day of my departure came, we all gathered in the living room to say our farewells. I had one last thing left to do in Miami.

Communications between Cuba and the United States were broken, which made it impossible to make a phone call directly to the island. The only option was to make a three-way connection via Canada, which required a reliable friend to the north. I now had one, and I called my friend William in Montreal to give him the phone number of my neighbor Delia.

Everyone in the Miami living room waited, curious to know what I was up to. My grandmother was sunk in gloomy silence on her sofa, and Mireya kept looking doubtfully into my eyes. Corairis was sitting beside her boyfriend. Roberto was in his toolshed as usual.

Suddenly the phone rang, and William said my mother was on the line.

"How are you, son?" she asked, but I did not answer her. I took the phone and passed it straight over to my grandmother.

For a moment, the old woman maintained her inscrutable expression. Then her eye twitched, her lips puckered slightly, tears began to roll down her face, and her body began to quake like a quivering bird, until finally she spoke. "My daughter . . . my darling daughter . . . forgive me, forgive me, forgive me for abandoning you!"

I find it hard to describe the scene, though I remember it vividly: an old lady with barely the strength to live sobbing like a child; a sister covering her head to shut out the ghosts of the past; a young couple blocking their ears so that they would not have to hear my grandmother's cries; and, at the other end of the telephone, my mother's suffering connected to ours by a cable routed through Canada.

I wondered if there could be anything worse than witnessing the weeping of an old lady for a daughter she could not see. I felt powerless at not being able to console my grandmother but, at the same time, liberated by the knowledge that my mother had finally spoken to her mother after all these years. It was what Mamá had wanted most in the world.

I was relieved to return to London after my week in the United States, but I could not stop thinking about my divided family, and I had trouble concentrating on my dancing.

I had just finished a rehearsal of *The Spectre of the Rose;* my clothes and ballet shoes were soaked through with sweat, I went to practice a jump with my friend José, and I never took off. My foot slid out from under me, and the full weight of my body came down on my right ankle.

José ran to lift me up from the floor. The other dancers, who had also seen what had happened, did the same. I told them to leave me sitting down. I took off my shoes and leg warmers and slowly rotated my right ankle. It hurt and was swelling rapidly. I signaled to my friend to help me get up off the floor to see if I could bear the weight of my body on both my legs. The pain grew stronger. José went with me to the physiotherapy department, where they put my foot in a bucket of ice. The ice did nothing to help the pain, and the following day I went to get an X-ray.

"You have a bone spur," Dr. Strong, the company physician, explained when he saw me the next morning. A piece of bone had become detached and had lodged itself in my right ankle joint. Apparently it was very common among ballet dancers, especially those in the U.K., and I need not worry. He advised that I required a simple operation, followed by eight to ten weeks of recovery before I would be completely healed. But from that moment on, the winter in London seemed interminable to me.

They operated at the end of March. When I came round from the anesthetic, I found myself in a ward full of empty beds and with seven stitches in my ankle. The rain slid rapidly down the windowpane, and the few trees that were visible in the distance were bent double by the wind. Outside, a multitude of people bobbed around under a sea of umbrellas, their arms and hands weighed down with bags from John Lewis or Top Shop or Selfridges. Rain was no impediment to the serious business of shopping. The indistinct babble of voices seemed to float up and lodge itself in my head.

The worst thing that can happen to a dancer is to wake up and discover he cannot move. I kept fooling myself into believing that nothing had happened, and I had a tremendous desire to get out of bed and dance the variation from *The Corsair.* I would sense the music inside me and hear the applause; at once my chest would swell with the joy and exhilaration that dancing inspires in me. Then I would remember that I was prostrate on my bed, like a prisoner in a cell.

I started to think like a bored prisoner, to stroll in my imagination through the streets and places where I had once been happy. I got used to not hoping for anything. The only glimmer of happiness I had was when Lourdes Novoa visited me (which she did, religiously, sometimes canceling rehearsals on all kinds of pretexts in order to come to see me), but I was depressed again when she left.

I began to think weird thoughts. If I could get used to not dancing, then perhaps I could get used to anything. I might be able to get used to living in a wardrobe, for example. I spent a month without ballet, recuperating in my flat, and I noticed that when I looked at myself in the mirror and tried to smile, my reflection remained serious. I heard voices call out from beneath the sofa and chairs, voices in every corner of my room. Yet I knew I was on my own in the flat. I opened the window for some air, and the voices continued to laugh wickedly. I covered my head with a pillow, but I could not silence them. And then I recognized my own voice among the babble. I realized I had been talking to myself and swore I would never speak about it to anyone.

Eight weeks went by, and I still could not flex my foot. I was not worried about the pain so much as the fact that I still had not recovered any movement. It was as though the piece of bone were still lodged in my ankle joint. I followed the instructions of Dr. Strong and the physical therapist to the letter, but I developed keloids both inside and outside of the scar, and the pain was more intense than ever.

In June, I returned to ballet classes once more, with my foot in worse shape than ever. The doctors said I should be patient, but the pain was extraordinary. I could not dance *The Spectre of the Rose* and was given a part in *Les Sylphides* and the slave role in *Scheherazade,* because they did not require much jumping. I was nineteen years old, but I looked about forty. I was taking all kinds of sedatives and anti-inflammatory medication to keep the pain away. I tried to save my energy, hoard my reserves so that this show would not be my last, but deep down, I knew my days with the English National Ballet were numbered—it was no use continuing to dance in pain, giving less than my all. And yet I had many dreams I had hoped to realize with this contract, like moving my family in Cuba to a bigger house. I knew I would have to decide between dancing in a mediocre manner for money and allowing myself to perform only at my very best, even if this meant having to take more time off. It was a terrible decision to make.

To make matters worse, the voices in my head would not let me think clearly. They appeared at all hours. The wickedest said that this was the end. I thought about my sister Berta; she, too, had heard those voices. Perhaps they had persuaded her to run out naked into the street, and maybe they also told her to throw herself from the motorbike. I began to wonder whether I was schizophrenic, too, and that was truly terrifying.

One day during the English National Ballet's season at the Royal Festival Hall, one of the dancers became ill, and there was no one to replace him in *The Spectre of the Rose.* As I had learned the role before, Ivan Nagy asked me to dance. I did not hesitate; I downed all kinds of painkillers, smothered my ankle with Voltaren ointment, and went out onstage, dancing with all my might, jumping as never before, taking no notice of the pain. I laughed at my ankle and at all the voices in my head and took flight in a way I had not done for ages. In retrospect, I do not know what possessed me. After the show, Ivan Nagy congratulated me, and I was proud of myself, but right there and then, as the effect of the analgesic drugs gave way to the most terrible pain, I knew this was the end.

When I got home, I put all my clothes into two suitcases and the presents I had bought for my family into a third. José and Lourdes immediately sensed what was going on.

"Don't worry, everything will be fine," said Lourdes. We hugged each other so tightly that for a moment I thought she was my mother and found it very hard to disentangle myself from her embrace. José said good-bye to me with a promise that we would see each other again.

And so it was that I finished with the English National Ballet, a company that will always have a place in my heart.

The following day I limped my way to the airport and caught a plane back to Cuba.

Chapter 14

A YEAR WITHOUT DANCING

As usual, there was nobody waiting for me in the airport. Because communication with my family was virtually impossible from afar, ever since I had gone to school in Pinar del Río I had fallen into the habit of turning up unexpectedly. Months would go by and my family would receive no news of me; then suddenly I would appear unannounced at their door.

When I arrived back in Los Pinos, there seemed to be some sort of party going on at our house. Two men were sitting on the little balcony above the entrance, and shadows of different shapes and sizes patterned the light on the living room wall. The music pouring out of the open windows could be heard from a block away, so when the taxi drew up in front of the house, I tried to get the attention of the revelers inside by shouting, "I'm here, it's me, Yuli! I've just arrived!"

Nobody heard me. I paid the taxi driver, who helped me unload my suitcases onto the pavement. At that moment, Marilín came out onto the balcony and, spotting me, shouted, "Look, Mami! Yuli's here, Yuli's here!" She ran downstairs and flung herself upon me at the speed of a runaway horse.

All the people who were indoors, including my mother and father, came outside, and the two men on the balcony came down to help me up with my suitcases.

"Hey, Yuli, meet my boyfriend, Yiyo, and his brother Jesús!"

We all shook hands. Yiyo's grip was firm, and his green eyes contrasted dramatically with his dark skin.

Marilín told me she and Yiyo were celebrating their first anniversary as a couple as well as the end of Yiyo's three years of military service. The two dates happened to have coincided.

"You couldn't have arrived at a better time. Yiyo's mother has made some delicious pork crackling," said Marilín.

"What about Bertica?" I asked her as we went up the stairs.

Marilín assured me that our sister was much better, but that she had stayed at Eduardo's house because parties unsettled her.

It had been eight months since I had hugged my mother, and as I clung to her, I felt my legs giving way and heat rising up through my entire body to the tips of my ears.

"How have you been, Mamá?" I asked, but my mother could not speak.

Oh hell! I thought as I felt a lump constrict my throat.

We went into the living room, leaning awkwardly into each other, as my mother did not want to let go of me. She kept clinging to me even as I was introduced to Yiyo's mother, Caridad, and her husband.

My father remained seated in his wicker armchair. It had been eight months since our last terrible fight, and my position at the English National Ballet had helped to smooth things over between us. He was smiling, but his happiness seemed less easy and spontaneous than that of everybody else present. After Mamá managed to pull herself away from my chest, my father took the opportunity to come over and give me a kiss and a couple of little slaps on the back. Then he asked, "How did it go, son? Did you get on well in London?"

I told him that I had had a very good time, that I had danced in a three-act ballet for the first time, and that I was close friends with José Manuel Carreño and Lourdes Novoa. Before I could say anything else, however, my mother interrupted me to ask if I wanted something to eat. I said I did, so she went to the kitchen and returned with a plate of rice and beans and pork crackling. Everyone sat down, leaving me in the middle of the room. My father resumed his questioning.

"I can't believe that you've met Princess Diana," he said, as he drew his armchair closer to my seat while I told them all about that embarrassing encounter. Everybody except my father roared with laughter.

"Leave him be; his food will get cold!" said my mother, sticking her head out of the kitchen, but nobody took any notice.

They asked me about London. Were Big Ben and Buckingham Palace as majestic in real life as they appeared on television? Had I met Michael Jackson or gone to a soccer match? I answered their questions in as much detail as possible.

"I've heard it's a very lonely city and it rains a lot," declared Yiyo, as he went toward the refrigerator in search of another beer. As soon as my sister's boyfriend opened his mouth, my father's face grew hard.

"It's true, but there are other things that make up for it," I answered, then continued to tell everyone all the great things about London. They looked at me, rapt, as if I was somebody important, a minister or something, which I rather liked, so I went on, telling them about the winter, the darkness, and the rain, and inadvertently mentioning my operation.

"What do you mean an operation? Come on, let's see!" ordered my father. My mother left what she was doing in the kitchen to come look at my scar. I told them how I had injured myself, explaining that I had found the trip to Miami very emotional and afterward had found it difficult to concentrate in rehearsals and that I thought this was why I had hurt my ankle. I explained that after eight weeks of recuperating, I still was not completely better. My mother started crying again when she heard the word *Miami,* and Marilín went to comfort her. My father, however, was furious.

"How many times have I told you not to think about anyone else and to concentrate on your career? Now look what's happened; who knows when you'll be able to dance again!"

There was silence in the living room. My father had gotten up from his chair and was pacing around the tiny area. Mamá went back to the kitchen, and Marilín sat on her boyfriend's lap. Jesús, his mother, and her husband were listening with interest.

I took advantage of the silence to lift a spoonful of the food Mamá had prepared for me to my mouth. I did not want to get into an argument with my father after an eight-month absence. Anyway, there was nothing that could be done. The seven stitches had already been in my ankle. I took a deep breath. At the precise moment the spoon was hovering in front of my mouth, my father burst into speech.

"You're such an idiot! Sometimes I wonder if you deserve your talent. The only thing you know how to do is to complain about life, all that rubbish about how you miss your family, as though that made you the unhappiest person in the whole wide world. Let me tell you something . . ."

My old man sat down in his armchair again, but this time he positioned himself directly opposite me.

"I never knew my father. I lost my only brother when I was twenty and my mother when I was twenty-seven. In my day, blacks were shoeshine boys, stevedores, newspaper sellers, street cleaners. Our jobs were the most inhuman, humiliating, and degrading, but even so we managed to live without this constant pessimism. We cleaned those streets for a pittance, put up with the beatings from the police and all the other humiliations, because, when all's said and done, that's just how life was. You are lucky enough to live in an age where talent is rewarded, and you have a God-given gift. But what do you do? You squander it, and you complain about what you don't have, instead of being happy with what you do! What's the use of a family if you can't breathe, if you're discriminated against? Don't look a gift horse in the mouth. This is your time, not mine. I only wish it were the other way around. I know that I would put all my energies into serving my talent and forget about everything else."

Nobody moved. My father continued to fix his dark eyes on mine. My mother had come out of the kitchen and was watching us silently.

How could my father speak to me like that after not seeing me for eight months, and in front of all those people I had only just met? We eyeballed each other defiantly; then something came over me.

I threw down the spoon, which bounced and clattered to the floor, and leaped to my feet, shouting: "You always criticize me! You never lose an opportunity to make me feel like shit. Tell me something, why do I have to be like you? I wouldn't do to my children what you did to me. Get it? There's a thing called freedom, and you've taken it away from me!"

"You're wrong," answered my old man. "How many people here can talk about Big Ben in London or the Leaning Tower of Pisa? How many have had the freedom to travel and to see these things? The television will be the nearest that I'll ever get to London—"

"And did you ever ask yourself if it would make me happy?" I countered. "Perhaps my happiness was never meant to be in London but here with my family; with you, for instance, loading up fruit. You never listened to me when I tried to tell you what I wanted to do with my life! You just put me into ballet and to hell with it. Now I'm supposed to be grateful, to be strong, and to forget about all of you, to concentrate on my career because that's what you would have done. But I am me, and my life is my life. I don't know how you can be so insensitive!"

"Sensitivity is for weak men," replied my father, waving his arms in the air. "In the midst of this jungle called life, sensitivity will kill you quicker than a stray bullet. That's what I've been trying to teach you all these years!"

"Let me die then. Better to die young with a heart than to live on for years without one," I answered him.

You could have heard a pin drop. The neighbors had turned down the volumes on their televisions and radios so as to better follow the argument. My mother was crying again as my father walked slowly over to the balcony in search of some air. I sat staring at my untouched plate of food upon the table.

"Well," said Yiyo cheerfully, trying to alleviate the tension. "I had an operation on my ankle once, and it didn't cause me any major problems. I was walking again after six weeks, and I wasn't left with any lasting damage. You'll soon recover, you'll see."

My father looked at Yiyo out of the corner of his eye and then strode toward him. "And are you by any chance a dancer?" His eyes betrayed his murderous intentions.

Yiyo swallowed his smile and shrank back.

"Listen to me, Papi!" said Marilín, standing between Yiyo and my father. "Yiyo and I are celebrating our first anniversary, and Yuli's just arrived; so don't you go ruining the night for us. Leave them both alone!"

"I'm talking to my son. Anybody who doesn't like it can leave," said my father, waving his hands angrily in the air.

"This is my house, too!" cried Marilín.

My mother rushed over to try to calm the situation, as did Yiyo's relatives. I stared at the floor, thinking about those black stevedores and shoeshine boys that my father had spoken of, then left the room. I climbed up to the roof, where the last of the pet pigeons I had kept as a child cooed at me sympathetically. With the echo of insults and threats fading in my ears, I opened the cage door, stroked its blue-gray feathers one final time, and let it go. It flew away and was soon swallowed up by the blackness. I watched the bird disappear into the night, wishing I could do the same.

Now that I was back home, it was impossible not to recognize that Cuba was going through a crisis. With the fall of the Berlin wall in 1989, the economy, which until then had been greatly dependent on help from the countries of the Socialist bloc, had fallen into a deep decline. Cuba had to develop strategies for its own economic survival. This was the beginning of the so-called Special Period, an experimental process aimed at maintaining the country's resources. This process brought with it an increase in the *apagones,* power cuts that could last for up to twenty hours a day. Dollars were illegal. When the police caught me with thirteen dollars in my pocket one day, I was arrested and released only when one of the officers at the police station recognized me. Instead, a new sort of money emerged. Issued by the Cuban government, *los chavitos* operated as a kind of check, a convertible currency given parity with the dollar. Cubans with *chavitos,* usually those who were able to travel abroad, had access to the hard-currency shops that sold electrical appliances, clothes, shoes, and food. In a desperate bid to obtain this convertible currency, people started to trade their gold and silver items at an outlet created by the government called the House of Silver.

Reforms were brought in to facilitate the development of tourism. Foreigners were allowed to invest in the country. The number of hotels and shopping centers grew, and the most exotic and beautiful areas of the island became exclusive tourist resorts. Overnight, tourism came to be the mainstay of the economy, overtaking sugar and tobacco. The emergence of the *chavitos* and the introduction of hard currency relegated the Cuban peso to second place. On the black market the exchange rate for 1 dollar was 120 pesos, almost the basic monthly salary for a worker.

I had been home for a month. When my injury did not improve with physical therapy, electro-acupuncture, and laser treatment, my father got it into his head that someone had cast a spell on me. He took me to see *su padrino,* his witch doctor, who lived in Párragas, a neighborhood close to Los Pinos. The man chanted something in an African language, sucked on his cigar, blew the smoke in my face, took a mouthful of white rum and spat it out all over me, threw conch shells on the ground, and concluded that, yes, I most certainly had been bewitched.

He instructed my father to buy a small ram, a small chicken, cocoa butter, palm oil, and toasted maize. We were told to return with these items and to bring a stone that I had chosen from a river, three candles, rum, and cigars. Only then could the spell be broken.

The ram cried like a human as its throat was slit with a sharp knife. It went on bellowing as if it were begging as the witch doctor mercilessly twisted its neck so that the blood could flow more freely. The red liquid stained the stone I had picked from a nearby river. Then, once the creature's soul had fled, the man cut open its stomach. He removed the organs, throwing them into a plastic bag, then cut off the animal's head, chucked that in the bag as well, and proceeded to skin the poor beast. He set the skin on fire, then scooped up the charred, pulverized result and mixed it with the cocoa butter, palm oil, and toasted maize to make a paste for me to rub on my foot every day. Not one to waste free food, he put what was left of the animal in the fridge.

Next, he quartered the small chicken and placed it next to the river stone. He lit the three candles and, chanting again in an African language, spat rum over the stone and over my face. He did the same thing with the cigar, blowing smoke over me till my eyes stung. Then he charged us 200 pesos for his services, which my father paid willingly, and told us we could go on our way free of worry because the spell had been lifted from me.

I spent a whole month rubbing that gruesome ointment on my foot. Every time I took the bus, people couldn't stop looking at me.

"Have you got a dead animal or something on your shoe, my boy?" an old lady asked me one day, covering her mouth to stop herself from vomiting from the stench.

But the ram and the chicken lost their lives in vain. My ankle showed no signs of improvement.

It was becoming increasingly obvious that I would have to have another operation, a realization that plunged me into a black hole. I was cheered up only by chats with my friend Rafael. He was one of the few in my year who had joined the Cuban National Ballet. He was now living in Los Pinos in a garage close to the neighborhood bakery. Every afternoon I would pass by his house, and we would talk about ballet.

One day I told him that I had met a girl in town.

"Rafa, do you remember Estefania, the dancer? Wow! What a woman! She's good enough to eat!"

Rafael's eyes opened wide. "Listen to me, Junior; forget about her. You don't want to get involved."

I looked at him in surprise. "Why? Why shouldn't I?"

"Julio Ariel had a thing with her, and he had to escape faster than a bullet. He says she's absolutely lethal."

"Lethal? What a load of bull."

"You think she's as harmless as a dead mosquito, but you've no idea. . . ."

"Well, anyway," I told him. "I've got a date with her this weekend."

"Okay," said Rafael. "But don't say I didn't warn you!" He gave me a mug of coffee. "And I wish you the best of luck with your conquest."

That weekend, I took Estefania to the Coppelia ice-cream parlor. She was tall, with black hair that reached to her waist and long, shapely legs. Her nose was narrow, slightly hooked, and her eyes were black and warm when she smiled. She loved hearing about my adventures in London.

"What a career you've had!" she said, as we stood in the queue for a table. "You must be so happy!"

"It started really well," I told her. "If it wasn't for this damn foot, I'd be preparing to tour Australia with the English National Ballet right now."

Estefania looked sympathetically at my ankle.

"Does it hurt a lot?" she asked.

Before I could answer, we managed to get a seat. Estefania ordered a strawberry sundae, and I ordered a chocolate one. When the waiter brought us our order, my foot gave an agonizing twinge. Estefania noticed me wince and, with a glance at my ankle, told me to take off my shoes. I thought it was a little inappropriate to take my shoes off in a place where people were eating, but Estefania insisted, so I humored her, propping my now bare foot on her knee. Bringing her hands together around my foot, Estefania breathed deeply with her eyes closed. People were staring at our table, but I kept my foot on Estefania's lap. With her eyes shut her face had a sweetness about it, and I thought it was very kind of her to help me before tasting even a spoonful of her ice cream.

"You have a lot of stress, and your stress is reflected in your foot," she told me, speaking like a clairvoyant. A few seconds later she opened her eyes and said, "You'll be fine. You'll continue your career without any problems."

"You've felt it in my foot?"

"No, I've felt it in your energy."

I did not know what to say—I had never met anyone quite like her. Looking into her jet black eyes, I dug my spoon down into the sundae glass, where my ice cream had already turned to soup.

Later, as we walked down L Street, I became more and more convinced that Rafael must have been mistaken about Estefania. How could this intelligent, shy girl be "lethal"? She was curious about me, inquiring about my family, even asking if my parents had ever hit me, because she said she detected a certain sadness in me. Nobody had ever shown so much interest in me. I felt my heart thumping in my chest, and I took her by the hand. Estefania looked at me in surprise, and we continued walking, her hand in mine.

At the intersection of L and 19, we walked by the school where I had started ballet classes. There was an enormous poster of me on the wall and a caption underneath that read CARLOS JUNIOR ACOSTA, WINNER OF THE LAUSANNE GRAND PRIX AND THE PARIS GRAND PRIX, STUDIED AT THIS SCHOOL. When I stuck my head inside, people recognized me and greeted me as if I was a celebrity and not the boy who had been expelled. Children crowded around me asking for my autograph, while Estefania hung back, watching with a delighted expression on her face. Then one of the teachers who had been there in my day came over and said, with a smile as artificial as a clown's, "Our glories can erase our memories!"

The proud feelings that had surged through my chest when the children had flocked around me were abruptly extinguished. I felt like walking straight back out of there, but, instead, I looked the woman in the eye and said, "If there are any memories that are never likely to be erased from my mind, they're the ones from this place."

We stared at each other in silence for a moment.

I had wanted the chance to tell someone how I felt about my

unhappy years at L and 19 for a long time. Now that it was off my chest, I felt as though my body was rising up high, and suddenly, as if by magic, the bitterness that had been living inside me had been cast off. I walked toward the door, almost flying because I felt so light. I seized Estefania by the hand and, at the bus stop, I kissed her. It was the start of one of the best relationships of my life.

Soon, though, I began to see what Rafael had been talking about.

Estefania loved to have sex in public places—in public buildings, on the Malecón boardwalk along the sea, at the baker's, at the dry cleaner's—and nearly always standing up. She made an exception only when we stayed at my parents' apartment in Los Pinos because I had no desire to make love outside in one of the dark corners or alleyways where people urinated, nor was I keen for the marksmen of the area to use us as target practice. Estefania was excited by the painfully sharp springs in the old double bed, and she was always keen to explore all sorts of sadomasochistic fantasies. When I went into the hospital for my second operation, during which a piece of bone the size of a grain of maize was extracted from my ankle, she came to see me every day after her contemporary dance class, and she always wanted to have sex. She did not seem fazed by the fact that I had just had an operation—it did not stop her wanting to make love standing up in a corner of the ward. One night we were moving around my hospital room to give my ankle some exercise, and when we reached the corner she put her hand down my trousers so that I felt my body shiver. The pain in my foot was intense, but the pleasure was even stronger. Estefania started to get excited, always a danger sign, and pulled a strap out of her bag, asking me to hit her on the back with it.

"Damn it, Estefania! There are enough sick people in this hospital," I told her, but she had already climbed on top of me and had the object of sin inside of her. "Ouch! Ouch! Let me sit down!" I yelled in pain.

"Hey! Just what do you think you're doing?"

The nurse caught us in flagrante. Estefania clambered down from me, put the strap away, tucked me back inside my trousers, straightened herself up a bit, and led me by the arm back to my bed as though nothing had happened.

As well as an adventurous lover, Estefania was a great friend who became almost a part of the family and had the unique ability to act as an intermediary between my father and me. My father had refused to speak to me since hearing I would have to have another operation. His silence was a way of punishing me, though Mamá said he was going through a period of reflection that had nothing to do with me. She said that he often did not speak to her either and that the same thing had happened with Marilín—that I was imagining most of the resentment anyway. But it was not my imagination. His silence was like a kind of water torture, slowly dripping away on the same old spot. I would rather my father had beaten me with the thick cable he kept under the bed or attacked me with his machete instead of inflicting this brutal silence upon me. But he did communicate with me via Estefania. When she told me in no uncertain terms that I must be sure to make a full recovery so I could dance with the English National Ballet again, I knew it was not really Estefania speaking.

After I came out of hospital, I bought a car and asked my father, through Estefania, to teach me to drive. He accepted, only on the condition that he would give me instructions via my girlfriend. This method was a complete disaster. The three of us went to the Cuatro Caminos, a deserted road. The car stalled as soon as I tried to move it.

"Tell him that he must not take his foot off the clutch so abruptly," my father explained to Estefania. "Clumsiness in life is paid for by ankle operations."

The car stalled again.

"Tell him that he must concentrate. If he could manage to remember that, then perhaps he wouldn't injure himself. . . ."

I had had enough.

I turned to my father and told him it was my foot and my operation, and it was bad enough not being able to dance without getting grief from anyone else, then I got out of the car and started to walk along the Cuatro Caminos. It took Estefania a good ten minutes to persuade me to get back inside the vehicle, where my father continued to ignore me. He spent a total of five weeks not talking to me, only breaking his silence once, two weeks after the ill-fated driving lesson, on the day I was caught driving without a license through the Bay Tunnel and had no other option but to ask for his help. He came to my rescue without hesitation. Five days later I took my driving test, and the examiner, the bastard, failed me.

———

The hospital was a long way from our house in Los Pinos, so despite my lack of a license I drove myself there when I had to go in for physical therapy. However, I did not want to run the risk of my Volkswagen being stolen if I left it unwatched on the street while I was in receiving treatment. One day I had the idea of asking Marta Ulloa, the principal of the National School of the Arts, if, while I continued my rehabilitation, she might let me live in the mathematics classroom at the back of the school, as from there I could easily take a bus to the hospital. Marta agreed, and so Estefania and I carried out all the tables and chairs and gave the place a good scrubbing down. Next I got Guillermo, the neighborhood blacksmith, to make me a tall, square pair of iron window frames and a door, also iron, for the entrance. I transported everything in my neighbor Eddie's truck and arranged for a builder, also from my neighborhood, to assemble it all. I had a wooden bed made by a carpenter over in Marianao. I painted the walls, glazed the door, and bought blue curtains for the windows and moved into my new accommodation.

Six months flew by. I had never gone for so long without dancing and, oddly, it did not bother me in the slightest. I got used to sleeping late in the mornings, to seeing sunshine, to attending parties, and to living a life free from physical pain.

One evening, as we were lazing on the wall of the Malecón, watching the sun go down, I said to Estefania, "Do you know something? I don't want to go back to dancing."

"Are you crazy?" she replied. "Ballet is your life, and you know it. Anyway, your father would kill you!"

Estefania was right. My father would kill me, or, worse, he would stop talking to me forever. And when I thought about all the problems at home, about my sister Berta and our divided family, I knew I could not let them down. We did not need any more unhappiness. I lay back on the wall, lost in thought, watching the sun as it sank into the water. At my side, Estefania kissed me, understanding that my silence was a change of heart.

Chapter 15

BEGINNING AGAIN

On my first day back in the dance studio, when I put on my leotard and saw my body in the mirror, I was horrified. Rolls of fat had accumulated around my waist. My back and abdominal muscles had completely disappeared. My thighs were like two long strips dangling from my hips. My body was one ball of flesh with another smaller ball on top, with chubby cheeks and a wild Afro. My God, what a sight! My athletic figure was gone. I took off my leotard, put on my street clothes, and told Chery, who had offered to give me classes to get my body used to exercise again, that I had a headache and it would be better to leave things until the next day. The following morning I dressed myself in track pants and a loose top to hide the flabby body I had seen in the mirror.

Chery had gotten it into her head that I should talk to Alicia Alonso, the director of the Cuban National Ballet, to see whether I could join the company. I was not so sure this was a good idea—what if they were still bitter about my going to the English National Ballet?—but Chery said that Cuba was my country and that the Cuban ballet company was, therefore, also my ballet company. It was not like I had defected or made statements against the government.

"You had the opportunity to join a highly prestigious company as principal dancer at the age of only eighteen. That doesn't happen to everyone, and it is not only an achievement for the Cuban Ballet School but also for Cuba itself," she reiterated stridently, her voice surprisingly vehement.

Alicia Alonso is not only one of the most celebrated personalities in the world of ballet, she is also, together with her ex-husband, Fernando Alonso, responsible for the emergence of the whole Cuban ballet movement. Thanks to these two figures, the methodology of the Cuban Ballet School exists—a single system practiced in all twenty-five ballet schools on the island. To the outside world, Alicia is a legend; within Cuba, she is a figure of such importance that her power could be compared to that of the president. One word from Alicia can change your future.

When I came knocking on her door, she treated me imperiously, allowing me to join the company but awarding me only the status of soloist, four categories below a principal dancer, which I had been with the English National Ballet.

Even though I had debuted in three-act ballets and received good notices in the British press—one of the reviews even described me as the Cuban Nijinsky—in my new position I began to feel insecure. I asked my teacher if she really thought that I was any good.

"Please, Junior, stop being so silly," Chery replied. "Just keep on working as hard as you always have."

And so I worked. I worked unceasingly. My foot was starting to hurt me less, so I quickly lost all the weight I had put on. My legs were soon toned again, as were my back and stomach muscles. Many of the dancers who had inspired me when I was a student were still with the company, so it was easy for me to get my focus back. Each challenge was stimulating, and each drop of sweat was for good. The greater the effort I made, the more quickly my strength came back. I had to try by every means possible to reinvent myself, to give birth to another Carlos Acosta. It was the only way to show everyone in Cuba that I really was a principal dancer—in fact, if not in name.

In June, when I had just turned twenty, I made my debut with the company, exactly a year to the day after my last performance in London. I danced *The Corsair* with Alihaydee Carreño. When the curtain came down, the audience gave us a loud ovation, but I knew my performance had not been up to the standard of other *Corsair*s I had danced. Nevertheless, after a year without performing, it was not a bad start. The most important thing was that I was dancing again.

Next came the third act of *Coppelia* with my friend Lourdes Novoa, who had also left the English National Ballet to rejoin the Cuban National Ballet. This time I felt stronger and more at ease with myself.

My family was there. It had been years since they saw me dance, and for the first time in many months my father seemed calm, one might even say content. My mother wore an elegant dress, and the pride on her face was evident. Marilín looked like a queen, although her boyfriend, Yiyo, had a rather uncomfortable expression on his face. When I asked him if he had enjoyed it, my sister took me to one side and explained that her boyfriend had spent the whole show snoring, to the annoyance of a lot of people in the audience.

I was growing stronger all the time and was thrilled to see my name on the cast list for the ballet *Oedipus Rex* by Jorge Lefebre. I had long dreamed of interpreting the title role made famous by Jorge Esquivel. I immediately phoned Chery to give her the good news and when, later that night, I met up with Estefania at the Diploclub in Miramar, we toasted my success. I discovered only the next day that I would not be dancing the role of Oedipus, but that of the old man who is charged with killing him. I was disappointed, of course, but I told myself that sometimes the secondary roles are as good as if not better than the principal ones. Take Mercutio, for example, in *Romeo and Juliet,* or *Manon,* in which Lescaut is at least as strong a part as Des Grieux. Surely the old man in *Oedipus* would be one of those roles, a part with technical and dramatic complexities, a character that would enhance my repertoire?

So I was horrified to discover that there was no dancing to the role at all, no leaps or pirouettes. They put a white wig on my head, painted my smooth young face to look like an old man of eighty, and dressed me in rags. I came onstage pushing Oedipus with a stick, mimed sparing him his life, and, at the end of it all, Oedipus hanged me. That was it.

The worst thing was not the other dancers joking that I looked like the ancient salsa singer Celia Cruz but that everyone who was important to me was in the audience: my family, Estefania, Chery, all there watching me limping onto the stage, a twenty-year-old geriatric. I wanted the stage to open up and swallow me. It was humiliating.

When I complained about my lot to Chery, she said I should not let it bother me so much. "Look, Junior," she said, sitting down on one of the wicker armchairs in her apartment. "Some things in life don't turn out quite as we expect."

"But, I mean, walking like an old man! My father could have done it better!" I protested.

"That's just how things are," answered Chery. Beckoning me over to sit down next to her, she began to tell me a story.

"I once had a friend who dreamed of being a carpenter. He was young and very good-looking, although you couldn't tell, because he was always unkempt and had an enormous beard. The only features that stood out were his kindly green eyes, which looked like a cat's when it's asking for food. He didn't care about his appearance, or what people might think, because wood was his whole world. Unfortunately, he was one of many siblings, and money was tight in the family home. Nevertheless, my friend was a dreamer, and they say that where there's a will there's a way, so one fine day he managed to raise enough money to buy several meters of lovely timber—mahogany, cedar, and some strips of *majagua*. He set up a workshop in the patio of his house. Some of his siblings became ill from breathing in so much sawdust, but he convinced them that his dreams would make their fortunes and went on sawing wood and assembling furniture.

"After a while, my friend got a stand on the market up by Cuatro Caminos, where he displayed a huge variety of the most luxurious pieces of furniture: tables, wardrobes, sofas, bedroom suites, all in different styles. His Louis XV reproduction drawing room suites were identical to the originals and his modern sofas were better in quality and design than anything the shops could offer, but, strangely, nobody bought his wares. From the first day that he came to the market, the other carpenters had bad-mouthed him, criticizing him and his furniture. And any customers who did take the trouble to go over to his stall were put off by his unkempt appearance and would continue on their way. But my friend wouldn't admit defeat. He improved the quality of his furniture even further, painting each piece with new details, perfecting ever more intricate designs. He was convinced that, sooner or later, his work would be rewarded. Back at home, with no money coming in, the rumbling of empty stomachs grew louder.

"One day a new customer appeared, and my friend enthusiastically showed off his vast collection of three-piece suites, beds, and wardrobes. The customer didn't buy anything, but he said that he would return the next day, if my friend would agree to a curious request: Would my friend please shave off his beard? He didn't object, and the next day he went to his stall with a smooth face and well-combed hair. The customer arrived at the same time as the day before, but this time he showed no interest whatsoever in any of the furniture. After staring for a long time at my friend's physique, he offered him a modeling contract. Nowadays my friend lives in Paris and enjoys a lucrative modeling career. . . ."

For a few minutes, I did not know what to say. I tried to understand the significance of the story that I had just been told. "Are you trying to tell me that someone might offer me a modeling contract?" I asked ingenuously.

My teacher's smile lit up her huge blue eyes. She went into the kitchen and brought out two cups of coffee. "What I'm trying to say is that, along the way, you are going to meet a lot of jealous, spiteful people, like those furniture sellers who maligned my friend. But you will meet others who will give you opportunities, like the modeling agent. Sometimes it's better to dance the role of an old man just to remind yourself that you don't always deserve everything. I know that you feel bad, but perhaps it's some consolation to know that you participated in a performance that moved hundreds of people. Everyone played their part, and it fell upon you, this time, to take on the role of the ridiculous old man. But there is nothing nobler than to sacrifice your ideals for the benefit of others. . . ."

Chery could always find a way to make me feel better. Suddenly I did not mind that I had danced the old man in *Oedipus Rex*. And when, two weeks later, I danced *The Spectre of the Rose*, wearing a costume that made me look like the Pink Panther, that did not matter either. I was no longer worried about what people might say or bothered by the jibes of the other dancers.

On this occasion and many others, I often wondered if Chery was psychic. I do not know how she did it, but I swear her thought processes influenced events. Three weeks after my performance as an old man, I received a letter quite out of the blue from Ben Stevenson, the choreographer I had met in London, formally offering me a contract to work with his company in Houston.

I immediately phoned the number on his letter. When I got Ben on the line, he asked me if I liked his offer, and I told him that I did. He wanted to know if I might be able to travel to some other country to apply for the visa I would need to work in the United States, since obtaining a U.S. work visa in Cuba would be virtually impossible. As luck would have it, in July and August I was scheduled to be in Spain with the Cuban National Ballet.

The following week, Ben stuck his head around the door of the room where the male Cuban National Ballet dancers were having their class. He was wearing a multicolored shirt, similar to the one he had worn when I had first met him at the studios of the English National Ballet, and a pair of dark green trousers. He shook my hand and said he would wait for me to finish my class.

Everyone wanted to know why Ben Stevenson had come to Havana. Still reeling from the speed with which things had happened, I told them the truth: that we had worked together in London and that he wanted to give me a contract. At the end of the class, many of my fellow dancers went to greet him, thronging around him like a sort of all-male chorus. I smiled. Who wouldn't want a modeling agent to turn their dreams into reality?

I offered Ben a lift to his hotel in my car, but as we climbed into my beat-up old Volkswagen, he looked terrified. It was probably the first time he had been in an old, rickety car like that. He asked me if I had car insurance, and I asked him what that was. After that he did not ask any more questions, which was just as well because I still did not have a driver's license. Instead, I kept the glove compartment of the car well stocked with bars of soap. At the time, soap was scarce but I managed to buy it in the shops where they accepted *chavitos.* If I was stopped by the police and asked for my license, I would hand over a bar or two of soap, and was usually allowed to continue on my way. Some of the police officers knew me by now, and if they needed a wash or a present for their girlfriends, they would trail me around to get their soap. With the money that I was spending daily on fines and bars of soap, I could easily have bought another car.

I had never been inside the Hotel Riviera because back then a Cuban could enter only with a foreigner. Crossing the lobby with Ben, I was entranced by the elaborate decor and by the view of the sea from the windows.

We took an elevator to the top floor, where there was a luxury restaurant with a panoramic view of the city. Ben ordered me a filet mignon and then took some programs from the Houston Ballet out of his bag so that I could read about all the company members, about seventy dancers in all. The average age of the dancers was twenty-five, and most of them were graduates of the school Ben had founded. As I leafed through the programs, I got a clear idea of the company's varied repertoire, the impressive sets, the sumptuous costumes, and I could also see from their faces that the dancers were young and happy. I knew it was the ideal company for me.

Ben put a blue paper envelope on the table, which turned out to be a letter of endorsement for my visa. He explained that I had only to present it at the consulate of the U.S. Embassy in Madrid and, with a little bit of luck, they would grant me the visa. My filet mignon arrived, and Ben watched as I devoured the piece of meat, staring at me intently, as if he was trying to work out what was going through my head.

As I chewed the last of my meal, Ben placed another document on the table. I opened it and started to read. Forty-four weeks of work a year on average, medical and dental insurance, two paid weeks in which I could dance with other companies . . . My eyes suddenly stopped on a line where there were a lot of zeros. A piece of steak got stuck in my throat. I started to cough. Ben got me some water and thumped me on the back. He asked if there was something in the contract that I did not agree with. I could not speak for choking. Never in my life had I dreamed of earning so much money. When I eventually got my breath back, I told him I accepted the contract and signed it there and then. It was only years later that Ben Stevenson discovered that my salary at the time was 138 pesos, about 1 dollar a month.

My father, Pedro Acosta, and his first wife, María. When I studied at Pinar del Río many years later, I would spend weekends with María and my half brother Pedro.

My mother, María Quesada, on her fifteenth birthday.

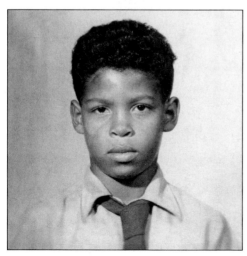

My first picture, age seven, and the only image that exists of me before ballet entered my life.

My first stage appearance, in the mazurka. Experiencing the lights, the music, and the applause for the first time was a revelation.

Posing proudly with Grettel. She was my first love, but I thought she was far too pretty to bother with someone as rough as me.

An early school photo. I'm wearing the white shirt and blue kerchief that are part of the uniform for all primary school children in Cuba.

The cast of *Dreams of Sailors,* with our teacher, Lupe Calzadilla. I am on the far right, but I missed so many classes that I never performed in this ballet.

Chery. Much more than just a teacher, she became like a second mother to me.

My first class at the Prix de Lausanne was easy, but on the second day the teacher nearly finished us off. (© *Philippe Pache*)

Performing *Tocororo* in Lausanne. I had not realized the danger of watching all the other competitors perform until it was too late. (© *Philippe Pache*)

Don Quixote at the Prix de Lausanne, the performance that changed my future. (© *Francette Levieux*)

The winners of the Prix de Lausanne. I am in the middle; the impeccable Victor Álvarez is on the far right. It was not until I looked at my medal that I realized I had won the Médaille d'Or. (© *Francette Levieux*)

I arrived in London to join the English National Ballet at the age of eighteen, not knowing a word of English.

Rehearsing *Don Quixote* with María Teresa del Real before a gala for English National Ballet patrons. Ivan Nagy, the company's director, took great pains to teach me the art of partnering.
(© Adrian Gray)

Back in Houston, Lauren and I began rehearsing Ben Stevenson's new choreography for *Don Quixote*. It was an exhausting experience, but also incredibly rewarding. (© *Jann Whaley, courtesy of Houston Ballet*)

The debut of *Don Quixote* was one of the most unforgettable nights of my life. The only thing missing from it was my family. (© *Jim Caldwell, courtesy of Houston Ballet*)

After five years in Houston, I was getting rave reviews for performances in ballets such as *The Rite of Spring,* but I needed to know if I was good enough to dance with the major-league companies. (© *Drew Donovan, courtesy of Houston Ballet*)

In London for the second time, I made my debut with the Royal Ballet in *In the Middle, Somewhat Elevated*. Once again, I had to earn my place, starting from scratch. *(© Angela Taylor)*

Frederick Ashton's *La Fille Mal Gardée*. After my first performance in Colas's banana yellow tights, I felt like giving up ballet altogether. *(© Angela Taylor)*

I was honored to be asked to represent Nureyev, dancing *Le Corsaire* at the opening gala for the Royal Opera House. *(© Angela Taylor)*

Rehearsing *Manon* with Gillian Revie. *(© Angela Taylor)*

The first black Romeo in Covent Garden, with Tamara Rojo as Juliet. (© *Angela Taylor*)

A dream come true. The opening night of *Tocororo* at Sadler's Wells, with Veronica Corveas in the leading female role and my family watching from the audience, was the happiest night of my life. (© *Angela Taylor*)

My family: Marilín's husband, Elisardo; my nephew Andy; Marilín; my mother; Berta; my nephew Yonah; me; and my father.

My father, Pedro Acosta, at home in Cuba.
(© Angela Taylor)

Me and my mother.
(© Angela Taylor)

Chapter 16

MADRID

Do you remember the time that I bumped into you in a studio at the García Lorca and I told you that I wanted to be like you . . . ?"

"No. No, I don't remember."

"It would have been around 1988. I think you were dancing in *The Three Musketeers*. Don't you remember?"

"Junior, even if you torture me I'm still not going to remember. . . ."

Alberto Terrero wandered off into the bathroom of our hotel room with two plates in his hands. He disconnected the current from the homemade cooker we had fashioned from recycled tins, coat hangers, and cables pulled out of electric irons, then lifted off a frying pan containing two delicious-smelling pork chops. He added white rice and fried potatoes to each plate, and we sat down on our respective beds in the tiny room to enjoy our meal.

The chops were extremely tasty. The day before, we had eaten two tins of Asturian bean stew. Terrero and I had been put together as roommates in Madrid. To save money, we bought our food from El Corte Inglés and cooked it on this improvised hot plate. All the other dancers in the company were doing the same. There was even a famous story in the company about a guy who had once secretly served dog food at a birthday party. Everybody he invited leaped at the chance for a free meal, so they all went and ate what they thought were meat and potatoes. At the end of the party the host showed his guests the empty tins that had contained the food they had just eaten—and while some people felt like vomiting, others swore that the very next day they would go out to buy more of that delicious dog food.

"The truth is, your memory is smaller than a mosquito's," I said to Terrero. "I told you that I wanted to be like you, and you and Domingo laughed."

"I should have been flattered," said Terrero.

"That's what I thought," I told him. "The first time I saw you dance was in Pinar del Río, in *Flower Festival in Genzano.* You leaped so high that I thought you were held up by wires."

"It's true, I did have a good jump in those days—" Terrero began, when there was a sudden knock at the door. I got up, looked through the peephole in the door, and saw the hotel receptionist.

"What's that smell?" said the good gentleman. "You wouldn't be cooking in here by any chance, would you?"

"In here? You must be joking!" Terrero replied calmly. "No, nothing like that, sir. I can assure you the smell comes from the restaurant on the corner. I can't sleep a wink because of it. I feel like running out and saying to the chef, 'Please, have mercy, let me sleep, I have to work in the morning!' But as you can see, the torturous odor persists, and the only remedy is to bury one's nose in the pillow."

The fellow looked at us both dubiously. Terrero, the rascal, had pronounced every *s* during the course of his little speech with a lisp, like the Madrileños do. I could hardly contain my laughter.

"Christ, Terrero, you're a genius . . ." I said, after the receptionist had left.

We got our plates of food out of the bathroom and sat down on our beds again.

"That was nothing, man, fooling people is an art in itself, and if there's one thing that I have more than enough of, it's the talent to survive."

"If only I had your talent," I told him, finishing my last piece of meat.

Terrero suddenly stopped chewing. He put his plate down on the bedside table and looked across at me. There was nothing of the joker or the actor about him now.

"Shall I tell you something, Junior? I'm the one who'd like to have your talent."

Then he picked up his plate and started eating again. I remembered when I had seen him dance for the first time, that night at the Saidén

Theatre in Pinar del Río. Who would have thought it? Alberto Terrero, the dancer who had inspired me, eating a plate of pork chops at my side?

After two months in Madrid, the bodily exhaustion we all felt began to show on our faces. It was not just that we were getting up at eight o'clock in the morning for classes and rehearsals all day, then dancing six shows a week; we were also up all night. After the performances we would head to the salsa club Ozone, where the manager let us in for free, and dance until six in the morning, returning to the hotel only for breakfast, then going to ballet class and starting the whole routine again.

In my case, however, the most exhausting thing was not the dancing but the stress of knowing that, sooner or later, I was going to have to have a serious talk with Alicia Alonso about the Houston Ballet. Before signing the contract with Ben, I had told her of my intention to dance in Houston for eight months, not quite a full season. She had given me to understand that she was in agreement but that nothing was certain, and I was dreading having to talk to her again. If Alicia were to oppose my contract, I would have to decide whether to become an independent dancer and go to Houston anyway, which would signify a split with the National Ballet, and probably mean I would never dance in my country again. Alternatively, I could stay with the National Ballet as a soloist, earning a dollar a month and losing the thread of the international career that I had only just begun. Everything was in the hands of Alicia.

Anxiety pervaded every area of my life. To make matters worse, I discovered that my debut in *Giselle,* one of the most complicated and subtle ballets, was to open without a dress rehearsal. The career anxiety that was clouding my mind, combined with the lack of a dress rehearsal, made it impossible for me to focus, to the extent that during the show, my one-time teacher Lázaro Carreño, who had kindly agreed to dance Hilarion, had to dictate the choreography to me. A few days later, when I argued with a female friend and found myself wanting to strangle her, I realized this had to stop. The stress was making me crazy. I could no longer put off the conversation.

Fara, Alicia's secretary, opened the door of the director's dressing room in the Albéniz Theatre. I went through to a white, brightly lit vestibule and sat down to wait. The silence that followed after Fara left the room made me even more nervous. I looked around, watching a line of termites crawl down from the ceiling and wondering if there was any way they could be related to the termites in our Los Pinos apartment. My thoughts were still wandering when, after five minutes, Alicia called me through. I went in and closed the door behind me.

I came out of that meeting about fifteen minutes later, still anxious and bemused. I had been left with the strange feeling that the last four years of my life had been a lie, as if all my achievements had been nothing more than a stroke of luck. No matter, I told myself; Alicia had given her blessing to the contract, and that was what counted.

There was still another hurdle for me to jump, however: the interview at the embassy for my visa. I made my debut in the ballet *Don Quixote*, again without a dress rehearsal, and at seven o'clock the next morning I arrived at the U.S. Embassy, an imposing white building with black railings all around it. The queue was short, barely twenty people. Ben had left everything ready for me, including a completed visa application form, and as the queue moved rapidly, I soon found myself at the front.

"Next!" said a woman of about forty with reddish hair.

My hands would not stop shaking after so many days thinking about the possibility of failure. I was at the mercy of this woman, who had the power to reduce me to nothing, to snatch away from me the hope of a better future. Could she have even the slightest idea how drastically my life could be changed by that visa?

I put my passport through the window with the application form and the blue visa endorsement from the U.S. government. The woman looked me straight in the eyes, then she studied the documents meticulously, just like the officials in Miami International Airport had done.

"Are you Cuban?" she asked.

"Here we go again!" I said to myself. "Yes, I'm from Havana," I replied nervously.

"You have a work contract for the United States?" she asked incredulously.

My tongue was sticking to the back of my throat. I managed only a nod. She continued examining the documents with an impassive face.

"They're not going to give it to you!" shouted the voices of my insecurity. By now, my whole body was trembling. I thought about my father and how his hopes for me would crumble to dust if this visa was denied me.

"I'm sorry, Papito, the saints know that I did everything I could," I whispered under my breath, lowering my head hopelessly.

"It says here that you're a dancer," the woman said suddenly. "You're not by any chance the same lad who danced *Don Quixote* last night at the Albéniz, are you?" The change was remarkable. Suddenly her face was that of a mother looking at her son.

"Yes, yes . . . it's me," I said desperately.

"Consuelo, look who we've got here; it's the boy from *Don Quixote*!"

The woman got up from her chair and fetched her fellow worker, Consuelo, who greeted me shyly, as if I were a rock star. They went to get the consul, a tall man with a dark complexion, who by coincidence happened to have the program from the show with him.

"You were absolutely fantastic," he said, as I signed his program; then he asked me to come back the next morning after he had assessed my case.

Twenty-four hours later, I found myself at the exit of the embassy, holding in my sweaty hands my passport. Inside was a U.S. work visa, valid for one year.

Chery and Estefania were the first people I told after I returned to Cuba.

"What did Alicia Alonso say to you?" Estefania wanted to know.

"Okay, I'm going to tell you, but first you need to answer me this. Do you think that the color of my skin isn't suited for ballet?"

She looked at me, disconcerted, then, with her characteristic warmth, replied, "No, your color is beautiful!" and burst out laughing. With that, I knew I did not have to say any more, and the memory of that awkward interview faded from my mind.

Estefania seized me by the arm and stuck her hand down my

trousers. I kissed her moist lips and bit her warm neck. I could feel her heart start to pound against my chest like the hooves of wild horses. She crouched down and reached for her bag, but I stopped her just as she was putting her hand inside it.

"Estefania, tonight we're going to do it in bed like normal people," I said. She smiled and slipped out of her clothes, stretching her voluptuous body out on the bed. The moon coaxed the hint of chocolate in her skin to give off a shimmering light, and the room filled with a wonderful, seductive aroma.

"Come here," she whispered softly. And there, at last, in the mathematics classroom beneath a glittering full moon, we finally made love in the normal fashion.

We almost fell in love that night. We sank so deep into each other that the heat from her body tore at my throat. Looking into her eyes, I realized Estefania would have liked to stay in that place, where the only thing to see was each other and the only thing to hear were her cries. She started to weep, perhaps because she saw that same desire reciprocated in my own eyes. At heart, we both knew that our relationship was destined to live on only in our memories, but my throat still aches whenever I think about her.

The following day, I went to Eduardo's house to tell my sister Berta the news that I would be leaving.

"I'm very happy for you, my little brother, Yuli," she said, her eyes lifeless and blackened. "God told me that he had a lovely surprise for you. God is the only one who matters. Dance for Him."

I realized that she wasn't even looking at me. Her eyes were still, transfixed by a crucifix on the wall. I left her house in tears.

When I told my father, he clapped his hands together so hard that it sounded like a bear roaring and hugged me so tightly I could hardly breathe. When he managed to control his emotions, he led me over to a corner of the sitting room and whispered something in my ear: "Remember, don't give in to nostalgia. Forget everything. To reap, you first need to sow, sweat, and suffer. I want people to know your name, to look at you with respect. I want anyone who sees you dance to feel fortunate, and for other mothers to be jealous of your mother. Of course, she doesn't want you to leave, but you have to be strong. Men are born into the world to fulfill their destiny, and yours isn't here. We're the ones who were born to live and die in Los Pinos. Your future lies elsewhere. However much you want to"—he took me by the shoulders and fixed his gaze on my eyes—"never look back!"

PART THREE

1993–2003

Chapter 17

FEARS AND INSECURITIES

I arrived at Houston Intercontinental Airport in October 1992 and was detained at the border. After looking at my passport, immigration officers took me into a room and fired questions at me, just as they had done when I visited Miami.

"I come here to work," I protested, but they did not believe me.

They made me take everything out of my hand luggage: ballet shoes, makeup bag, the photograph of my sisters, and an amulet that my father had given me. One of the officers picked up the little chain with the hen's foot on it and examined it closely.

"Be careful, my father says that charm will protect me and nobody must touch it *except* me," I told him.

I have never seen anyone drop something so quickly.

Houston is a huge city, home to more than 5 million people, many of whom spend more time in their cars than in their own homes. During rush hour those 5 million people pour out onto the freeways like impatient ants, and it is easy to lose what seems like days stuck in a traffic jam on one of the bridges. The city's few buses run only on some of the main streets, and taxis are used simply for getting people to and from the airport. Many of the inhabitants have emigrated from various regions of Latin America, the largest proportion coming from Mexico. There is a small Cuban community, which holds festivals annually to celebrate significant dates in the country's history.

Ben Stevenson, an Englishman who had been a dancer at the Royal Ballet Company, arrived in Houston in the 1970s to develop a ballet company in the region. Houston then was synonymous with NASA, rodeos, and oil. There was virtually no tradition of ballet in the city. Yet within a few years the company base increased, and Ben began an academy that could supply dancers for the company. The repertoire expanded rapidly under his direction and the company gained the recognition of the national press. When I joined the Houston Ballet, sixteen years after Ben had assumed the role of artistic director, it was thought to be the third most important regional ballet company in the United States—after the San Francisco and the Boston ballet companies.

Although I was just nineteen when I arrived that October morning, one thing was quite clear: ballet, like any other art form, is competitive. We all make comparisons between people because we all want to find a hero to worship. No matter how supportive colleagues might be, critics ensure that such categories as "the best" and "the worst" exist, and this constantly makes artists prey to insecurity and frustration. Chery used to try to counter these fears by telling us that each of us was unique in our own way, and therefore nobody was "the best" or "the worst."

"That ballerina is taller and has a better physique; that other one is more musical and has a better jump. So which one is the best, then?" Chery would ask me, her eyes wide as an owl's. "All art is subjective, and of course it is only natural that people would have different tastes and preferences. However, if someone tries to tear you down, remember that they can never deny the fact that you have come out of nothing and have turned yourself into a principal dancer. Even ten bad performances can't blot out that achievement. Maybe some people won't like the way you dance, but no one can take away what you have achieved. One day, when you've retired, someone will want to have their photo taken with you, and you will realize that in their mind, you are still dancing. This is the best way to live on, in someone's memory."

In reality, however, we dancers will do almost anything to win medals in ballet competitions, putting forth the effort and determination of Olympic athletes. Some people even resort to placing nails and tacks in potential rivals' ballet shoes to cause them injury. In a profession like ballet, where time treats all dancers with equal contempt, and where opportunities to perform are always contested, it is very difficult not to feel jealous of the competition.

When I arrived that morning at the Wortham Theater, however, I was convinced that nobody would ever be good enough to really threaten me. Most of the dancers welcomed me in a friendly manner, and I was not alarmed by the few menacing looks I received when I walked into the studios.

In those days, the company had ten principal dancers, male and female, but the two most popular stars were undoubtedly Li Cunxin and Janie Parker. Ben had brought Li over from China when he was barely out of boyhood. Li was an exceptional dancer with great technique and artistic ability, and, above all, he was a good partner. He was also an eloquent speaker and a kind person. In the partnership of Janie Parker and Li Cunxin, Ben found the inspiration for much of his choreography; it was during their heyday that the Houston Ballet enjoyed its glory years. The relationship between Ben and Li had once been almost like that of father and son, but by the time I arrived at the Houston Ballet, things had cooled and the company was divided, supporting either Li's side or Ben's.

I was to make my debut dancing in *The Nutcracker* with Martha Butler. She was one of the most renowned dancers with the Houston Ballet and was in Li's camp. When I arrived, I was ignorant of the company's internal politics, and everybody inevitably jumped to the conclusion that I was in Ben's camp.

During our first rehearsal, as we were practicing one of the promenades, Martha said to me bad-temperedly, "What are you doing? You are putting me away from my leg."

"Okay, give me time. Remember, I have never danced with you before," I replied.

We repeated everything.

"You see what I mean; you're clumsy!" Martha said.

I replied once more, "Give me time. I just got here."

We spent the rest of the rehearsal like a cat and a dog, at each other's throats. Unfortunately, we were going to be dancing nearly everything together: *Swan Lake, La Bayadère, Etudes.* I tried not to let it bother me, telling myself she was probably just stressed out.

The next day the situation grew worse.

"No, no, no, this has to stop. You are such a bad partner!" Martha said to me, and ran down to the studio below to find Li and ask him to instruct me.

"What I do is take her by the waist and her armpits and put her waist a little bit forward," said Li, as he marked out the movement with Martha.

"Okay, let me try."

I did it again, correcting my movement the way Li had shown me, but the results were not good.

"You see what I mean, Li. He's just not a good partner," said Martha.

"I know I'm not the best partner in the world," I protested, "but I am a hard worker, and with time we can figure it out. We are going to be dancing a lot together, and it is not good to be fighting like this. But if you want to fight, that's fine by me."

After that things improved. Three weeks later, I made my debut with the company. During the show Martha and I gazed at each other as though we were in love, beaming happily the whole time. Nobody could have guessed that the prince, given half a chance, would have done anything in his power to make the princess break her ankle, and that the princess would have been happy had the same fate befallen the prince. Appearances are often deceiving.

The reviews were good, and there were numerous articles in the press about the Cuban in Houston. Every time I found a piece with my name in it, I cut it out and saved it to show my parents and my sisters.

Ben Stevenson had generously offered to accommodate me in his home until I got used to the confusing reality of living in the United States. It was a two-story house on La Porte bay, miles and miles away from the city center. There were four bedrooms and a garden with a jetty that jutted out into the waters of the bay. The whole house was carpeted and had huge glass windows; a television set with a screen at least sixty inches wide stood near the fireplace; and there was a shelf by the stereo with hundreds of CDs and videocassettes on it. There were paintings, photographs, and books; and there were at least five cats, running about or lying on the cushions and in the wicker armchairs as if they were the true owners of the house. To me, it seemed like a palace. A Colombian dancer, José Herrera, and his wife, Sonia, were also living there, and it was not long before they became great friends of mine.

As soon as I arrived in Houston I got in touch with my aunt Mireya in Miami and told her I had a contract with the Houston Ballet Company. I spent at least an hour telling her about everything that had happened during the year and a half since we had seen each other, and she in her turn filled me in on their news. My grandmother was hardly able to walk now, and they were very hard up.

"They must have offered you a lot of money to leave London and go to Texas," Mireya said.

I promised her that when I got my first paycheck I would send her $200. She promised she would write to my mother, and we signed off from each other with a kiss.

It was at Ben's house that I celebrated Christmas for the first time. In Cuba religious festivals are either unmarked or observed in silence. It was only in 1998, after Pope John Paul II visited the island, that Christmas started to be celebrated once more in Cuba; however, since the custom had been dead for many decades, nobody really had any idea what to do. Instead of a fir tree, some people decorated mango bushes with empty beer and Coke cans. The food was the same as always: roast pork, cassava, fried plantains, and white rice with black beans.

I had no idea about Christmas traditions and had to ask José who was the old bearded guy dressed in red. One day we got back to La Porte and found a huge fir tree in the sitting room; and Ben arrived home that evening with dozens of multicolored balls and decorations. An hour later the tree had stopped being a tree and had turned into a carnival float.

On the day itself, lots of people, most of them strangers to me, stopped by the house, and the tree was soon surrounded by a huge number of presents. I was embarrassed because I had bought gifts only for Ben, José, Sonia, and Humberto "the Skinny," who had recently arrived from Colombia and joined the Latin clan at La Porte. José told me not to worry, that I was not expected to buy presents for everyone. The quantity of food was phenomenal. Everyone laughed, told stories, opened presents, kissed one another, ate, and drank; the joy was free-flowing and felt never-ending.

When Ben called me over to give me a box wrapped in burgundy paper, I opened it enthusiastically to find a very expensive leather jacket inside.

"This is too much!" I exclaimed in surprise.

It was the most expensive present I had ever received. In Cuba, people did not have the luxury of spending much money on gifts. I was

used to getting a postcard or a pair of socks as a birthday present. In
Cuba, I might have saved enough money to buy myself a similar coat
after twenty years of dancing with the Cuban National Ballet. I could
not help making comparisons, and the more I did, the worse I felt.
More money had been spent on this party than a surgeon in Cuba
could hope to earn during his entire lifetime. I told José and Sonia how
I was feeling, and they said they had felt the same way when they first
arrived from Colombia. They told me that the world was topsy-turvy
and that nobody could do anything about it, but for my own peace of
mind I should try as much as possible not to compare the situations of
the two countries.

Sometimes, though, it was hard not to notice the differences. The
Houston Ballet Company had a two-story building with space enough
for six studios, costume storerooms, numerous offices, a physical therapy department, a gymnasium, at least three changing rooms, and various rooms for just hanging out. One day, after the Christmas holidays,
José and I arrived to find the whole company gathered together in the
main communal area on the second floor. I asked José what was going
on, and he told me it was a union meeting to discuss the state of the
floors in the dance studios. I did not understand what my friend was
talking about, because as far as I could see, the floors were in perfect
condition. José said the dancers had been complaining for months
about the sticky linoleum, which made it difficult to turn. The whole
thing seemed ridiculous to me.

In Cuba, we danced on uneven wooden floorboards or on rough
sheets of plywood, with nails that ripped our dance shoes, and nobody
ever complained. Much of the wood in the studios was riddled with
woodworm, and, as linoleum was prohibitively expensive, it was just
another part of a distant utopian dream. Exercises were done in any
spare corner. To strengthen our arms we did push-ups; to increase elasticity, someone would stretch your legs open or push you down to the
floor by the shoulders; to correct your insteps someone would push
against your feet, forcing them to point.

In Houston, the gym had Pilates machines with numerous kinds of
weights, enormous exercise balls for doing sit-ups or for stretching back
muscles, running machines, and bicycles. The whole place was air-con-
ditioned and lined with mirrors. The dancers in the company had med-

ical and dental insurance, and workers' compensation in case of injury. It was inconceivable to me that a member of a company such as the Houston Ballet could have anything to complain about.

Of course, everyone has the right to ask for better working conditions. At the Cuban National Ballet nobody complained because they were afraid, particularly of losing the privilege of traveling the world. However, it is one thing to complain about a floor full of nails and broken floorboards and quite another to get upset about a piece of sticky linoleum that probably just needs a good cleaning.

Sometimes obstacles can become the very things that motivate us. When food is accessible and abundant, when options are endless, then art becomes a hobby. I believed that if I had had everything, I would have lost interest in dance after only a few years, abandoning it to pursue a university degree, or to open a business. But when art is the only way out, the only means of supporting loved ones, when the practice of your art is the only way to make yourself seen, heard, distinguished, then art is never just a hobby. Art is a means of survival; passion is more intense, the nails and the broken floorboards nothing more than an excuse to work even harder and become even better. Perhaps that is why there are no Beethovens and van Goghs these days, because we live in a world that is relatively easy. Genius needs despair, and despair comes out of cruelty, hunger, and pain.

All these thoughts were going through my mind as I sat in a corner of the room, wondering if these dancers had any idea just how fortunate they were. I thought about how unjust the world was, how some people had everything and others had nothing, and I felt a profound sadness creep over me.

Gradually, I began to settle into the city, becoming acquainted with the best clubs and restaurants, the different shopping centers, cinemas, and museums. Even after I had been working there for more than two months, however, some of the girls in the company were very reluctant to greet me. In Cuba, it is customary to kiss female colleagues on the cheek as a way of saying good morning. Every time I bent to kiss one of the girls, I would receive a look of consternation, and they would do their best to avoid me when they saw me arrive. A few of them found my appearance and my body odors amusing, and that made me insecure.

"You'd better give those warmers a good washing," a ballerina said to me one day; and during the dress rehearsals, some of them would gather into groups and laugh uproariously whenever they glanced in my direction.

On top of all this, Ben Stevenson was continuously correcting me, in every exercise, every day. He would grab my arms and shake them until they relaxed, and suddenly I would become the center of attention in the room. My fears and insecurities had nowhere to hide.

Conquering the roles of princes was the greatest challenge for me. I had never had any problem portraying characters such as Basilio in *Don Quixote,* who is a barber, or Ali, the slave in *The Corsair.* They were people of humble birth, like me and the people I grew up with, so I instinctively knew how to play them. Roles like Prince Igor, Solor in *La Bayadère,* or Acteon were vehicles to express masculine power and virility through powerful leaps and turns, and I was well equipped for these by my training at the Cuban School. Truly becoming a prince, however, was a nightmare for me.

"You have to stand and run like a prince would," Ben said, as he prepared me for my debut in *Swan Lake.*

He demonstrated with some flourishes of his hand, and I imitated him, but when I looked at myself in the mirror, I saw a man who was born in Los Pinos, with a truck-driver father and a housewife mother. The popular conception of a prince is someone blond and elegant, someone who captivates all the women in the kingdom, but the guy in the mirror was a mulatto with unruly hair, who was more likely to be the palace cook. If my teacher Chery had been there, she would certainly have said, "Dance like a prince, and you will become one. Convince the audience that you were born in Buckingham Palace and you will be crowned. A lot of people look like princes and dance like peasants."

The prince in *The Nutcracker* is purely a dancing role—his interaction with the other characters is minimal—but princes such as Siegfried in *Swan Lake* or Florimund in *Sleeping Beauty* have a story to tell. In *Swan Lake,* I had to converse with my mother and my tutor, tell the enchanted princess Odette that I loved her, swear my love in front of a large assembly of guests, and then commit suicide by throwing myself into the lake. And I had never taken an acting lesson in my life! It took me a long time to learn to play the princely roles, but, after a lot of guidance, I finally got the hang of standing and drinking wine in the refined manner of an aristocrat. I was grateful for Ben's support; he used to tell me, "Carlos, to me you are a prince, and that is why I am casting you in this ballet."

Ben's artistic vision was apparent in the way everybody danced, as if each one were connected to him by an umbilical cord. Much of his experience came from his country of origin, England, and the Royal Ballet School that Ninette de Valois had founded in the 1930s. The little that I knew, I had learned in the Cuban School, which was influenced by the Russian tradition and was quite distinct from the English style. While I was with the Houston Ballet, I came to understand that the art of dance is something more than jumping very high or raising your leg up over your head. After a few months I stopped getting annoyed when Ben corrected me; I incorporated the new teaching into my dancing without jettisoning what I had learned in Cuba. But the insecurity that I had felt since my arrival in Houston continued to plague me.

Eventually, I came to the conclusion that I was anxious because I lacked a circle of friends, so I went about changing that. I met Kentaro in Elvia's Cantina, a popular Latin restaurant and dance club in the city. We hit it off straightaway. His father was a famous Japanese karate master, and his mother was Cuban. Physically, he looked very Japanese, but his Cuban side was revealed in the way he danced salsa and the way he spoke. As he did not have a car or a driver's license and I now did, on the weekends I would pick him up from the university where he studied. He would always bring at least seven people with him, most of them beautiful women. Because of our salsa moves on the dance floor and the beautiful women who accompanied us, we were nearly always the center of attention in clubs. Going out with Kentaro was a guaranteed party, and so I was always impatient for the weekend to come around.

I met two other Cubans, Luis and Wicho, at Elvia's as well. They had both left Cuba at the age of ten, but they felt just as Cuban as I did. Shirley, a girl whom I had met in Lausanne, was now dancing with the

Houston Ballet and joined my circle of friends, which expanded further with the arrival of Johnny Warren and Lury, and the Mexicans Raúl and Celina. My friendship with José and Sonia had become so strong, the three of us decided to rent a new apartment near the company base. Kentaro helped us to carry the few pieces of furniture that we owned, and I realized then that it could not be a lack of friends that was causing this strange feeling of unease that still bothered me.

Houston was just as sunny as Cuba, the vegetation was just as green, trees lined the avenues, there were roses in the gardens, and everything was very clean. I was with an excellent company, with an enviable corps de ballet and exceptional soloists and principal dancers. The audiences were extremely warm. On the day of my debut in *Swan Lake,* which I was again dancing with Martha, I received an ovation unlike any I had ever experienced before. There was no doubt that I enjoyed working in Houston. But this thing, whatever it was, kept tormenting me. At night, when I had time to think, I felt even worse. Only when I remembered Estefania did I find peace. I thought how good it would be to have her by my side and to show her the city, the Moody Gardens, NASA, the downtown area. And then I imagined Estefania asking me to make love to her on the ice rink in the Galleria and to whip her with hundreds of people watching. Maybe it was better that we were separated after all.

The problem was obviously that I needed a girlfriend. What else could it be? No sooner had I had this thought than I received a phone call.

"Ciao, Carlos, quanto tempo!"

It was Mela's voice. I had not heard anything of her since the last time I had been in Turin, three years before. We chatted about old times and people whom we both knew. The situation at the Teatro Nuovo was not great, and she was thinking of moving elsewhere. It was only after about half an hour of chatting that Mela casually threw in her question. "Do you think they'd let me study there?"

I sat up in bed like a shot. "I'm sure there won't be a problem, I'll talk to the director."

The next day I spoke to Ben, and he agreed that Mela could take classes at the academy.

She arrived from Italy on a Monday, at eight o'clock at night. She was far too thin, her face was pale, and when I hugged her I had to take care not to crush her frail frame. Her smell immediately took me back to the days of the Teatro Nuovo di Torino, that tour of Venice and our first embrace in a hotel room. From the moment I had met her, I had seen something in her eyes that I had never sensed in anyone else, and I knew that she was saving whatever it was just for me. In those days, however, my feelings had been reserved for Narina, and there was nothing left over to share with anyone else. Now Mela's shining eyes were in front of me again, looking at me the same way they had years before. By her second day in Houston, we were already boyfriend and girlfriend. The way she loved me was something new for me, and each minute we spent together she took me further into her confidence. She told me that her mother had died from a terrible illness and that her family had sold their house in the mountains because her mother's spirit still prowled every corner. Mela's grief had taken its toll on her body, and her cheekbones were as sharp as blades. I suspected she might be bulimic, something that was later confirmed when we dined in a restaurant and she came back to the table from the toilet with a bile stain on her white blouse. I did not know how to help her, so I kept quiet and acted as though nothing had happened.

Time passed more quickly now that Mela was with me. Even though deep down I knew this relationship was not going to take me anywhere, Mela's company, even if it did not completely cure me of all my ills, did seem to erase that curious sense of unease.

The papers started to compare me to Baryshnikov and even to Nureyev, the owner of the island I had seen in the Gulf of Positano before I even knew who he was. I cut out the articles as always and put them into an envelope with the others.

In March, I danced *Etudes* with Li Cunxin and Martha Butler, who by this time had become great friends of mine after they realized that I didn't want to take sides between the dancers and the director. Later on, I danced the shadow scene from *La Bayadère*. *Coppelia* followed, and Ben included me in some of his new creations. I received some bad reviews, but I kept only the good ones. I felt that I was earning my place in the company and that I was not a stranger there anymore.

Everyone thought Mela and I made a lovely couple, except Kentaro, who told me I would be better off with somebody who could dance salsa and was more down to earth. I explained that our relationship was not serious. Nobody believed me, but it was true. When Mela hugged me, the only thing I felt was the warmth of affection. Her fire did not reach right down inside of me. I liked having her around, eating breakfast together, finding her stretched out on the bed. I became very fond of her. But it was not love.

"So, you've got a girlfriend. How long have you been together?" asked my aunt Mireya on one of our telephone calls.

"She's not really my girlfriend. We met in Turin three years ago. We're just friends," I told her.

Mireya laughed mischievously.

"Be careful, or you'll end up having more children than your father," she said. My father's many children from his relationships with women before he met my mother were the source of lots of jokes in the family.

"Have you written to Mamá?" I asked.

"No, no, I haven't been able to write to her. I haven't had time with all my problems." She explained that she and Roberto had decided to get divorced. "I don't know how I'm going to pay the mortgage. I'm extremely worried about it," she added.

I couldn't believe what I was hearing. If in two years Mireya had not found twenty minutes to write a letter to my mother, it was clear she was never going to. I thought about my trip to Miami and my regular phone calls since being back in the States. Had it all been a farce?

"Yuli, I wanted to ask you something. You couldn't lend me three hundred dollars until next month, could you? Hey, Yuli? Yuli, are you there?"

I hung up, realizing that my efforts to unite the family had been in vain.

I spoke to my friend William in Canada so that he could get me a three-way connection with Los Pinos, but the lines were worse than ever. When I finally managed to get in touch, I learned that my sister Berta had had another crisis. They had found her naked in the street again. Eduardo had rushed her to the Almejeiras Brothers Hospital, where she had been admitted to the psychiatric department, and she was now doing better. The news from the neighborhood was that power cuts were now lasting for twenty hours a day. At night, since they could not turn on the electric fans, nobody could sleep for the heat. People were throwing themselves into the sea on rafts to try to reach the United States. Many of them were childhood friends like Denei, Papo, Roli, and the fat kid I used to raise pigeons with. Fortunately, they were all safe and sound, but others had not been so lucky. Thousands of Cubans had perished trying to get out.

"And how are your grandmother and your aunt?" my mother asked. "What news of them?"

"Mami, there's something you ought to know," I said. "Granny, Auntie, and Corairis . . ." I hesitated for a few seconds, not knowing how to tell her that her own sister and mother did not care enough about her even to write. Mela was gesturing to me to be quiet, and in that instant I decided she was right. It was better not to give my mother any more problems to think about. "They're all fine. They miss you a lot," I said, with a lump in my throat.

That night I went to bed thinking about Berta and about the Cuban rafters; I could feel the knots forming in my shoulders. My body became as hard as an iron girder. Mela gave me a massage, and I felt happy to have her by my side.

We had been living together for a while now, and I had come to realize that she was not just a pretty face. Beneath the radiant dark brown hair was an intelligent and cultured girl. She loved literature, but her favorite subject was the Bible and everything related to God.

"Do you believe in God?" she asked me once.

I told her about my sister Berta's illness, and how I did not understand why God had not protected her from schizophrenia. "The thing is, I'd like to believe in God, Mela, but what I see around me doesn't inspire me to," I said.

She tried to explain to me that having faith was the most important thing, but we would end up arguing every time we talked about religion. Mostly, though, we spent our time laughing or remembering our years in Italy. She teased me about the gap between my front teeth, which had disappeared with my first visit to a Houston dentist.

"I liked you better before," she mocked me in the laid-back, ironic way I loved.

Sex was a lovely game in which I was the driver and she was my passenger. Every night I took her on a different journey, and she would follow me to all the wild and crazy places I chose to take her. She liked to try new things, but whenever we did, I had to cover her mouth to muffle her cries of pleasure, as José and Sonia could hear her shouts from their bedroom next door. Even when we decided to make love under the shower in an attempt to disguise the madness beneath the sound of running water, José and Sonia looked at us wickedly when we emerged. They had no choice but to get used to the hurricane that lived in our shower.

Love arrived for me in the same way that pain arrives, unexpectedly. I did everything possible not to fall in love with Mela, but as time passed, her smile and her femininity worked their way inside my body. One day I woke up and discovered that Mela possessed nearly all of me. She had gotten nearer to that terrifying point than either Olga or Narina had done before her.

Just a week before my twenty-first birthday, Ben invited us to a party at his house. Mela was not feeling well; she had a bad headache and said she would stay in our apartment. I wanted to stay with her because I was not in the mood for a party, but Mela insisted that I could not do that to my director and that I should go with José and Sonia.

When we arrived at La Porte, the party was already in full swing. There were people on Jet Skis in the bay, dancers in the new Jacuzzi that Ben had bought, and sunbathers stretched out in the garden.

José and I sat down to watch a film that was showing on the television in the living room. It was the story of one of the many Mexican families that migrated to the United States in search of a better life. Ironically, they had settled in Los Angeles. California had been part of Mexico up until the Mexican-American War of 1846–1848, so in a way they were immigrants in their own country. The children were "Chicanos," born of Mexican parents in the United States.

Ben came over to us carrying two plates heaped with food, then went to fetch his own plate and sat down beside me.

He asked me if I liked working with the company.

Barely looking away from the screen, I told him that I did.

"That's good, because I would like to invite you to dance with us next year as well," he said.

The film had gotten to the part now where the two rival gangs of Chicanos had a fight in a club. They were the sort of tough guys I used to hang out with in my youth, the kind of guys who had been at that break-dance competition in Almendares Park.

"Of course, that's assuming that you want to and that Alicia lets you come," Ben added.

I smiled at him, still with one eye on the screen. He rolled his eyes and went out into the garden.

The film was getting more and more interesting. One of the brothers, the gang leader, was killed by the police in a hail of bullets. His father wept with despair as he held the bloodstained body of the poor boy.

"What for, Maria . . . what for?" the father cried. "What was the point of leaving everything to live life as a foreigner? We came here looking for a better life and look what we got . . . the death of a son! I'm going back now. I'm going back to our world, the one that we left behind."

A woman in the film also started to cry. The brothers of the dead boy lifted up his body and carried it away in silence.

I stared at the screen, feeling I had experienced an epiphany. Something dormant in me had awoken. Suddenly I knew that this was the thing that had been troubling me so much, the unease that I had been unable to put my finger on. It was not a lack of friends, the new city, the rigors of work, or the need of a girlfriend. It was a terrible fear that, just like the Mexican family in the film, I would be a foreigner for the rest of my life.

I, too, had emigrated within my own country, moving to Pinar del Río to follow my father's exotic dream, and now I was an alien to my family in Miami, and even to a certain extent in my own home. Now I was being offered the chance to extend my contract with the Houston Ballet, which would mean another year away from Cuba. This had to stop! I had to end my contract in Houston and return to Cuba, where I belonged. I would put up with the power cuts, the lousy transportation, the Special Period; those problems could not last forever. Anyway, wouldn't it be worth going through it all, if, at the end of each performance, I could turn to my mother and my sisters, waiting for me, their eyes filled with pride? My life as a foreigner had to end.

I made my apologies to Ben. "Ben, I'm leaving. Mela doesn't feel well, and I think I'd better check on her." I asked him to let José know I was going and walked to my car.

But as I drove through the electric gate of the apartment complex where we lived, I saw something that disturbed me. Over in the direction of the swimming pool, two people were walking along, holding hands. The couple seemed familiar. I braked quickly and got out of the car to have a better look. Even from a distance, Mela and Kentaro looked happy, as though they had been together for years. She was not at all ill. In fact, she looked full of vitality in her blue bikini. Kentaro put his arm around her shoulders and leaned in to give her a kiss.

"Son of a bitch!"

Instinct clouded my judgment. I went back to the car and took my aluminum baseball bat out of the trunk.

When they saw me coming toward them, bat in hand, they sprang apart.

"Carlos, no, it isn't what you think!"

I raised the bat and they both jumped backward.

"Carlos, Mela told me she felt bad. I'm your friend. I would never do anything like that to you."

"Friend? What you are is a bastard!"

By now, people had started to gather around us. Someone called the apartment complex office, and security guards arrived.

"Put the baseball bat down! Don't do it, boy, don't do it!"

"Don't do it, Junior!" Mela repeated urgently.

Each time it looked as though I was about to hit Kentaro with the bat, the crowd of people all moved back and shouted, "No, don't do it, boy! Don't do it, Junior!"

The heat inside my head was becoming unbearable. Gripping the bat with both hands, I brought it down with all my force against the ground.

"I don't know what your definition of friendship is, but you never do that, even to your worst enemy. I'd like to smash your face in, but I prefer to leave you with one less friend," I told Kentaro.

The security guards picked the bat up off the ground and took me by the arm. "It's okay, boy, let's go home."

I looked long and hard at Mela's eyes, realizing that I was not her driver anymore. What she had been saving for me now belonged to Kentaro.

I turned on my heels and fled.

Mela returned to Italy immediately, and I spent my twenty-first birthday shut up inside my apartment, regretting not having smashed in Kentaro's face.

"Do you know what, José?" I told my friend. "I should have let him have it. Yeah, I definitely should have split that son of a bitch's head open."

Only one thing cheered me up: my contract with the Houston Ballet was almost up. I could return to Havana forever.

Chapter 18

BACK IN HAVANA

Almost as soon as I got back to Havana, I was asked to appear with my father on *Joven Joven,* one of the most popular television programs of the day. It was live, with a salsa orchestra and a large audience. We were told to arrive around eleven in the morning so we could have makeup applied and meet the interviewer. Leaving the house at nine-thirty would have got us there with time to spare, but my father was up at five A.M. brewing the coffee. When I awoke, he was standing in front of the mirror, dressed in a suit and tie, looking as though he were about to receive an Oscar. He had shaved, and the smell of his cologne pervaded not just the house but the whole neighborhood.

"Papito, you should wear something lighter. You'll die in this heat."

In Cuba, the humidity and heat of July are almost unbearable.

"Too bad. I must pay homage to the star," my old man replied, preening in the mirror.

"Pedro, where do you think you're going?" my mother asked when she woke up. "It's not your son's wedding, just an interview."

My father ignored her and sat down on the bed to pull on the cowboy boots I had brought him back from Texas.

"Papito, no! The boots don't go with the suit. Why don't you wear these, you'll be more comfortable," I said, reaching for a fashionable pair of Kenneth Cole shoes.

"Who told you that? Those dress shoes hurt my corns," my father answered. "This is how we wore them in my day, and this is how I'm going to wear them now."

"Don't worry, Yuli," my mother intervened. "Let your father wear whatever he likes."

It was a Saturday, and many people were off to the beach. On the number 13 bus we were squashed together, shoulder to shoulder, like bunches of bananas. Nearly all the men were shirtless and the women were wearing bikini tops. In among these scantily clad people we stood—my father in his best suit and cowboy boots and me in a smart pair of trousers and a long-sleeved shirt, both of us drenched in sweat. I could see that people were laughing at us, but my father smiled as if it was all part of the show.

When we arrived, we asked to cool off in front of an electric fan. When the interviewer came to meet us, I wiped the sweat from my forehead and introduced us both.

"I'm Carlos Acosta, and this is my father."

The woman's gaze rested on my father's boots. "It's a pleasure to have you on the program," she said eventually.

Television cameras have always terrified me. As soon as they started rolling, I spoke very little, hesitating over each answer.

"Life in Houston was good. The sun shines a lot," I responded as the interviewer waited, microphone in hand, for me to elaborate.

"So, you've had a nice time. And what about London, how did you get on there?"

"In London, I met Princess Diana and had an operation on my ankle," I answered, my hands clammy with sweat.

"So you had some success but also some misfortunes. Let's talk about your misfortunes."

"Well, my misfortunes, the misfortunes were . . . nothing. I don't want to talk about my misfortunes."

The interviewer realized that she was wasting her time with me and turned toward my father.

"Tell me, sir, how do you feel about your son's success?"

"I feel like Gutamber of Maguncia's ray of light," he told her.

She was clearly astonished, but my father was just warming up.

"Art belongs to all of us. It isn't something that exists in a separate world," he expounded. "Talking of misfortune, I'd say it's a misfortune not to be an artist. Take pigeons, for example: you feed them, you take them out every day and put them in a place where they can see their surroundings and get used to their new home. After a while you set them free, and they don't leave. Art is the same. You dedicate time to it, you nourish it, even though in doing so your health might be affected and you might not see immediate results. One day a child asks you for your autograph to frame and hang at the head of his bed. That's when art completes its cycle. That pigeon will want to return time and time again, and one day, that child, already, strictly speaking, an artist, will begin the process again with another bird."

Everybody looked at one another as if to say, Where on earth did they find this truck driver?

"I'm obviously speaking to the voice of experience," said the interviewer. "Your wisdom is as unquestionable as your love for pigeons."

"No, no, I can't stand pigeons," my old man said abruptly.

There was silence, then the interviewer repeated, "So . . . you can't stand pigeons?"

"That's right, pigeons are ugly. I like ducks. And showgirls who wear lots of feathers."

Some people laughed. The interviewer was disconcerted, clearly unsure how to respond to my father's answers. After a long pause, she said, "Good . . . good . . . um, and now, everybody, here's the group that's number one in the hit parade, NG La Banda!"

And that was that. But as soon as we came out of the television studio and started walking down the street, a man came up to me. "Excuse me, aren't you that dancer, the truck driver's son?" he asked.

I nodded my head.

"See, Marta, I told you!" he exclaimed delightedly. "I recognized you because of your father!"

My father smiled, smug as a peacock displaying its lovely plumage. Then he regaled the couple with stories about his childhood, about meeting the workers' leader Lázaro Peña, and, inevitably, about how he had crept into the cinema to watch the film about ballet only to be kicked out for being black.

These people looked at him as if they wanted to adopt him. Two more arrived.

"Look who it is! The dancer's father. You are a model father," they said admiringly.

Nobody told me that I was a model son.

"Papito, let's go now, we'll be late back," I said, tapping him on the shoulder, but my father launched into the story of his life from the very beginning, accentuating each anecdote as though he were an actor. We got home very late that night.

Two days later an article appeared in the newspaper *Granma* entitled "The Medals That My Father Won." The next day in the newspaper *Juventud Rebelde* another appeared entitled "The Golden Mulatto."

Now it was my father who cut the articles out to put together with the ones I had brought back from Houston.

One day there was a knock at the door of my apartment in Los Pinos. When I stuck my head out, I saw a small man with a muscular body, prominent teeth, and a freckled face.

"Hi, Yuli, when did you arrive?"

"Opito!" It was the first time he had ever knocked on the door of my house. His eyes betrayed the frustration of a person unfulfilled, and his seriousness surprised me. It was as though he had lost all connection with the kid he used to be.

"How's it going, Opito? I got here two weeks ago. How are you?"

"I'm fine," he said. "Look, Milli, Chinchán, and the others are sitting on the wall. We wanted to know if you'd like to come down and talk to us for a while?"

His tone sounded friendly enough. I shouted to my mother from the living room that I would be at the wall on the corner, and I went downstairs.

The breeze coming from the north stirred the trees around Zoilita's house, making the mangos fall down onto her roof and then roll to the ground. The late afternoon sun was lazing around in the sky and turning a deeper and deeper orange. Tonito was trying to climb the fence to steal some of Zoilita's mangos. As I came around the corner, someone whistled, and Tonito turned to look in my direction, gave up the idea of the mangos, and came back to sit on the wall. Everyone stopped what they were doing and waited in silence.

"How's it going?" I greeted each of the seven men, slapping their hands as I used to do when we were kids. Most of them had beards and mustaches and permanent wrinkles. Half of Chinchán's middle finger had been shot off in a fight, and you could already see the hollows in Milli's face.

"How's it going, Yuli? We saw you on *Joven Joven* and in the papers," Chinchán said, offering me the hand with the stumpy finger. "I didn't know that Pedro could speak so well."

"My father? Oh yes, he always steals the show. I wish I'd inherited some of his charisma!"

They made some space for me to sit on the wall.

"Hey, is it true that Papo left on a raft?" I asked.

"Yes. Nelda, his sister, got a letter the other day. They're all being held in a camp while they find places for them to go. He says they're fine. . . ."

"How come you haven't defected?" Milli asked me.

"I don't want to live so far away from my family," I replied. "Anyway, life outside isn't as easy as you think. . . ."

Suddenly everyone looked at me as if I were a member of the Cuban State Security.

"Ha, Yuli, you've got to be joking!" said Milli. "Don't give us that stuff. Things over there must be better than they are here. Let's see, how many times a day do the lights go off in London? And the people in the States, do they have ration books?"

Everybody laughed, including me.

"No, Milli, but you have to pay taxes, and there's the cold and the isolation. You mustn't think that everything's rosy, or that it's paradise like people claim. Nobody's going to give you a car or a house. You have to work like a maniac day and night in order to get anywhere, and no one will help you because they're all struggling to succeed, too. It's true that things here are terrible, but when you leave you'll realize what you've lost, and you'll miss the things that I missed: the meetings on this wall, the Los Van Van concerts, even the Camels . . ." I said, remembering the huge, humpbacked buses that transport hundreds of people.

"Hey, bro, leave it out," said Chinchán, raising his stumpy finger in the air. "First, nobody, absolutely nobody, could ever miss the Camels, and second, or rather, one and a half," he said, this time also raising his index finger in the air, making us all laugh, "it's easy for you to say that because you're allowed to travel. You've been to Paris and London, and when you have kids you'll be able to tell them about the Eiffel Tower and all that. If I stay, the only things I'll be able to tell my kids about will be the Popsicles that Quenia makes, La Finca, and the power cuts, because I'm not even allowed into a fucking hotel here. That's why the next raft out of here will be mine. I'm tired of the politics, of how we've all got to be like Che, when the only thing I want to do is to earn a living making shoes. That's what I want to do, open a shoe shop. That's my dream; that's why I'm going."

"Dreams! You know what I think about dreams?" I said, smiling. "Dreams are like those lights you see on a motorway; they approach slowly and when they arrive they start to move away again. I dreamed about being a soccer player, and now I'm a ballet dancer. If I were you, I wouldn't depend on them."

Everyone was quiet. Then Bobe, a tall, muscular black guy, spoke. "Look, brother, you should be grateful to your dad for getting you into ballet; otherwise, you'd just be here wasting time like the rest of us. Maybe you'd have been the first to leave on a raft. Or perhaps you don't appreciate your life?"

"No, man," I said, jumping down off the wall. "What I was trying to say was that often dreams don't measure up to reality. People dream about paradise, but the truth is that here you can have heart surgery free of charge, while in the States you could die of a stomachache if you don't have health insurance. Here they don't let you have money because we've all got to be equal, and there you can get to wherever your talent and ability take you. Understand? It's all relative. There are good things and bad things. The only certain thing is that, in the end, they'll screw you up there as much as they do here. So isn't it better to be screwed up in your own country?"

"Screw that! I'd rather be messed up by Uncle Sam," replied Pedro Julio, and we all laughed again. "Papo said in his letter that if anyone around here wanted to leave, he'd be happy to put them up. Well, as soon as he has a house, that is, because he doesn't know how long he's going to be detained."

"So, Chinchán," said Bobe, jumping off the wall, "save me a place on your raft, because I'm leaving, too."

Opito was sitting just over to my right and still seemed slightly withdrawn.

"And what do you think, bro?" I asked my old dancing partner.

"That politics is shit whichever way you look at it. It's better to talk about something else."

"Too right, so let's drink to the good times!" concluded Tonito, as he got out a bottle of "train spark," a kind of homemade rum very popular in the 1990s, and started pouring the drink into three plastic cups.

We chatted on, discussing the local gossip about how Gerardo "the Hat" had been stabbed and how Chino was still in prison for robbery, and from there we fell to talking about our childhood memories.

"Do you remember that competition in Lenin Park, Yuli?" asked Pedro Julio, and I noticed that Opito looked a little uncomfortable.

"How could I forget? It was one of the happiest moments of my life," I answered.

"And that time when we were playing Eat Mud and a black car came looking for you because you'd left them in the lurch and they couldn't start the show without you?" Pedro Julio continued.

"Of course! We were fighting because you didn't want to eat mud. Do you remember how I rubbed the mud ball all over your face?"

We all clapped our hands and cheered, but Opito remained serious and withdrawn.

"Man, do you remember that break-dance competition in Almendares?" Now it was Tonito who spoke.

"Shit, of course! Opito saw off everybody that day. He did at least ten head spins. Do you remember how they stabbed Tar Ball?"

We all started laughing again. I realized that I had missed these guys as much as I missed those days when Los Pinos was a paradise on earth, when the owls still hooted at night and grass did not grow out of the holes in the streets. The Los Pinos that I now saw before me had been going downhill for years. Its residents were old and neglected; they did not paint their houses or cut their lawns anymore. Most of the trees had been violently hacked down in an attempt to clear more land to build on. Even my friends sitting there on that wall looked the worse for wear; they were still young, but nearly all of them had lost many of their teeth.

"Yuli, do you remember when we caught you by that wall on the corner and Opito gave you two black eyes? Do you rem—"

"Hey, you shut your mouth!" Opito jumped down from his perch angrily, not allowing Milli to finish. "I knew you were going to open it sooner or later. You're so full of shit."

We all instinctively jumped down to quiet Opito.

"Calm down, Opito; it's nothing," said Pedro Julio.

"Calm down? No! You lot are always talking crap. The past is the past. You should concentrate on the present and leave the past alone."

We gazed at each other uncomprehendingly, then looked back at Opito, but he had already turned around and was walking toward his house.

"Opito, Opito, come here!" I shouted, running after him.

I caught him up, but he did not seem to want to stop; he just walked even faster.

"Opito, what's the matter, bro? All that happened a long time ago." He kept ignoring me.

"Hey, listen to me, man!" I grabbed hold of him tightly by the arm. "Look, what happened between us was kid stuff. Don't feel bad because of that. I can hardly even remember it."

"You don't remember it?" Now it was his turn to grab me by the arm. "Well, there isn't a night goes by when I don't remember. Yes, that's right, so forgive me, then. I want to hear you say it."

"Opito, don't fuck about!"

"Go on, say it. Say it, damn it."

He stared at me fiercely. Still without understanding, I pried his hand away from my arm and, looking into his eyes, said, "I forgive you. Okay?"

Opito exhaled as though a great weight had been taken away from him. The anger cleared from his eyes. He smiled, and I suppose he must have been pleased.

"Now tell me about yourself. How are your brothers?" I said, to change the subject.

He flashed me his yellow teeth in a grin and, after giving me a couple of pats on the back, turned on his heels and disappeared down the long dark passageway that led to his house.

"Hey! Opito, come here!" I called after him in vain.

Some while later, I found out that his exit visa to Spain had arrived, and I realized that he had been saying good-bye to me with those two pats on the back. It also went some way toward explaining his strange behavior: before going away forever, he wanted to leave his past behind in Los Pinos, the place where he was born.

———

Although I was not aware of it, Chery had put my name down on the list of artists who needed housing, and a month after arriving back from Houston, I was given the keys to an apartment on the fifth floor of a building on Décima Avenida and Calzada, just ten blocks away from the headquarters of the Cuban National Ballet. I paid the bank the sum of 8,000 Cuban pesos, something in the region of $800, and the apartment was mine. I bought a lamp, a table with four folding chairs, and an electric cooker, then transported my bed, my videos, and my stereo over. Good-bye, mathematics classroom!

As soon as I had my apartment neat and tidy, I called Estefania.

"Junior! What a surprise! When did you arrive?" She sounded very happy to hear my voice.

"I got here a month ago, and do you know what? They've given me an apartment in Vedado, on Décima Avenida. You've got to come over and see it."

I had a lot to tell her and a lot that would be difficult to say over the phone, so we agreed that I would collect her at four o'clock the following afternoon from outside La Pedrera restaurant, after I had finished my rehearsals of *Raymonda* at the National Ballet.

My Volkswagen stopped in front of a pair of extremely long legs.

"Estefania, I have to say you're just as lovely as ever," I said, getting out of the car to have a better look at her. "Turn around, let me see what I've been missing."

"It's you who haven't changed. You're as cheeky as ever! Anyway, nobody changes in just nine months."

We hugged tightly, then, when we had disentangled, we looked into each other's eyes. She let out a sigh, and we got back into the car.

Twenty minutes later we were in my apartment.

"Wow! You can't complain now; you're an independent man with a car and a house," exclaimed Estefania as I opened the door. She went straight to the bathroom and examined everything.

"What a shame you don't have a water tank like the one in Los Pinos!" she said mischievously.

"I do have one, but it's in the kitchen."

Estefania began to lick her lips. She was wearing a tiny miniskirt, and her smooth legs seemed to be inviting me to touch them. I imagined my hands inside her skirt, feeling that delicious treasure hidden beneath the fabric. I walked toward her, but the little tease sidestepped me and moved toward the bedroom, where she started to sniff the bedclothes.

"New sheets. Where did you buy them, in Houston?"

My erection was extremely visible. Estefania looked at the bulge in my pants, licking her lips.

"Houston's set you up." She smiled.

I was not listening to a word she said. I sat down beside her and began to stroke her thighs.

She looked me in the eye. "You haven't left a girlfriend over there?"

"No. There's no one," I said, as my hands slowly worked toward their destination.

"And when are you going back?" she asked.

"Never," I said, feeling as though I was about to explode.

"What do you mean, never?" She stood up abruptly and strode back into the living room.

"Estefania, what's the matter?"

"I asked what do you mean, never? Didn't they give you another contract?"

"Can we change the subject?"

"What about your career?"

"Forget my career! I've decided to make my life here. I don't want to travel anymore."

Estefania looked as though someone had just thrown a bucket of cold water over her. "You're crazy! What are you going to do here? This place is going to the dogs!"

I felt myself gradually losing that fabulous erection.

"At least this is my sun, my sea, my wine," I said.

"Oh, Junior, wine or no wine, stop being so sentimental and so foolish! Make the most of your glory days, because they're not going to last forever. You're making money over there and when you retire you'll have a pension. What are you going to have here? Why do you think people are throwing themselves into the sea on rafts? Keep on chasing the money; otherwise, it's going to be too late."

"You're just like Chinchán, Milli, and all the other people in Los Pinos who don't know what they're talking about," I told her. "You have no idea what it's like to arrive somewhere and make a new life for yourself, all the time struggling to speak English. You don't know how frustrating it is when nobody says hello to you in the morning, when no one could care less about you. The worst thing is when they criticize Cuba to your face and you have to keep your mouth shut and your head down, because it's thanks to the fact that you are there that your parents have a better life. But everybody thinks of you as just another foreigner! Well, I'm sick of all of it, of not even being able to crack a damn joke that makes sense. Are you listening, Estefania? It's so easy for you. You've got your family to come running to your side every time you've got a pain. Well, I also want that luxury."

My erection had completely subsided. The heat I felt now was of a different sort than what I had been feeling a few seconds before.

"And have you told your father?" Estefania asked, sitting down on one of the chairs at the table.

"Not yet. I'm going to speak to him very soon."

We remained silent for a few minutes. Estefania looked as though someone had punched her in the stomach.

"You know what's going to happen when he finds out, right?"

"Yes, I know. I'll think of something."

Estefania got up, picked up her bag from the bed, and walked toward the door.

"Why don't you stay a bit longer?" I asked her.

"No. I've got to go."

"Do you want me to take you to your house?"

"No. No, I'm not going there."

I walked with her down the stairs. At the exit she kissed me on the cheek and, looking at me sadly, said, "Do you know something? I was wrong when I told you that nobody changes in nine months."

We looked at each other for a few seconds, then she kissed me softly on the lips, turned on her heels, and walked off in the direction of Linea Street.

I stood for a long while watching how her long black hair gently bounced against her miniskirt, and how the neighbors turned their heads to proposition her.

And to think that glorious body had once been mine!

———

Seven days were enough to change my life, because a week after my encounter with Estefania, my sister Berta asked if she could move to my apartment. She and Eduardo had split up shortly after her last episode.

"Of course, Bertica, come and live with me," I told her, and soon afterward my mother also moved in to look after her.

Marilín was still living with her boyfriend, Yiyo, and my father was left on his own in Los Pinos.

I was very happy. I had a car and a house, and my mother and Berta were living with me. Everything was going well at the National Ballet, too. I was scheduled to participate in the summer tour to Spain in August, and I would be dancing in many ballets that were new to me. The only thing that bothered me was the fact that I still was not a principal dancer. Dancers moved up a category only after an annual evaluation at which all the teachers met and agreed on who should be promoted. I had still not been evaluated, which meant that, technically, even though I was dancing principal roles, I was still a soloist. And that, not unnaturally, irked me.

One day, I had just gotten home from rehearsals when I met Berta coming down the stairs from the apartment. "How are you?" I asked, giving her a hug.

"Today is a special day. I feel better than ever," she replied.

I rapidly ran through a mental list of birthdays and anniversaries in case I had forgotten an important occasion. "Why is it a special day?" I asked, perplexed, as I walked with her to the exit of the apartment building.

"Don't worry, you'll soon realize why."

The shadows in the passageway obscured her expression, but once we reached the exit, the sunlight illuminated her face, and my instinct told me that something was wrong.

"Berta, what's the matter? Have you taken your medication? Where are you going?" I asked her in alarm, holding her by the arms.

"Let me go, Yuli; nothing's the matter!" she shouted furiously. "I'm going to take a walk on the Malecón. I want to get a bit of sea air. Wait here for me. I'll soon be back."

"Wait . . . don't go. Look . . . let me go with you!" I said, trying to catch her by the hand, but she walked away from me, shaking her head.

Schizophrenia was written all over her face, and I let her go. I was left alone, standing on the street like a fool. Slowly, I turned and went upstairs to have something to eat before returning to rehearsals.

All over Cuba at the time, people were launching themselves upon the waves with their children, their grandparents, even their dogs. The government had said anyone who wanted to leave could, and so they went—on wooden rafts, on the inner tubes of truck tires, on whatever they could find. The same police officers who before would have arrested people for trying to leave, now helped to push off rafts and wished emigrants good luck.

Other people threw themselves into the sea for different reasons. Some just wanted to cool down, some wanted to fish, and very soon the Cuban waterways became a free-for-all. Nobody could be sure who was leaving, who was fishing, and who was bathing. One thing was certain, though: everybody cried. The waters of the Malecón mingled with the tears shed by hundreds of families, mine included. For among all those people leaping into the sea, there was one who leaped straight onto the jagged rocks of the Malecón: my sister Berta.

When I arrived at the accident and emergency department at the Calixto García Hospital, my mother and Marilín came running to meet me. They were crying so hard they could not speak.

"Mami, what's happened? Just what has happened? Marilín, stop crying a minute and tell me what's happened . . . damn it!"

Marilín told me that Berta had thrown herself onto the rocks. She had done it looking at the sun and holding on to her ankles, landing on her knees in a free fall from a height of twenty feet. Now she was in the operating room, where they were inserting metal rods to knit her broken bones together: the tibia, the fibula, and the kneecap of her right leg and the elbow of her left arm. Her breasts were purple with bruises and her stomach was scratched all over.

"Oh my God . . . Why did she go and do that?"

I sat down on a bench. With my head in my hands, I started to tremble. I realized then that when she had said she was going to the Malecón to get some sea air, she had left with the intention of killing herself. I should have tied her up forcibly, held her back at all costs. Instead, I just stood there on the street and watched her go. Now she was in the hospital, and it was all my fault.

"I'm to blame for all of this," I said, my voice cracking. I began to sob.

I told my mother and Marilín what had happened that morning. They tried to comfort me, to convince me it was fate, but inside my head I knew I was the guilty one.

"Berta told me that today was a special day, Mami. Understand? For her it was a special day," I shouted, the snot running down over my lips.

I wept to think that my sister had thought the day of her death was a special day, when it would destroy our whole family. Schizophrenia has to be the most horrific illness in the world.

My father joined us a little while later. He sat down beside me in silence and put his arm around my shoulders. My mother and Marilín had calmed down and were now sleeping quietly. The four of us spent the night in the accident and emergency department, waiting for someone to give us some news about my sister's condition.

I felt so terrible the next day that I could not go to class. Marilín woke up early and bought some bread and milk for our breakfast. About eleven in the morning a male nurse asked if we were the family of Berta Acosta and took us to where my sister was. The ward was dirty and hot and smelled of urine and medicine. The paint was flaking off the walls. There were people of all ages—children, elderly men and women—with broken arms and amputated legs, who cried out in agony like the mournful chorus of a funeral mass.

My sister's moans were part of this dismal music. Her right leg was slightly raised, with metal rods buried along its whole length. Her left arm also had rods in it and a white bandage that covered her hand. She muttered incoherently about God, Franz, Eduardo, and Satan, and she pleaded with Aunt Lucia to come to fetch her. When she noticed us, she gestured with her healthy hand for us to come over. Then, when we were all gathered around her bed, she told us in a macabre whisper that she wanted to die, that Aunt Lucia had come to get her, and that we should not cry.

My mother fell to her knees on the floor. "Oh, don't say that, my daughter!" she implored.

Marilín hung on to my shoulders. My father helped my mother up and led her outside. The young man with the amputated leg in the next bed started to scream with pain, and a nurse came running up with a syringe to sedate him. They told us that Berta remained unsettled because they could not give her any of her regular medication while she was still under the effects of the painkillers.

I felt numb, as though I was in a kind of trance. I was looking at Berta, but my mind was far, far away, confused by dozens of conflicting emotions. I kept thinking that I could have prevented all this, but it was too late.

"Yuli, listen to me, son. Don't let this put you off track. Don't think yourself unlucky. It's just how things are. The moment you think you've got it all under control, life always springs a surprise on you. It happens to everyone. At least we have you. There are some people who don't have any hope to hang on to, and their suffering is eternal. Don't let this put you off track, son."

My father shook me gently, and I realized that the distant voice I had been hearing was his.

I looked around me. My mother was sobbing on the nurse's chest, and Marilín had her arms around her protectively. A subdued and melancholy voice was murmuring behind me. "Dance for God, Yuli, my brother. Only God matters. I feel much closer to Him. Lucia says that she will take me tonight, and she'll keep a place for you when you are ready. One day, we'll all be reunited with God in glory."

I threw myself against my father's shoulders.

"I know, son, I know it's difficult, but you have to understand that it's all a result of that damned illness. No one wants to die just like that. You've got to be strong, Yuli. You are our light. Go to Houston, follow your path."

"But, Papito, how can you tell me to leave at a moment like this?" I asked, drying my tears. "I have to help you, help Berta; this is when you all need me most."

"You're not going to help her by crying. What we need is for you to be happy for all of us. Let us at least live with that comfort, son."

"But, Papito . . . I . . ."

"Listen, son." My father lifted up my chin and looked at me for a long while. Then he spoke: "Once you told me that you hated me, and that night I couldn't sleep for thinking I had failed. In the end, I realized that you were right to hate me. I was hard on you. I beat you just as my mother beat me, and I never went to visit you in the two years that you were in Pinar del Río. And believe me, Yuli, I also suffered, because even if I appeared not to have a heart, I didn't want to hurt my own flesh and blood. But if there was one thing that I couldn't allow, it was that you should go the same way as your brother Pedro and the others, who never listened to me and who chose the wrong path. You are my hope, my last and only chance to do something good before I die. By the time you have your own children, I may well be dead, and you can tell them all you want how cruel your father was to you. But you have to understand that we all come into this world with a specific mission, and mine was not to shower you with love, as you might have wanted, but to try to guide you and prepare you for life."

"But why does it have to be me?" I asked him.

"Because you are the one who's been given the chance, my son," said my father, lifting up my chin once more. "Go away from here. Make your life in the world. When people hear the surname Acosta, I want everyone to know that they're talking about you."

Then my father gripped me by the shoulders and, with his customary hardness, said: "Promise me that you won't look back."

"Papito . . ."

"Promise me!"

I wiped my eyes with my arm. My mother was looking at me from the door as if she had heard everything.

In a shaking voice I said to my father, "I promise you," and he hugged me once more.

"That's what I want to hear. You can't see it now, but one day you'll thank me. Go, my son, go, and don't look back!"

I stroked my sister Berta's forehead. She was still calling for Aunt Lucia. I hugged my old man, my mother, and Marilín, and with no more ado I walked out of the hospital. I heard the three of them calling good-bye to me from a distance.

When I showed up to the National Ballet that afternoon, people asked me why I had not been at rehearsals. I told them I felt ill and went home. The next day, I told Alicia Alonso about Ben Stevenson's invitation for me to dance again with his company. She asked me a few questions about the Houston Ballet and finally agreed to the invitation.

That same afternoon I telephoned Ben and told him that in three weeks' time I would be going on tour to Spain with the National Ballet, just like the year before. We agreed that he would send me my contract and a letter of endorsement for the visa I needed, as well as an airline ticket to Houston from Madrid. I would not be going back to Havana after the tour.

Before leaving for Spain, I danced at the García Lorca Theatre in *The Flower Festival in Gensano; Rhythmics,* choreographed by Ivan Tenorio; and *Prologue to a Tragedy,* by Brian McDonald. The applause echoed in my head like never before. The decor took on a rosy hue of nostalgia. These performances would be the last I would give in this theater for a very long time.

Three days before I left, we moved Berta back into my apartment. She seemed like a different person, gingerly touching the rods in her leg and asking my mother how she could have done this to herself. My mother and Marilín dabbed the sweat from her brow and comforted her, telling her she would soon be back to normal, while my father fetched her a glass of mango juice. I stood in the living room, watching them all in silence, scanning their faces, memorizing even the most insignificant detail. I wanted to remember everything about this moment. Then I left.

I went down the stairs to take a last look at the people in the neighborhood, the gardens, the houses, the trees, the animals. I walked all over Los Pinos, to La Fortuna, with its lovely forest, and to the stadium, where I used to escape to play soccer in my childhood. I went to L and 19 and to the National School for the Arts, my old schools. I went as far as Old Havana, with its cobbled streets, and sat in the middle of Obispo to watch the crowds. I walked along the Malecón and looked for the place where Berta had thrown herself off. I shed a few final tears and drew a deep breath of all the heady fragrances of my beautiful city. I wanted to remember my world as it was, the world I would be leaving behind.

Chapter 19

THE WORLD WILL BE MINE

I arrived back in Houston in August 1993. In the time I had been away Li Cunxin had moved to Australia, so I started to dance the opening nights. At the end of November, I danced *The Nutcracker* again with Martha Butler. When the performance was over, we were taken to the green room to sign autographs, and I noticed many Cubans.

"Thank goodness we have someone in the company to represent us at last," said one elderly man. "We're from Matanzas. This is my wife, Caridad."

I wiped the sweat from my forehead and kissed his spouse on the cheek.

"We used to go to the ballet in Cuba very often," he went on. "We saw Alicia dance many times, in her golden days. It was the closest thing to heaven. But since we moved here, we hadn't been to the ballet for twenty years, until you turned up. Thanks to you, we're reliving the old days."

I had no idea what to say to this man, who was gripping my hand with such devotion. A little stunned by his words, I signed his program and posed for a photograph.

"Don't you recognize me?" another lady asked. "I'm Monica Isla's aunt, Sonia." Monica and I had started at L and 19 at the same time. "Monica always said you would go far, and she was right. You were phenomenal! Nobody expected you to end up in Houston, though."

"Houston is a long way from Havana," I replied, smiling.

"You must come over to the house and eat some proper rice and beans. We're at your disposal if you need anything, so no need to feel lonely," she said, and I wondered if she had said this for the sake of something to say, or whether my loneliness was written all over my face.

I put my towel around my shoulders and walked toward my dressing room, aware of some pain in my right ankle.

"José, the ankle I had the operation on is hurting," I said as I came through the door of the house.

José took a look. "It's swollen. Sonia, can you bring a bag of ice here, please!"

Sonia asked if I had hurt myself during the show.

"The show was fine, but after I'd cooled down I felt this pain," I replied, holding the bag of ice to my foot.

"You've probably just pulled some ligaments," said José. "It'll soon be better."

The next day the pain was still there, but despite the discomfort, I was able to jump and do pirouettes, and it did not stop me from performing.

A few weeks later, Ben Stevenson said he would like to create a new *Don Quixote* for me and Lauren Anderson, a black American ballerina at the Houston Ballet with whom I had a happy and successful partnership. I was thrilled because I had always dreamed of taking part in the creation of a three-act ballet.

"When do we start?" I asked the director, keen to get going straightaway.

"As soon as *The Nutcracker* and *The Merry Widow* are over," Ben said. "Just try not to get injured in the meantime."

"Great," I replied, rotating my ankle slightly; and, as soon as Ben had disappeared into one of the studios, I went to put some ice on my foot.

At the beginning of 1995, Lauren and I were invited to dance at a gala at the Bolshoi Theatre in honor of the legendary Russian dancer Olga Lepeshinskaya. I had never imagined myself dancing in Russia, the birthplace of classical ballet. Hardly able to contain my excitement, I asked Ben for his permission, promising that we would be absent for only three days. We would leave on a Thursday night, dance on Saturday, and be back in the studio by Monday. Lauren and I rehearsed *The Corsair* in our spare time.

Russia was in a period of transition. The communist legacy was still evident in people's mentality and in their clothes, which looked very traditional and free from the influence of the fashions of other countries. There were images from Russian folklore everywhere. Ladas and other Russian cars, which were also a familiar sight in Cuba, still filled the streets, with only the occasional Mercedes-Benz gliding by with a foreign flag on the hood. The capitalist multinationals were just starting to make their presence felt, but there were still no McDonald's or Toni & Guy hair salons. The cold was unbearable.

The theater was very grand and showed no sign of ever having been modernized. It was as if we had taken a journey into the past. The candelabra in the middle of the auditorium appeared to be almost two hundred years old, and the hard, rough wooden boards of the stage looked like they had been that way for centuries. Everything was so old and yet so magical that it felt as though the ghosts of Pavlova, Lavrovsky, and Messerer were still trapped there, dancing in the corners. We knew that it was a privilege to be invited to this theater and that we would have to dance to the very best of our abilities. Lauren and I were the only black people, not just on the stage but in the entire theater. It was as though we had landed from another galaxy, and, although it made us nervous, it was certainly stimulating. I took all the painkillers I had brought with me, put ice on my ankle for fifteen minutes, and then went out to give it my all. My jumps were high and precise; Lauren's turns were swift and in perfect time with the music. As our performance finished, the audience gave us a thunderous ovation.

Once we had changed back into our clothes, we went to the reception that followed the performance, and the next day we took the plane back to Houston. The show had been a triumph, and later in the year we would return to dance in another gala at the Kremlin.

Back in Houston, my foot was continuing to trouble me. I went to see the company physical therapist, who told me that there was a lot of scar tissue as a result of my two previous operations, and she recommended an ultrasound. I was terrified I would have to have another operation, and I did not want to have anything to do with hospitals.

"Do you think it's serious?" I asked her.

"I wouldn't say that, but you need to take care of it. Don't force it," she advised.

I needed to be in top form for *Don Quixote.*

The creation of a new choreography involves hours and hours of rehearsal, and endless repetition of complicated and innovative lifts.

"Repeat that step, but this time with your arms in fifth position," Ben would say. "No, no, that doesn't look good, there's too much tension in your arms. Try and do it as though it were no effort."

No effort! Just turn twice while two meters up in the air, keep my legs in one position, smile, and make it look easy!

Sometimes after we had spent hours rehearsing a particular sequence, Ben would decide he did not like it and the next day he would change everything and we would start from scratch, repeating the lifts, correcting steps, until at last he was satisfied. It was an incredibly exhausting process but, at the same time, the most enriching experience a dancer can have. At the end of rehearsals, my clothes were soaked in sweat, and I would drag myself, dripping with perspiration, to the physical therapist to ice my ankle. Once my body had cooled down, I would limp in pain to my dressing room, take a shower, and limp out to my car. When I arrived home, I would have just enough strength to exchange a few words with José and Sonia, raise some food to my mouth, and fall into bed to be ready for the following day when it would all begin again.

Huge photographs of Lauren and me went up on billboards all over the city, and every morning I would make a detour in order to go past one of the sites. Sometimes I would even stop on the shoulder and look up, unable to believe that the dancer suspended in midair was me. Once, I was sitting there gazing up when I recalled the moment in the Saidén Theatre when Terrero had leaped toward the sky. The thought brought back all sorts of memories of Pinar del Río and Los Pinos, and it suddenly occurred to me that I had managed to block my longing for my family out of my mind. I had programmed myself to live in the present. Now it was just me flying through the Houston sky.

The production of *Don Quixote* began to take shape. Day by day, the company dancers became more like the street sellers and artisans of La Mancha. The choreography accentuated the Spanish style of dancing. Lauren and I had developed a great rapport. We could do the lifts without difficulty and brought freshness and humor to the roles of the principal characters. Ben allowed me to incorporate the jumps I developed in my spare time, which had never been used before. I had spent my life imitating other dancers. Now, when others danced the Houston *Don Quixote*, they would have to imitate me.

In March, we premiered *Don Quixote*. The theater was full to the rafters, and the applause was prolonged and deafening. My foot hurt me during the performance, but I disguised it behind the pranks of the charismatic Basilio and it did not stop me from jumping like a gazelle. Lauren was phenomenal, as was the rest of the company. Afterward, there was a party at the mansion of one of the company's sponsors in River Oaks. We danced, ate, and laughed as though we were one big happy family. I demonstrated salsa to my fellow dancers, danced a little merengue with Shirley, and even did some break dancing. It was an altogether unforgettable night for me.

The reviews were ecstatic. An article in *The New York Times* called me the lethal weapon hidden inside the Houston Ballet. Other articles referred to me as the Parachute or the Flying Cuban, and placed me among the myths and legends. I wished then that I could phone my family and tell my father how well I was doing, but calling them would mean looking back, and I had promised my father I would not do that.

Television producers wanted to make documentaries about me. The first arrived shortly after the company had returned from a tour of China.

The producer from a program called *First Impact* was named Florinda. She was friendly and eager to put me at ease.

"Sit down as though you were at home. After all, we Latinos are one big family," she said, showing off her white teeth.

I went to the bathroom and smoothed my hair down with water and applied a little gel. I was as nervous as hell, and wished that I had inherited a bit of my old man's eloquence.

Florinda asked me before we started whether there was anything I did not want to talk about.

"No, it's all okay," I told her. "But could you leave politics out of it?"

We spoke mainly about my years as a student, and after filming was over, Florinda told me when the program would air and shook my hand, saying it had been a pleasure.

The next Wednesday at eight o'clock on the dot, José, Sonia, and I were sitting in front of the television set. The program makers had also interviewed José.

"Carlos is a really hard worker," he said. "That's what's made him the dancer he is. He's a great example."

Sonia covered him in kisses and told him that television made him look years younger.

"Thanks for not mentioning the times that I've left the plates unwashed in the kitchen," I said, raising a beer.

"If people knew what a lazybones you were at home, there'd be no more documentaries and even your career would be in trouble," he replied.

We all roared with laughter, but our eyes remained fixed on the television screen.

Then suddenly the interviewer said something that stunned me. "Before starting this interview, Carlos told us that he didn't want to talk about politics. He doesn't want to be described as a communist."

"What a bitch!" I stood up from the sofa with my hands on my head. "I'm going to call her right now."

"Don't take it to heart," said Sonia.

"But she's going to get me into trouble. If the people from the Cuban Consulate see that, what are they going to think?"

"That's just the way it is, Carlos. Reporters are only interested in causing controversy and keeping people's eyes glued to the screen long enough to sell them cars, houses, and all the other shit they flog in the commercials."

"But she can't say something against my will! That's unprofessional."

"Don't worry. Anyone who's seen it will have forgotten all about it by tomorrow," Sonia said, as she went into the kitchen to prepare the evening meal. I continued watching, realizing that I would have to be more careful with the press in the future.

The story of the Cuban ballet dancer, son of a truck-driving father and a housewife mother, did the rounds in the United States. It was broadcast on *Sunday Morning* and CNN. The questions got more and more complicated. They were no longer about how high I could jump or how many pirouettes I could do. Suddenly no one was interested in how well I danced *The Nutcracker* or *Don Quixote* or anything else related to my art.

"Do you consider yourself an example of why the United States will have to lift the embargo against Cuba?" one journalist asked.

"I think Fidel Castro or Bill Clinton could answer that question better than me, but if you want, I can tell you how I feel dancing *Swan Lake*," I told him.

"Are you saying that you are not interested in politics?" he persisted.

"I am saying that politics is for politicians; I am just a dancer."

"No, you're not just a dancer; you are a Cuban dancer."

"Well, my friend, if you don't want to talk about Tchaikovsky, I'm out of here." I got up and strode toward my dressing room.

When the article appeared, it stated that, with all the atrocities in the world, we needed role models who would help to inspire our young people, but that I was indifferent to all of this. From that moment on, I understood the true implications of being an artist and the responsibility that success could bring.

My career continued to bring surprises.

The Latino edition of *People* magazine listed me as one of the sexiest Latinos in the United States, which shocked me because I had never thought of myself as an attractive man. Since the days when sex and love stopped being words and turned into hormonal necessities, I had known one thing for sure: the tall, elegant, pretty girls whom the whole world lusted after were not interested in me. My first relationships with Olga and Narina as well as others had only served to increase my insecurity around women. I treated them all with extreme caution and never suspected I possessed any qualities capable of attracting them.

One day, the company manager called me to tell me I had been awarded the Princess Grace Kelly Prize in the dance category. I would have to travel to New York to collect the prize and appear before members of the royal family of Monaco.

When I was a child, I never even dreamed of leaving Los Pinos. When the airplane that should have taken me abroad for the first time exploded, I agreed with my father that a miracle had occurred. Clearly, all his stories about Changó, Ogun, and other African gods must be true—look how lucky I had been! Not only had I been saved from the plane crash, but the rebellious boy who used to break-dance and play Eat Mud managed to leave Los Pinos behind for the developed world. Now, at twenty-one, I had been on many planes to Europe, Latin

America, and Asia. The excitement I used to feel when I traveled during my student years had waned. But this was special. This was not Turin, Houston, or Venezuela. This was New York, the capital of the world, and it looked exactly as it did in the movies, with skyscrapers that blocked out the sun, avenues that went on for miles, and thousands of people of every nationality in the streets.

Even though I always tried to stop myself from dwelling on the people in my past, I could not help thinking about my sisters as I walked through Times Square. Why could they not be here with me in this city? Now that I was earning enough money, why couldn't I bring my family over to see me dance? A dark shadow seemed to descend on me, and I started to hate myself. I kept telling myself to remember that I was one of the sexiest Latinos in the United States and was about to receive a prize from a royal family, and, gradually, reluctantly, I tugged myself back to the present.

There were fifteen artists receiving prizes. For the photo, I was placed between Princess Caroline and Prince Albert, to the left of Prince Rainier. I remembered a previous brush with royalty, when I met Princess Diana in London, and wanted to be as careful as possible not to do anything stupid. Luckily, this time I did not even have to open my mouth. We were all given diplomas, the Houston Ballet was given some money, and that was it. They told us they would send the photo to us by post the following week, and then we were taken to dinner.

I was seated at a table with about thirty spoons and forks, eight knives of different shapes and sizes, and many wineglasses, tumblers, and assorted pieces of crockery for my place setting alone. By the time the food arrived I was very hungry, so while they were serving the starters, I grabbed a piece of bread from a small plate by my side.

"Could you pass me your bread, please, because you are eating mine," said the lady sitting to my right.

I passed her the bread with profuse apologies.

So everything on my left is mine, I thought, and started to drink the wine and the water on my left.

"Excuse me, son, you're drinking my wine," said the older lady to my left.

I looked at her, nonplussed.

"Look, son, do you like cars?" she said kindly.

"Yes, I do."

"Well, then, think BMW."

I looked her in the eye. Was she drunk?

"It's easy. *B* for bread, *M* for meat, and *W* for wine. That's the order."

The lady smiled and ate a piece of bread.

Now there were only the thirty forks and spoons and the knives to deal with. I waited for everyone to pick up their knives and forks so it would be clear which cutlery was mine. I imitated the couple sitting opposite me, taking hold of the knives and forks in the same order, and wiping my mouth on the white linen napkin when they did.

"This is also very easy," said the lady to my left again; she was at least sixty. "Do you like sex?"

When I heard this, I dropped my knife to the floor with a loud clang. "Excuse me, but—"

"Don't be ridiculous, I'm not inviting you to have sex with me," she said. "I'm old enough to be your grandmother. I mean, do you like sex in general?"

"Of course!" I replied, leaning down to pick up the knife from the floor.

"In that case, think about taking the utensils from the outside to the inside, just like you do with sex."

I was dumbstruck, unable to believe that this lady, apparently a member of the royal family of some country or other, was talking about sex at the dinner table. She watched me proudly as I cautiously picked up the cutlery on the outside and worked my way inside over the course of the meal. From time to time, she winked at me, and I had the distinct impression that she would have liked to teach me a thing or two that had nothing to do with the dinner.

When the photograph of me with the royal family arrived, I hung it at the end of my bed.

Someone once said that in order for society to function and the economy to prosper, human beings must go on wanting more and more, until their desire devours them. Until now, that desire had remained dormant inside me. It was not that I didn't want things, but, for me, quality was more important than quantity. I preferred to have a few true friends than many false ones. I knew that material possessions did not bring happiness, and, most important, that one should not put the quest for "more" ahead of the love of one's family.

But around this time, spurred on by all the acclaim I was receiving, I began to crave more success, more fame, and more money. It was as though that dormant greed had been woken up by an alarm clock. Suddenly, the desire to have more of everything began to overshadow my humility, and, worst of all, I started acting as if the world would very soon be mine. To put it plainly, I became greedy in all aspects of my life.

In my spare time, I worked tirelessly, going to the gym, using the machines to stretch my ligaments and improve my elasticity. After each class, I would stay behind to practice new jumps, and sometimes I would shut myself up alone inside a studio and work late into the night. Nobody was going to sabotage my focus. When my foot hurt, I would repeat to myself, "The world will be mine; the world will be mine," and the pain would disappear. My technique improved. I was impressing everyone with my performances. Signing autographs soon became routine, as did meeting my many admirers in the green room. I was given the nickname "Air Acosta" by the newspapers, which compared my jumps to those of basketball star Michael Jordan.

"If I'm a star, I have to dress like one," I told myself, and enlisted my friend Luis Ortis to help me find outfits appropriate for my celebrity status. He bought me a subscription to *GQ* so that I could peruse the latest fashions each month. On weekends, we would go shopping in the Galleria to buy expensive suits and shoes: Prada, Kenneth Cole, Armani. I also bought gadgets: an electronic organizer, and a gold and sapphire Cartier watch worth $4,000.

I put on my Prada suit, my Cartier watch, and looked at myself in the mirror, thinking, Now I really am a star.

When I totaled up the cost of what I was wearing, it came to $6,000, enough to buy a three-bedroom house for my family. I willed myself not to think about it.

"Where are you off to?" Sonia asked me.

"I'm going to Elvia's Cantina," I replied, still admiring myself in the mirror.

Sonia looked at me curiously. Nobody went to Elvia's Cantina in a suit. But I was not just anybody. I was Air Acosta, the star of the Houston Ballet.

"What's happened to the Carlos who I know?" Sonia asked.

"I'm still the same person, just a more sophisticated version," I replied.

At Elvia's Cantina, I did not dance. Stars always keep an air of mystery about them. They do not mix with people who are not at their level. I must have looked like a solitary $10,000 bill stuffed into a beer glass.

"Carlos, what's up?" Wicho called from the dance floor, but I did not answer him. I continued to watch disdainfully, as if I were the proprietor. People started looking at me as if to say, "Where did they find that penguin?" Some recognized me from the ballet and came over to talk about which of my performances they had seen. Angelucho's band was just playing "El cuarto de Tula" when Kentaro came through the door with his chorus of university women. I downed what remained of my beer and left.

I no longer spoke of my past, except to José and Sonia and a few very close friends. I became a master at hiding my emotions. I was like Neanderthal man: powerful but remote and self-absorbed, hiding behind my fame and my expensive clothes, sheltering myself in the artistic cave that was ballet. Slowly, I turned into a man without a past; needing no one and nothing, I was selfish and lonely, continually telling myself, "The world will be mine; the world will be mine."

Just before my twenty-second birthday, I awoke in the early hours of the morning from a terrible nightmare. My sister Berta had appeared with the rods for her broken bones protruding from her body. My mother and Marilín were staring at me. They had different faces, faces I had never seen before, faces that were accusing me. I got out of bed and took a sleeping pill. Then I searched for a photograph I had of my sisters and looked at it for a long time. Marilín was about twelve. She was wearing a white cotton dress with orange flowers, and her hair was drawn back in a ponytail. Berta looked about sixteen; her hair was long, and she wore a bandana across her forehead. She was smiling mysteriously like the Mona Lisa. I went back to sleep again with the photograph pressed to my chest.

The next night the same thing happened, but this time, my two sisters threw themselves together onto the rocks of the Malecón. I got up, went to the bathroom, and stuck my head under the shower. It took me ages to get back to sleep.

The nightmares continued, and then, during my birthday party at my old friend Johnny Warren's house, as I was about to blow out candles on the first birthday cake I had ever had, something very strange happened.

Everybody was singing "Happy Birthday" when suddenly my aunt Lucia appeared outside in the corner of the patio.

"Oh my God!" I jumped to my feet with a start.

"What's the matter, Carlos? Don't you like the cake?" asked José.

"No, no, it's nothing," I replied, smiling, and then I blew out the twenty-two candles. When I went out onto the patio afterward, I found nobody there.

A few days later, I was buying food at the Kroger supermarket when I heard someone calling my name. I looked up and there was Lucia again, standing among the crowds of people. I put the basket down on the ground and ran to meet her, but instead found myself standing in front of an old lady shopping with her grandson.

The nightmares were haunting me even when I was awake. My guilt would not let me live in peace. I had tried with all my might to get rid of my memories because they made me weak, and men of iron should not have any weaknesses. But I could not manage it.

Worst of all was when my sister Berta, full of rods, with her face disfigured, appeared before me, saying, "It's your fault. Accept the consequences."

Nothing could take me out of my own personal hell. Even though I had turned myself into a man of steel, I was unable to control my nightmares. And then, during one of those sleepless nights, a plan suddenly came to me. I would bring my mother over so she could be reunited with my grandmother. Then, surely, the nightmares would cease.

I spoke to the company lawyer, Charles Foster, who had become a good friend, and had helped me become an official resident alien. I told him how important bringing my mother over for a visit would be to me. Charles agreed to try, but he said it would take a huge number of calls. Eventually, he spoke to Texas congresswoman Sheila Jackson-Lee, who told him that before deciding whether to help, she would have to meet me in order to verify that my mother had no intention of remaining in the United States and that I would have to sign a document to that effect. I went to the meeting, and the eloquent black woman who received me asked me a lot of questions, after which I signed the paper. Now all I had to do was to wait.

I made a three-way telephone call via Canada and got through to my family. As always, the first few minutes were taken up with family news. My mother told me Berta was now walking with crutches and seeing a psychiatrist regularly. After we had caught up, I mentioned my plan.

"Mami, don't start getting excited yet, because it's virtually impossible, you know."

But my mother was already crying. "Since the day that I spoke to your grandmother, I have dreamed so many times that I would see her again, and now that you tell me this, I'm sure it will happen. God wants us to be reunited once more. We must have faith!"

"Yes, Mami, but it's much better not to get your hopes up. Look, I have to go! We'll talk again soon!" I said, and hung up. My mother's weeping was unbearable.

I went straight to see my new girlfriend, Tica, to give her the news. Her face lit up with the same delight as the day I had declared my love to her.

I had liked Tica since joining the company and had confessed my feelings about her to José, but she was one of those girls whom the whole world lusted after, a beautiful blonde from California and a principal dancer with the company. On top of which, for six years she had been seriously dating a rival of mine: a tall, elegant, good-looking man. When I first arrived, the distance between Tica and me was so great that sometimes I could swear she did not even know my name. But in December, someone decided to put us together to dance in *The Merry Widow*. From that moment, we grew closer. I was fascinated by her and wanted to find out about the experiences that had shaped her, so in each rehearsal, very subtly, without expecting much in return, I let her know something of my intentions, hinting at friendship. Very soon, however, I stopped being able to look at her as a friend, or even as a romantic interest. My feelings changed to raw desire, and I would undress her with my eyes, imagining that I was controlling her, pulling down tightly on her hair, passionately kissing her breasts and her neck. She did not seem to want to engage with my unbridled lust, and her eyes always slid away and refused to make contact with my own.

One day we were dancing in Beaumont, a small town south of Houston, and I caught her looking at me the way I looked at her. On the way back to Houston, when I sat down beside her on the bus, I had the feeling that she had been waiting for me.

She started to speak, but I stopped her.

"Let me tell you something before you say anything," I said, looking at her seriously. Then I spent ten minutes talking about me and her, about Houston, Cuba, the sun, paradise, until, in the end, even I did not know what I was talking about.

Her blue eyes were as big as saucers. I was sure she was thinking that Cubans were very strange people.

"What I am trying to say is that I like you," I finished hurriedly, then got up and fled to the back of the bus. But that night I slept peacefully, knowing I had at last told her everything I wanted to say.

Four days later she asked me if we could talk and arranged to meet me in the Café Express. I thought I knew what was going to happen. I had said so many things to her that I had probably offended her without realizing it.

Now it was her turn to talk.

"I have been thinking about what you told me that night on the bus."

"I'm sorry," I said. "I said too much, and I am really sorry. It was a mistake."

"Oh no, no!" said Tica. "I wanted to tell you that you're right. Perhaps we should get to know each other better."

I could not believe it. "How? What? I mean you . . . you really think so?"

She smiled and left me there with my mouth wide open in the middle of Café Express.

Finishing a relationship of six years is never easy, so I had to give Tica space, but it was difficult, because each time I touched her slight, shapely body, I was on fire, and I would have to stamp down firmly on my imagination in order to stop myself from getting an erection.

Two weeks after I received the Princess Grace Prize in New York, I took Tica to Crystal Nightclub over on Hillcroft and Freeway 59. Tica still looked anxious, but I knew that this particular spot was designed to soothe troubles away. There were palm trees and a fresco of Caribbean beaches painted along the length of one wall, tanks full of

tropical fish, soft lighting, and discreet corners for insatiable couples
who were not content to simply dance. As soon as you walked in, the
music entered your body, stirring up overwhelming heat that slid
slowly down your legs and up to your head, inspiring such delicious
delirium that you soon forgot all your cares and woes.

"Would you like a drink?" I asked.

They were playing a song by Oscar D'León in which the singer
compares his relationship to an old shoe.

"No, thanks," she replied.

"Do you want to dance?" I said, taking her by the hand.

"No, I'd just like to watch."

I started to sing along with the song, unable to contain the urge to
move with the music.

"What do the words mean?" Tica asked.

"Our love is like an old shoe," I replied.

Tica stared at me.

"I didn't mean *our* love is like an old shoe . . . not that we are in love,
but . . . I mean, I am in love, but . . . but you, shit . . . what I am trying
to say is that—"

Tica reached up, pulled my face toward her, and silenced me with a
kiss. We gazed at each other for a moment or two before I snapped out
of my joyful trance and remembered to wave the waiter over for cele-
bratory drinks. Tica quickly drained her glass, and no sooner had she
finished her screwdriver than she grabbed me by the hand and dragged
me onto the dance floor.

"I feel like dancing now," she said, ecstatically flinging herself
about, jabbing people in the ribs with her elbows and treading on toes.

"Let me show you how to merengue; it's very simple, and it takes
up a bit less room," I suggested tactfully, but with every step she landed
on the corns on my feet.

"Ouch, ouch . . . shit!"

"What's wrong?"

"Nothing, I'm just singing!"

She led me back to the bar for more drinks.

"Why don't I take you home? It's kind of late," I suggested, but she
was having none of it. She drank screwdrivers, then a mojito, and
finally I ended up carrying her, almost unconscious, back to my house,

where she vomited an evil-smelling pool onto the carpet. After cleaning up, I stopped to look at her beautiful blond head fast asleep on my
pillow. In her innocence and vulnerability, she looked just like an angel,
with her fair curly hair spread across her face, hiding everything but her
red lips. For a moment, I wanted to kiss those lips, but I did not dare
to disturb the sculpture before my eyes. I went to get a couple of sheets
out of the closet, then headed for the sofa.

As I undressed, however, I felt in all four of my pockets and began
to panic. I searched Tica's handbag, ransacked the house, went through
my pockets once more, but I still could not find it. I drove to the club
and paid the entrance fee again. I looked in all the places we had been
and asked all the bar staff, but nobody had seen it. In shock, I eventually returned home and sat on the sofa, unable to believe what had happened. The electronic organizer, the only place where I had stored the
contact details of my family in Miami, was gone.

At midnight on a Saturday in July, my mother arrived in Houston. Tica
and I collected her from the Intercontinental Airport. She was wearing
a white cotton dress with red polka dots. Wrinkles were etched permanently into her forehead now and were starting to spread around her
eyes. Her hair was red in patches where she had dyed it, but the roots
were showing through, white against her scalp. She looked much older
than I remembered. In her tiredness, her eyelids were only half open,
which emphasized more than ever the customary sweetness of her face.
She put her suitcase down on the ground and hugged me tightly.

"Mami, this is Tica," I said to her.

She greeted my girlfriend with a smile and kissed her on the forehead, then we all linked arms, walked toward the estate car that a millionaire friend of Tica's had kindly lent us, and headed off for a house
that the same friend was letting us use during my mother's stay.

It was about a forty-five-minute journey, and my mother remained
silent, looking out the window.

"Do you think it would be too late to call them now?" she asked as
soon as we arrived.

My heart missed a beat. I still had not found my electronic organizer.
"Not now, Mami, you're tired after the journey. You should sleep a bit."

I took her to the largest of the bedrooms. She stopped in her tracks when she saw the enormous bed.

"All that bed just for me!" she exclaimed, stroking the silk covers on the pillows.

She wanted to see the kitchen and asked what every electric appliance was for. "You mean the plates wash themselves?" she asked disbelievingly.

I filled the Jacuzzi and threw in some relaxing Epsom salts. My mother stuck her head around the bathroom door.

"What is that?" she asked suspiciously.

After a long explanation of what a Jacuzzi is, she agreed to get in. When she got out, she fell into bed and did not wake up until twelve o'clock the following day.

"Why don't we call them now?" she said as soon as she opened her eyes.

"Mami, there's plenty of time. The main thing is for you to enjoy yourself a little," I answered.

I arranged for Tica to take her shopping at the Galleria, and to visit the hairdresser and have a manicure. Meanwhile, I was racing around like a madman, doing everything I could to contact my family in Miami. Desperate, I asked my friend Luis Ortis for advice. He said it should be easy to find them by their surname, but when I told him that my aunt had been married and changed her name and that I did not know her husband's surname, he said there was very little that could be done.

"That's just how it is, Carlitos. Without a surname, it's impossible. You could go to Miami and try to remember where their house is, but Hialeah is big, so it might take you some time."

I thought about doing this, but I could not. The end of the season was coming up, and I could not leave my work.

When Tica and my mother came home that afternoon, Mamá looked radiant. She suddenly looked more like thirty years old, rather than forty.

"Mami, you look like a queen, Caroline of Monaco herself, in person," I said, lifting her up in the air as Tica took a photo of us.

"And when are we going to phone your grandmother?" asked my mother repeatedly.

"There's plenty of time, Mami."

"But when? I've been here for days," she replied, getting a little agitated now.

"I tell you what we're going to do," I said. "First, I'm going to take you to see me rehearse and to meet Ben. Then we'll go out for a day, and after that we'll call them. Okay?"

She agreed reluctantly, and the next day I took her to the company studios.

"See how lovely it is, Mami?"

When I introduced her to Ben, she threw her arms around his neck, covered him with kisses, and refused to let go.

"That's enough now, Mami, leave him alone," I said, gently prying her arms away from the director's neck.

Ben asked us what we were doing that night, and when I told him we did not have anything planned, he invited us all out to dinner with José and Sonia.

All through rehearsal that afternoon, Mamá watched me closely. Whenever I executed one of my extraordinary jumps, she covered her mouth with her hand, just like she had done when she watched me through the glass in the door that time she took me to L and 19 for my first audition. Suddenly I was a child again, hungry for her attention. I wanted her to understand that her son was now a principal dancer, that she was seeing all her efforts repaid. There was no one else in that room for me but her. It was as simple as that: no makeup, no costumes, no lights, just my mother and me. At one point she smiled at me with creased-up eyes. I knew then that she felt proud of me. It was one of the happiest moments of my life.

Later that evening, in Carrabba's restaurant, she wanted to eat rice and black beans.

"Mami, this is an Italian restaurant. There's no Cuban food here."

That night we stayed at José and Sonia's house. We were awake till the early hours, swapping tales of Cuba and Colombia and drinking rum.

The next day we went to the three-dimensional cinema at Moody Gardens to watch *T-Rex,* a film about dinosaurs. When the enormous beast on the screen turned toward us, my mother screamed and leaped up from her seat.

"Hurry, hurry, it's going to eat us!"

I pulled her back down by the arm and explained to her that it was only a film, while people all around us whistled and shouted at us to sit down.

"Mami, don't worry; it's not a real dinosaur."

"No, no, let's go, son, let's leave this place!" She would not be convinced, so we left in the middle of the film and went to visit Galveston instead.

When she saw the gray, stony coast, she said, "I thought all beaches had blue sea and white sand."

"It might not have white sand, but at least there are seagulls. There aren't any of those in Cuba," I told her, pointing out the flocks of birds perched along the shoreline and flying through the air.

"Who says there are no seagulls in Cuba?" she snapped at me. "I can see you don't know your country."

We parked at a Starbucks that had a great view of the bay. I ordered a caramel macchiato, a cappuccino for Tica, and a café latte for Mamá.

"This coffee doesn't taste of anything, and there's enough here to fill an elephant," said my mother.

"You have to add some sugar, Mami. It's in those little brown packets over there." Much to Tica's disapproval, my mother and I took a total of fifteen packets of sugar from the counter. There was a terrible mess on the table when we left.

We drove by the mansions at River Oaks, and my mother stared openmouthed, unable to believe these were private homes. Tica explained to her that Houston was the city with the most oil in the United States, and that many people had made their fortunes from it. Mamá wanted us to take a photo of her in front of one of the houses, but as we were setting up the shot, a Mercedes-Benz turned into the driveway. The driver frowned at Tica and me, then looked across at my mother.

"That's enough, Mami; come on, let's go!"

But she insisted on posing for the photo, despite the driver's disapproving glare.

"Mami, let's go. . . . We are sorry, sir. We are leaving! Mami, get a move on."

As soon as we walked through the door of the Kroger supermarket, my mother burst into tears. Never in her life had she imagined such abundance, all those different types of cheese and ham.

"My God, so many people with nothing to eat, and here the food goes to waste!"

"Try not to think about Los Pinos; just try to enjoy these moments," I urged.

"How can I, when I know how little some people have compared to all this?" she answered.

We returned to the house in silence. For me, every second was hell because every meter we advanced led me deeper into the prison I had created for myself. There was no escape. I was going to have to face my mother and tell her the truth.

How could I have been so stupid as to lose that organizer? Why on earth had I not written their address down somewhere else after transferring it to my ridiculous new gadget? How could I have squandered the chance to give my mother what she had been waiting for all her life?

I asked Tica to give us some time alone.

My hair stood on end, and an icy feeling spread through my lungs.

"Mami, I need to tell you the truth. . . ."

"What's the matter? Has something bad happened? Don't tell me that your grandmother—"

"No, Mami, it's nothing like that."

She sighed with relief but kept staring at me. My mouth was parched; the prospect of witnessing my mother's anguish was making it difficult for me to speak.

"You see, the thing is, I've lost the telephone numbers, and now there's no way of getting in touch . . ." I said in a rush.

My mother just stood there, staring at me as if she could not understand what I was saying.

"So what do we do now?" she finally asked.

I hung my head. "I'm sorry, Mami. I've tried everything, but there's nothing that can be done."

My mother's whole body seemed to sink, as though she was about to collapse. The hairbrush in her hand clattered to the floor.

"Mami, Mami . . . where are you going?"

She turned and walked slowly to the door, then continued right across the front lawn and onto the street. I watched her fearfully from the bedroom. How was it possible that my mother's first trip abroad had turned out to be such a failure? Against all odds, I had managed to bring her to the United States. She was there with me. Was that not reason enough for her to feel happy? Had it not been her dream to see me dance in another country?

"Mami, wait!"

The night was dark, and a strong north wind was blowing. I ran as fast as I could until I caught up with her.

"Mami! Forget about it all for now. Why don't we go to NASA tomorrow, and you can see the spaceships?" I pleaded.

There was no response. It was as though she were somewhere else. Desperately, I tried to make her see the funny side of things.

"Look, I've got a joke for you. Are you listening? A man goes up to a woman who is breast-feeding her baby and says, 'Excuse me, madam, you're not going to believe this, but your son has invited me to dine. . . .'"

My mother's face crumpled up like a child's, her shoulders heaved up and down like hydraulic pistons, and her tears fell in torrents. As if the very elements were in sympathy with her, the sky grew dark, and it began to rain.

"Mami, don't cry! I swear to you I did everything that I could. Please forgive me!"

I tried to dry her tears, but her face was all wet from the rain, as if all the pores in her skin were crying. She walked away from me, staring at empty space. I followed her with my eyes, feeling my skin tighten and pucker as if there were no distinction between my flesh and her sorrow.

That night nobody slept, and the next day my mother asked me to change her ticket so she could go back to Cuba, without even staying to see me dance.

My mother never saw my grandmother or my aunt again. We still do not know if they are alive or dead.

———

As it turned out, even if she had wanted to stay, my mother would not have seen me dance. The pain in my foot had become so intense that I had to go to see an ankle specialist.

"I don't want to have surgery," I insisted to the doctor.

"There is no alternative. Something is stuck inside your ankle."

They operated on me on a Friday at ten o'clock in the morning. Lodged in the joint, among the cartilage, was a fragment of bone the size of a chickpea.

Chapter 20

GOOD-BYE, HOUSTON

The worst thing about undergoing another operation was that I had too much time to think. In the mornings I attended physical therapy sessions at a rehabilitation clinic in the Houston Medical Center, but from twelve o'clock onward I went back to my apartment on Buffalo Speedway and had no idea what to do with myself. José, Sonia, and Tica did not get home from work until around seven. With the worry that I might never dance again and the terror that my mother might never forgive me swirling around and around in my head, I took refuge in the kitchen, often eating the entire contents of the refrigerator. Sometimes when people are cut off from the things by which they usually define themselves—their jobs, their family, their friends—only the animal beneath the skin remains. Mine manifested itself in the form of a pig.

One day Sonia got home early from work in a very good mood. "Carlos, I've got some good news for you," she said from the living room. "I'm pregnant!"

"That's fantastic," I said, hugging her tightly. "Why don't we celebrate with some fried chicken wings or some pork crackling?"

"No, let's not!" yelled Sonia, blocking my way. "Enough of all this gluttony! Look at you! If you continue like this, you'll end up like Ben Stevenson."

"How can we celebrate without eating?"

"Very easily, with music and wine," said Sonia, pouring me a glass of fruit wine.

"I don't want wine. Give me some pork," I said indignantly.

Sonia grabbed me by the hand and sat me on the sofa.

"Carlos, you cannot go on eating like this. I'm not going to let you ruin your career."

"What career? I don't have a career. All I have are three hours of physical therapy daily," I said gloomily.

"Where's the Flying Cuban, the one in the photos and in the magazines?"

"I'll show you the Flying Cuban," I said, attempting to lift my right leg up to my head as I had always been able to. "I'm less flexible than an old man of eighty."

"Well, you'd better get your act together," said Sonia, "because my baby's not going to have a fat godfather."

"What?"

"You're going to be the godfather."

"You seriously want me to be the godfather? That's a huge responsibility. You should choose somebody else."

"Don't be ridiculous. You're like family. You're the ideal godfather!"

"Do you really think I'm like family?" I asked.

"Oh, for goodness' sake, stop being so sentimental, Carlos. Look, do me a favor: give me a hand to clear up your dirty dishes and forget the dramatics."

At seven in the evening, when José arrived home, Sonia threw herself upon him.

"Darling, you're going to be a daddy!" They fell to the floor and spent a long time kissing.

"And I'm going to be the godfather, so let's go to La Fogata for some nice pork crackling."

José looked at Sonia.

"Apparently, he's decided to eat until he explodes," said Sonia, smiling.

"Hey, Sonia, it's not a joke. You don't know what a fish feels like without water."

"Yes, I do know," said Sonia, pointing to a scar on her knee. "I do know what it feels like to have an operation." She had also been a ballet dancer back in Colombia. When she moved to the United States, she had taken up aerobics and was now an instructor. "And I know what it feels like to be a dancer, even though my career was more of an exercise in fooling the public. Not all of us have the luck to be able to dance really well like you do; some of us have to resort to a bit of trickery."

José and I laughed.

"You needn't think it's easy creating the illusion of being a good dancer; it's talent, you know," said Sonia mischievously, and the three of us hugged. They really did feel like another family. My Houston family.

That evening, I went to Tica's apartment in the Inverness Tower for a night of candles, incense, and multicolored veils. After licking and kissing each other all over, Tica whispered, "Let me blindfold you. I want you just to use touch and smell."

My body shivered defenselessly. I held an ice cube in my hands and rubbed it slowly over her swan's neck, her round breasts, taking it on a tender trajectory to each and every corner. The trembling of her body excited me. I spoke to her in Spanish, in words that she could not understand, tracing each curve with my hand and then with my tongue until finally she exploded into flames like a volcano. A sharp cry rang out that soared through the windows and echoed on to the end of the country. Moments like these were binding us closely together.

Gradually, her breathing grew lighter, until eventually it recovered its natural rhythm.

"I want to tell you something, Tica," I said.

She looked at me expectantly. The soft light from the candle flickered gently over the walls, letting love slip into the bedroom like a thief.

"I think . . . that . . . I am . . ."

Why can't relationships in real life be as simple as in a ballet? When I dance, I know exactly what's going to happen. I know if my partner loves me and whether the story will end happily or in tragedy. In real life, however, I had no idea what to expect. I had no idea if I was going to be betrayed or not. I thought that the best thing would be not to fall in love too deeply. But how is it possible to fall in love without surrendering to it completely?

My girlfriend was still waiting for me to speak.

"Sonia's going to have a baby," I said, turning my head away.

"Oh, that's nice. I'm pleased," Tica said, with a hint of disappointment that made me suspect that she had been hoping for the words I had such difficulty pronouncing.

Five weeks later I was back in the studios, having made a complete recovery. The company had changed during the past two years. Martha Butler was now a soloist with the American Ballet Theatre and lived in New York. Li Cunxin was still in Australia, and Janie Parker was to retire that season.

The Nutcracker accounted for half of the company's takings with an average of forty performances a year. The box-office receipts from this production ensured that the company balanced its books. This meant that the first ballet that I would dance that year, as ever, would be *The Nutcracker,* but this time I would dance the snow scene with Tica and the Sugar Plum *pas de deux* with Lauren. When Tica and I looked at each other during the performance, I felt that she was not just pretending for the sake of the show. Our onstage language was the same as the one that we practiced daily in our bed.

In Taco Cabana after the performance, I tried to ask her. "Tica . . . how did you feel during the show? What I mean is . . . did you feel the same as I did?"

She kissed me affectionately on the lips and whispered in my ear, "I love you, too."

A great warmth suffused my chest and surged up to the tips of my ears. I had rarely been so happy.

At the beginning of 1996, after all the seasonal festivities and celebrations were over, I received an invitation to dance with Lauren at the municipal theater in Santiago, Chile. On the way there, we spent more than four hours in the Miami airport, waiting for our connection.

"Miami is like a second Cuba," said Lauren. "Have you ever been?"

"Yes," I mumbled, not wanting to think about it.

We were in Chile for a short time, but long enough for us to become aware of the architectural beauty of Santiago. It felt great to be speaking Spanish again, and the dancers at the theater treated us warmly.

Whenever I dance *Don Quixote* I feel that I am in my element, as though I am back in Los Pinos. This shows in the way that I interact with the other characters, in my gestures, and even in my walk. When my oldest friends see me performing in that ballet, they say, "Shit, mate, you look as though you're dancing in the *comparsa* with the *guaracheros* from Regla!"

The performance in Chile was a great success, and they awarded me the National Critics' Prize, which was one of the sweetest experiences of my life.

Later that year, I went to Japan to dance with the Asami Maki Ballet. When I arrived, I went out looking for a little piece of Cuba, something I always do when I travel, but I did not find a single Cuban or even a Cuban restaurant. Someone recommended I try sushi, which consisted of a ball of rice and raw fish held together with a piquant green sauce and dipped, using chopsticks, into a little plate of soy sauce. The first time I tasted it, I leaped up from the table and ran to the toilet to be sick. I lost a lot of weight that first trip to Japan.

When I returned to the States, I started working on my debut as Prince Florimund in *Sleeping Beauty,* which would coincide with the retirement of Janie Parker, Houston Ballet's biggest star. Janie was forty-two, and I was twenty-two, so it was an enormous responsibility for me. In rehearsal I went over and over each detail with Ben. As usual, I found what the choreographer asked of me extremely difficult, but this time there was a whole new set of problems. In the part where the prince kisses the princess and breaks the spell, I attempted to kiss Janie like I kissed Tica.

"Carlos, when you kiss her, try not to eat her whole face. Do it more gently," Ben told me.

On the day of the first performance, when I stood in front of the mirror in full costume, I was astonished. I really looked like a prince. It was hard to believe that the man in the mirror was me. When the curtain opened, I came onstage full of youthful vitality and longing for love, just as the role required. It was easy because I was full of youthful vitality and in love myself. I never knew exactly who the audience saw: Prince Florimund or Carlos Acosta.

When we got to the part where Florimund finds the princess asleep on the bed, I approached and gave her a Russian kiss, no tongues. Janie awoke and looked into my eyes as if I were the only person in the whole theater. I offered her my hand to help her up from the bed. The king and queen agreed to our marriage with a regal gesture of approval.

The moment of the great *pas de deux* arrived. All the guests who had arrived from the four corners of the earth gathered together in this scene to admire the dance of the prince and princess. I gave Janie my hand, and she held it as she performed the intricate steps. Janie embodied all the youthfulness of Aurora, even though it was the last performance she would ever give. The performance so far had been flawless, and all that was required was one last effort. I spun her by her waist four times, threw her into the air, and, as soon as I had her in the fish-dive position, I opened my arms. The music stopped, and applause rang out around the theater. There was a bittersweet contrast between her career ending and mine just beginning. The whole stage turned into a sea of flowers. I took Janie by the hand and led her to center stage, where I left her. The members of the company who had not been in the show came out onto the stage in their street clothes and joined the thousands of people in the theater clapping and crying. A vast poster hanging from one of the balconies read YOU'LL LIVE ON IN OUR MINDS, JANIE, and when she saw it, she wept a river of tears. I watched her and imagined myself in her position. The moment when you have to retire as an artist must be terrible. But I was very happy to have accompanied Janie in her final hour, to have been the last prince for that fabulous princess.

As we walked back to the dressing rooms, Tica clung to me, crying. "Don't cry, Tica. That's just how life is." I tried to comfort her.

Janie's retirement meant more opportunities for the other female dancers, so, in fact, for many of them it would not be a negative thing at all, but Tica wept over Janie's retirement as though a family member had just died. The goodness and purity of her soul was one of the things I loved most about her.

In April, Lauren and I were invited to dance in New York at a gala to raise money for retired dancers. We danced the *pas de deux* from *The Corsair,* a particular favorite of mine because it displays the technical virtuosity and bravura of the dancer. We arrived a few days before the event and asked permission to take classes with the American Ballet Theatre, the most prestigious company in the United States. José Manuel Carreño, the Cuban friend I had lived with in London, was now a member of the company, so as soon as we arrived we sought him out. We found him en route to the dressing rooms.

"It's so great to see you, my friend. I'd heard that you'd been hired by the American," I said, giving him a big hug.

"Yes, I'd had enough of London, so I swapped it for New York. I've been here more than three years now."

"What about Lourdes?"

"She's at home. We live in New Jersey. She stopped dancing, and now she's pregnant."

Lauren stamped on my foot to remind me to introduce her to José.

"Oh, yes, this is Lauren. Lauren, this is José Manuel Carreño, the man who taught me what a bank is."

"Pleased to meet you," said my dancing partner, and she started talking to José.

"That's enough, Lauren. José, if you don't stop that woman, she'll be talking to you all day. We've got to get changed, or we'll be late for class."

Lauren jabbed me with her elbow, and we went to put on our dance clothes.

There were dancers of every nationality and style. The stars of the company were artists of world renown. This was the big leagues. Martha Butler, my ex-partner from the Houston Ballet, was also in the class. She looked happy, and her technique had improved considerably.

"So what do you think?" Martha asked, giving me a kiss.

"It's a great company," I said, as I admired the jumps of José and the other dancers.

"They would hire you just like that," she said, snapping her fingers.

"Do you think so?"

"I know so."

Martha continued with her class, and I remained in a corner, thinking that if I really did want to conquer the world, this would be the place to do it.

The next day we arrived early at Hunter College, where the performance was to take place. I did a short but efficient warm-up at the barre and immediately felt the sweat running down my body. When I went onto the stage to practice some jumps, I sensed a ripple of excitement.

"Look who's there . . . did you see him? There he is, Baryshnikov himself!"

I looked over and saw a small man in cowboy boots standing a few meters away from us, escorted by a throng of people. So this was the famous dancer the press was always comparing me to.

"And you, Carlos, aren't you going to say hello?" asked Lauren, heading toward the dancer.

"No, no, I can see him from here," I replied, and continued looking at him from where I stood.

For me, Baryshnikov's greatest achievement is not the films that he has made, his fame, or even his fortune, but the courage he showed in swapping the certainty of his old life for the uncertainty of a new one, knowing that by doing so he could never go back. How had he managed to bear his grief? What defenses had he had to construct to keep loneliness at bay? How did he manage to resign himself to living without a family? To be like Baryshnikov was everybody's highest aspiration. His name was synonymous with success. But was he really a happy man?

That day, I danced for Baryshnikov. I had no ambition to compete with him. I just wanted to pay homage to the man who was not afraid to burn himself in his efforts to reach the sun.

"Wow! That was amazing. Just like Baryshnikov!" people said to me as the curtain came down.

They were right. We were both foreigners.

"You actually saw Baryshnikov himself?" asked Tica when I told her.

"Yes. He's only this high," I said, lifting my hand up level with my nose.

"And did he see you dance?" Tica wanted to know.

"No, I don't think so. I think he left straight after his speech."

"What a shame. It would be nice to know his opinion of you."

"He'd probably be bored by my jumps," I said.

"No, no! Everybody has their time and their moment. Baryshnikov was big in his day, but now it's your turn. You're the new Baryshnikov," she insisted.

"Ah, Tica, don't be silly. The days of the Nureyevs and the Baryshnikovs are over now. The days of the Balanchines, the Ashtons, and the Macmillans, too—that era died with them. All we have now are bad imitations, and everybody knows that a copy just serves to highlight the quality of the original."

"So you don't think dance has evolved, then? Or are you not aware of the way in which you jump and turn? The quality of movement today is much better than it was in the past. If you need convincing, just look at a video of Margot Fonteyn and compare it with one of Sylvie Guillem."

"You can't compare Fonteyn to Guillem in either technique or style. They're two different dancers from two different eras."

"Exactly. That's precisely what I'm talking about. Baryshnikov had his day, and now you have yours," Tica insisted.

We started rehearsals for *Cinderella*. Even though Tica had danced the opening night of this ballet in previous years, Ben paired me with another dancer in the principal role and put Tica in the role of the Fairy Godmother. This made us suspect that Ben did not approve of our relationship. Tica arrived home almost in tears. I tried to reassure her that it did not mean anything, but later on, during the Houston Ballet tour to Washington, Ben and I fell out over the matter and said many things that we shouldn't have said. The resulting rift between us meant that from that moment on, the only challenge left to me in Houston would be to go on repeating all the ballets that I had danced already. Almost overnight, everything became monotonous, and my inspiration started to fade. The critics kept praising my work, but I began to wonder how good I really was. Being an excellent dancer in Houston did not necessarily mean that I was a great dancer in Paris, London, or New York. Was I ready to settle for this, or would I always ask myself what might have become of me if I had pushed myself further? I did not want to become one of those dancers frustrated by dreams they had never managed to realize—and so, with this in mind, I went to New York and asked for an interview with Kevin McKenzie, the director of the American Ballet Theatre. I told him straight-out that I wanted to join his company as a principal dancer, but he looked at me as if to say, "Who the hell do you think you are?" The meeting did not last even five minutes, and I never received a call from him, although I heard through the grapevine that he thought I was very pushy.

The doors of the American Ballet Theatre were closed to me, but giving up was not in my nature. I turned twenty-three, and in 1997, during the twenty-fifth anniversary of the Prix Lausanne, I was invited to participate in the closing gala of the competition. I danced the *pas de deux* from *The Corsair* with Diana Vishnyeva, a young ballerina from the Mariinsky Theatre in St. Petersburg, and I performed one of the most splendid versions of *The Corsair* I had ever danced. At the end of the show, I met Jay Jolly, a good-looking gentleman with graying hair, who turned out to be the director of the Royal Ballet School in London. I told him that I would like to dance with the company and gave him a folder with footage of my performances, reviews, and photographs, which he promised to pass on to Anthony Dowell, the director of the Royal Ballet Company.

The Royal Ballet called a month later to say that they were interested in me, but that I would have to take some classes with the company.

"I knew they would call you!" exclaimed Sonia, holding on to her now enormous belly. "You'll be farther away from your godson, but the Royal is the Royal. No one could miss an experience like that."

"Congratulations, buddy," said José, slapping my hand. "Now you're really going to fly!" We drank a toast together, and then I went to tell Tica.

"They called me to audition for the Royal," I told her the moment I saw her. She hugged me tightly, almost squeezing the breath out of my body, but both of us held back from talking about what the future had in store.

Tica was convinced that Ben did not like her, and she thought it was because he wanted her to lose weight. I wondered if that was why she had become a vegetarian. Trying to slim down, she had totally eliminated meat from her diet, something that I thought was dangerous for someone who did an average of six hours of intense physical activity daily. She arrived home each evening utterly exhausted, and it was taking her longer than normal to recover after a show.

At the beginning of May, I flew to London. The Royal Ballet was then based at the studios in Barons Court, in a cramped and uncomfortable building that it shared with the students from the Royal Ballet School. When I entered the studio, I recognized some of the dancers I had performed with at galas in previous years, but I could not see any of the directors anywhere. The class began, we finished our barre work, and still nobody had come to see me. I had almost forgotten that I was auditioning, when, just before the end of the class, a well-dressed man of noble bearing with expressive eyes, and a sweet-faced woman with completely white hair turned up. I was going to have to show them what I could do in the fifteen minutes remaining.

"Come on, you bastard!" I told myself.

I did the exercises as well as I could, the pirouettes and the jumps, and at the end of the class I walked over to the two people and stretched out my hand.

"Hi, I'm Carlos," I introduced myself.

"Yes, I know. I am Anthony Dowell, and this is my assistant director, Monica Mason."

They looked me long and hard in the eye and then led me into the director's office.

I was nervous. If I was not accepted by the Royal, I would have to remain in Houston, which I did not want to do. Worse than that, if neither the American nor the Royal wanted me, I would have to accept that I was not good enough to dance with the major-league companies, which would mean that all the accolades that the critics had piled up on me were lies.

"So, how do you see yourself in the company?" Anthony Dowell asked, once we were sitting in his office.

I told him that I had danced with the English National Ballet five years previously and that ever since then I had aspired to dancing with the Royal Ballet. I now felt I had sufficient experience to be a principal dancer with the company. I also added that, if it were possible, I would like the freedom to dance occasionally with the Houston Ballet, because it was a company that had done so much for my career. He listened to me carefully, then offered me a contract for the season that would begin in September 1998. I left the studios of the Royal Ballet flying with happiness. The Royal Ballet was not only one of the better-paying companies, it was also associated with one of the most prestigious theaters in Covent Garden—in short, it was one of the best ballet companies to work for in the world.

"Tica! They hired me and I start in September of next year!" I told my girlfriend once I got back to Houston. She gave me a big hug and then walked quietly into the kitchen of her apartment. I knew exactly what was going through her head: the contract with the Royal Ballet meant the end of our relationship. When I went, I would have to leave Tica behind, and my happiness would not be complete.

A few weeks later, my godson, Robert, was born. José came out into the corridor of the hospital with what appeared to be a big sausage wrapped in a towel. The sausage suddenly opened his eyes and looked at me as though he wanted to record every detail of my face. I had the most indescribable feeling, as though this was my own son and Tica's, too, and suddenly the idea of moving to London without her was inconceivable.

That night, I left the hospital and went to Tica's house, determined to reveal my feelings to her. I rang the bell. She opened the door, and, standing in the passageway trying to pluck up my courage, I said, "You know, Tica, I have been thinking for a long time, and I am ready to tell you that I . . . well, you know that I . . ." I still could not say it. Those three damn words were sticking in my throat.

My girlfriend waited unblinkingly.

"Well, what I want to say is that, *creo que te quiero* . . . and I think that we should leave here together."

Finally I had gotten it out.

Tica flung herself around my neck, and we both fell onto the carpet.

A neighbor found us kissing in the middle of the passageway, but we barely noticed him, and he had to clamber over us to get to the elevators.

Once we were inside the apartment, we began to plan our future together. We would both sign contracts to stay with the Houston Ballet until February 1998. After February we would dance freelance in galas in Mexico City and Brazil and in the Gala of the Stars on tour to Japan, Montreal, and Greece, a total of approximately twenty shows. If everything went well, we would move to London at the end of June, and after that Tica would audition for the Royal Ballet or the English National Ballet.

Now only the most difficult task remained: to tell Ben.

I knocked on the door of his office and told his secretary, Patsy, that I needed to talk to him.

"Come through, Carlos!"

I had so many reasons to be grateful to Ben. Telling him that I was leaving was going to be painful whichever way I put it, so I decided it would be better not to beat about the bush.

"Ben, I have been offered a contract with the Royal Ballet starting in September of next year. Tica and I have decided to move to London together."

When he heard this, the director got up from his chair, moving slowly, as if he were walking underwater. He lumbered toward me like a weary ox. I remembered the first time we met in London, in the studios of the English National Ballet, and then our next meeting in Cuba. I thought of all his jokes and his generosity, and these memories were as vivid in my mind as when I had first experienced them. I suddenly felt very sad.

"I will always be indebted to you for what you have done for me, Ben, but I have to know how good I really am," I said.

We looked each other in the eye for a long time, then Ben dropped his gaze to the floor and said in a voice that was gruff with emotion, "I always knew this day would come. First it was Li, then Janie, and now you."

"Ben, I'm—"

"Don't be. That's the way it goes. We all become lonelier. But the people we loved and the places where we were happy stay with us. Remember, this is your home, you know, in case you don't like it over there."

After he had spoken, he did not open his mouth again, just stood there, unmoving.

"Anthony Dowell told me I could guest with the Houston Ballet twice a year," I told him, but he did not respond, just looked at the floor.

I walked slowly toward the door. Before I left, I turned one more time and saw his tears splash down onto the carpet. It was like a stab wound to the chest, but, as he himself had said, that was life. We all have a destiny to follow, and mine was not to grow old in Houston.

After my godson, Robert, was baptized, I celebrated my twenty-fourth birthday. A week later, I traveled to Havana to give the news to my family in person. I arrived at the José Martí Airport around twelve midnight and caught a taxi to my apartment in Vedado. It was a Wednesday, and the moon was in its final quarter. The street was deserted except for four men sitting playing dominoes underneath a lamppost. I looked at the buildings, the washing strung across the windows, the dogs roaming the street. There was no mistaking it, I was home.

My mother opened the door. "Yuli, my baby! Quick, Marilín, Berta, Yuli's here!"

I hugged her tightly, savoring the smell of her. It was the scent of the countryside, as though she had been born among the orange groves. Nobody smelled like my mother. It made me feel as though I were nine years old again.

Marilín ran out from the bedroom.

"Let me see you! How white you've become! You've even got straight hair. Michael Jackson himself!"

Marilín kissed me twice and pinched my behind. She was as pretty as ever, with not a wrinkle in sight, and her teeth were still as white. I noticed the swelling belly beneath her blouse.

"Yes, that's right, I'm nearly seven months gone, and the oldest is two, but you never call, so I can't keep you up to date with my activities."

"You've got a child?"

"He's called Yonah, and he's the spitting image of you."

"Where is he?"

"His father's got him this week. You'll meet him on the weekend."

"Yiyo must be really happy," I said, dragging in the suitcases full of presents I had brought.

My mother and Marilín looked at each other.

"Yonah's father is called Roberto," Marilín replied.

I dropped the suitcases. "You finished with Yiyo?"

"And with Roberto, too!"

"Marilín, you're terrible! Who's the latest victim, then?"

"Elisardo is the father of this one in here."

My mother and Marilín laughed.

I walked slowly over to the kitchen. My things had vanished, and the whole place was so different from the way I had left it that it looked as though I had never lived there at all. I had a nephew I had never met and a nephew or niece whose birth I would not witness. I had spent so much time away from home that I felt the only thing that united me with my family was my unconditional love for them.

"And where's Berta?" I asked.

"Just coming," called a voice from inside the bedroom.

An obese woman weighing at least 250 pounds came out through the bedroom door, walking with a stick. For a moment I thought it was my grandmother, but when I saw the cold light in her eyes, I knew that it was my sister Berta.

"Berta, my God, what happened to you; where did you go?" I said, unable to hide my dismay. I glanced at my mother, who looked down at the floor.

"Don't worry about me, my brother. I'm fine." Berta let the stick fall to the ground in order to hug me. "The most important thing is that we're all together again, like in the old days, like when we used to live in Los Pinos. Remember?"

I tried hard to speak, but the words stuck in my throat. "Berta . . . but . . . how —"

"I'm so glad to see you," Berta interrupted, dragging me over to one of the armchairs so I could sit down. "Mami told me all about her trip to Houston, and we've seen the photos. When she got back, all she could do was talk about how beautiful it was. She told us about the Jacuzzi and how a dinosaur nearly ate her. We almost died laughing at her stories."

"She probably also told you how I lost Granny and Auntie's telephone number. Whenever I think about it, I can't sleep," I admitted.

"It wasn't your fault, son," said my mother, stroking my head. "You did all you could, and I really did have a good time. I'm the one who was selfish and who should ask your forgiveness for not staying to see you dance. The pain was too much, and it blinded me. Now I can see that there are some things in life that are better left where they are. Believe me, I'll always be grateful to you for bringing me to Houston."

When I heard that, I breathed a great sigh of relief, and my shoulders sank back into the chair.

"And when are you going to invite the two of us?" asked Marilín, smiling. "I don't know about Berta, but I'd also like to have straight hair, bathe in a Jacuzzi, and be eaten by a dinosaur."

We all roared with laughter.

"You'll see. One day we'll all meet up in another country. I still haven't given up the hope that you'll see me dance abroad."

"Well, if the Mambo King decrees it, then so be it. But let's stop dreaming for now. Come and have something to eat; you must be starving."

Marilín got up and went over to the kitchen. My mother kept stroking my head, and Berta continued to stare into my eyes. I looked at the ornaments, the photos on the wall, the faces of my mother and my sisters, and I was happy to be with my family again, in the land where I was born. That night I slept very comfortably on the floor. I did not dream about anything.

The next day the disillusion set in. It started from the moment I went downstairs and saw that the building was ugly and dirty and that people had different faces, older and careworn. I thought perhaps it was me who had changed. Nothing seemed to fit with my memories; the trees were stunted, the houses ruined; ragged vagrants prowled about on street corners. It seemed to me that people had relinquished any sense of decency in order to survive. Girls as young as sixteen walked along with tourists who were old enough to be their grandfathers. The worst thing was when children asked me for money, as if I were a foreigner.

I was not welcome inside the headquarters of the Cuban National Ballet because I had asked for leave to continue my career full-time in Houston. The few people who recognized me crossed the road to the opposite sidewalk, as if I were some kind of deserter. I was not a deserter. I had maintained very good relations with my country, but I felt like a traitor, someone who had abandoned his homeland and come back as a foreigner. A stranger in my own country.

In Los Pinos I found a neighborhood of overgrown gardens and dilapidated houses. There was no one there I knew. The children had become adults, the adults had grown old, and the old people had died. Most of my friends had left for the United States. Candida, our downstairs neighbor, and Yolanda, whose mangos I used to steal, had moved out of the neighborhood. Rene had died, and his house had become a doctor's office. The "Street Plan" competitions and the communal parties were no longer celebrated. The scissors sharpener and the other strolling street vendors had all disappeared. People no longer sold their homemade products, and the scent of ripe fruit, so characteristic of the neighborhood, had completely vanished. Now everything just smelled of old age.

I knocked on the door of our next-door neighbor, and a strange woman answered.

"Excuse me, is Ramona here?"

"Ramona died two years ago," she replied.

This had also been the fate of Juanito, the drunk.

I sat down on the edge of the pavement. It was as though the life I had once lived had been a dream. Then I had an idea. I jumped up from the pavement and ran up the hill, past the car-repair shop. When I reached the top, I could see in the distance some enormous warehouses belonging to the Caracol Company. I ran on, hoping that Cundo's house would suddenly appear, but Cundo, his house, the fiberboard caves, the streams, the forest, the pool had all completely disappeared. Gone were the owls, the myths and legends, everything that made Los Pinos the enchanted place it used to be. Vanished.

When I knocked at the door of my childhood home, a man of seventy-nine answered it. His hair was completely gray now, lending him a rather distinguished appearance, like one of the great prophets. He did not smile, but his ash-colored eyes, still as hard as ever, narrowed into slits, indicating that he was pleased to see me. A part of me wanted to hug him, but that was my weaker side. I squeezed his hands tightly and gave him a couple of pats on the shoulder. He remained silent, like the owls whose hoots had been extinguished. After I had given him his presents, we sat on the balcony for so long it seemed like a century of silence. We had so much to say to each other, but neither of us knew where to begin. As dusk began to fall and my eyes roamed around that unfamiliar neighborhood, my sense of displacement grew even stronger. The search for success had snatched away the most precious thing a person can ever ask for: a place to belong. Suddenly, my impulse to conquer the world was completely meaningless because my worst nightmare had been realized. I had become a citizen of nowhere.

The block was deserted. In the distance, I could see a few kids playing with the wooden scooters, or *chivichanas*, I had once played with. They looked about thirteen, the age at which I had already started, without knowing it, to grow apart from my family. The late afternoon sun had become as red as a ball of blood in the sky and my blood was boiling inside me. After so much thinking, there was only one thing left to say.

"I'm famous, Papito. I've traveled the world. They've made documentaries about me, and I've had my photo taken with princes and kings. I hope you're satisfied."

Tears pricked at my eyes, but I had resolved never again to cry in front of him. I picked my things up from the floor and got up out of the chair. My father did not try to stop me. He stayed silent, with a faraway look still in his eyes.

I gestured into the distance. "See those kids over there with the *chivichanas*?"

My father turned his head toward where I was pointing.

"I bet you that when I walk down the street, they'll ask me for money, without having any idea of how fortunate they are."

I walked slowly down the stairs. I had got halfway down when my father broke his silence.

"That's the fate of great men, Yuli. You belong to the world. Your art is your house, my son."

I stopped.

"Ah . . . my house . . . my house . . . maybe you're right."

When I got to the pavement, I turned toward my father one more time.

"You know what the difference is between me and you? You have spent your life talking to me about art when all I really wanted was a home. I'm sure I'll have many houses, but a house is not a home. My home was this one, and I lost it. You gave me life, and yet you're a stranger to me. But I'm famous, so we can drink to that! After all, I managed to do what you told me to, so we should at least drink to that, to the fame of the son whom you never see, the one who has the mark of a foreigner on his forehead."

I screwed up my face tightly to stop myself from crying, and said, "A house is not a home . . . eh, Papito! Remember that."

I turned on my heels and walked down that street with my father's shouts echoing around me. "Your art, Yuli . . . your art is your house, my son!"

"*Un peso, señor, un peso,*" said the kids with the *chivichanas*. I put my hand in my pocket and gave them all the money I had. More kids arrived asking me for chewing gum, anything at all, and I could not contain my grief any longer. Tears spilled down my face and ran down my throat.

Then, suddenly, a voice behind me said, "I don't want any money. I just want to get even!"

I spun around, and there was Pedro Julio. He had the Eat Mud stick in his hand.

"You didn't think I was going to let you get away with it, did you?" asked my old friend, the wrinkles on his face crinkling as he smiled.

I grinned at him and said, "Just because you saw me cry, don't think I'm going to show you any mercy, because I'm going to kick your ass!"

Chapter 21

THE LADY AND
THE THREE MUSKETEERS

When Tica and I arrived in London in June 1998, we rented a very expensive, spacious two-floor apartment in Earls Court, two blocks from the tube station. We brought all our belongings over by plane, fourteen suitcases between us.

The first days in a new company are always the most tiring. I started working the moment I arrived. At the time, the Royal Opera House was closed for restoration. Ninette de Valois, the founder of the Royal Ballet, had fought for decades for an English theater of the status of the Paris Opera or the Mariinsky Theatre, where opera and ballet could coexist, and at long last the Royal Ballet was looking forward to having a permanent home in the Royal Opera House, once it had been refurbished. In the meantime, the company was still in Barons Court, in a building consisting of one long corridor with various passageways and staircases leading off of it. I was informed that my first class would take place in the Big Studio, but I had no idea where the studios were, let alone which were the big ones and which were the small ones. I was told I could use one of the ground-floor changing rooms. But it was tiny, with only one shower and room for just seven lockers, and I found the claustrophobic atmosphere and poor light depressing.

Understandably, there were some malicious looks from dancers who saw me as potential competition. I had turned up out of the blue to occupy the place of another possible aspiring principal dancer. I told myself I was used to this sort of response, but that first day made me aware that the rivalry here was on a completely different level from anything I had experienced before. Few people came over to welcome me; those who did said hello and nothing more. The dancers were of the highest caliber, and I could easily distinguish the stars by the way that they dressed and by their air of superiority. I began to think that maybe it had not been such a good idea to leave Houston.

After class, I had rehearsals for *In the Middle, Somewhat Elevated,* a contemporary ballet by the choreographer William Forsythe. The rehearsal room was small compared to those in Houston, but unlike the other studios in the building, it was well lit by a number of skylights. The choreography was challenging, the music discordant, and I had to concentrate very hard to get the steps. I did everything that was asked of me, trying to retain my focus, but my head was full of the last words I had heard my father say to me: "Your art is your house."

If this was my house, then I was lost.

I discovered that my role in the ballet was not that of the protagonist but a secondary character and realized that, once again, I was going to have to earn my place by starting from the bottom. We finished at about four in the afternoon. I went to the changing room to get dressed and then left without speaking or saying good-bye to anyone.

Tica had flown off to take classes with the Stuttgart Ballet for a while, and the apartment felt too empty for me to stay in. I decided to take a walk down Kensington High Street, where I was surprised to find a Cuban restaurant called Bar Cuba. I sat down at a table and ordered rice and beans, fried chicken, fried plantains, and a mojito. The place was cozily decorated in warm, tropical colors. The food was not bad, but it was not Cuban food, and the mojito was a poor imitation made with too much mint, which got stuck between my teeth. Nevertheless, the music filtering through the speakers brought back memories of Cuba. I thought about how much everything had changed. My Cuba, the one of my dreams, was like the mojito that I was drinking in this restaurant: an illusion.

I could not help noticing a tall, imposing man at the bar ordering a mojito in a loud voice. He was black, his clothes were elegant, and he had an air of nobility about him.

"Hi, you're Cuban, aren't you?" I said.

"Othello, at your service. I hail from Regla, and you?"

"Los Pinos. My name's Carlos. I'm a ballet dancer."

"Ah, an artist!" said Othello. "I used to see a lot of ballet in Cuba, *Giselle, Swan Lake,* all that. . . . I was an artist, too. I studied theater with Perugorría, the one from the film *Strawberry and Chocolate.* I came here to study at the film school, and I've spent eight years in this gray country."

Othello looked out through the glass door of the restaurant to the sky beyond, sighed, and went back to his mojito. "So have you just arrived from Cuba?" he asked.

"I've been working in Houston for the past five years. Before that I was here with the English National Ballet, but it didn't work out."

"Then why did you come back? You won't be successful."

"Why do you say that?" I wanted to know.

"Because it's the truth," said Othello. "You should have stayed in the United States. Black people there are more united, and they even have their own record labels and film studios."

The last thing I needed at this point was someone making me feel insecure about my race. I tried to explain why I had come.

"You know when you get to a dead-end street? That's how I felt in Houston, and that's why I decided to come here. Today was my first day with the Royal Ballet. . . ."

"You're dancing with the Royal Ballet? Oh dear! Then it'll be even more difficult for you to become a principal dancer!"

"I already am one, but I know what you're trying to say. There's some serious competition. . . ."

"Do you know what the difference is between an artistic battle and the military kind?" Othello demanded, his six-foot frame looming over my head. "The difference is that at the end of a military battle, only the nameless corpses shattered by gunfire are left lying on the ground."

I stared at him uncomprehendingly. I thought he was the strangest Cuban I had ever met.

"Let me ask you a question. How many black dancers are there in your company?"

"Only two that I know of," I replied.

"They probably brought you over to play the jester," said Othello.

"I don't play jesters, my friend," I replied, flying into a rage. "I only dance principal roles. I am Romeo; I am Siegfried."

"Don't get angry with me; I'm on your side." Othello raised his hands in defense. "It's very simple. How many black Romeos have you seen at Covent Garden? None, right? While other dancers concentrate on dancing as well as possible, you have to do not only that, but you also have to concentrate on breaking down prejudices that have existed for centuries. Your battle is to make people see that black Romeos do exist, and somehow, I think that would be easier for you to achieve in the United States."

"There is no battle!" I shouted. "I came here to dance, not to fight with anyone! I'm not a black dancer. I'm a dancer, full stop. If there aren't any black Romeos, then I'll be the first one."

Othello stared at me with his trout eyes. Just as he was about to say something, another man spoke. He had very black hair and dark, Andalusian eyes.

"The great Othello, alias 'El Macua,'" he said sardonically.

"Ruswel, how's it going?" Othello grinned.

"Fine, and you? Where have you been hiding? Nobody's seen you for ages. I thought you'd gone back to Regla."

"I've spent a long time stuck inside my house thinking about what I'm going to do with my life," said Othello. "I have to get out of this country. I'm tired of living without sun, of speaking English, of seeing the same old faces every time I go to the clubs. I'm going to live in Spain."

Ruswel turned toward me, and Othello realized he had left me high and dry.

"Let me introduce you to . . . well, I shall call him Mandrake. He's a principal dancer with the Royal Ballet and a native of Los Pinos."

I offered Ruswel my hand. "Hi, my name's Carlos Acosta," I told him.

Ruswel stared at me, bewildered. "But it's him, the dancer I was talking to you about, the one in the newspaper article!"

"The one with the truck-driver father?" asked Othello.

"Why didn't you tell me that you knew him?" said Ruswel.

"Mandrake? I've only just met him now."

I felt the urge to punch Othello.

"What's all this Mandrake business? Is that your name?" asked Ruswel.

"No, my name's Carlos—did you get that, Othello?"

"Okay, whatever you say . . . Mandrake," he replied.

Bizarre though my new acquaintances might be, they were friendlier than my fellow dancers, and it felt good to hang out with some fellow Cubans. We spent the evening dancing salsa, and when we left, Othello said, "Why don't you guys come back to my house for a drink? You can stay the night, if you like. I've got a spare room and a sofa bed in the living room."

At loose ends without Tica to go home to, I agreed, and we headed toward his flat in Camden Town. It was like a greenhouse, with plants hanging from the ceiling, bright posters advertising Havana Club rum and colorful canvases on the walls, and wood carvings dotted about.

"Shit, brother, you've got the whole of Regla here just for you!" I exclaimed.

"This is my little Cuba," Othello agreed, pouring us each a glass of mango juice, with which we toasted our new friendship.

When Tica returned from Stuttgart few days later, I arranged with Monica Mason, the assistant director, for her to have an audition.

On the appointed day, my girlfriend got up earlier than usual. When the alarm went off, I turned to kiss her and found instead a half-twisted pillow tangled up in the sheet. I went into the living room and saw her sitting there ready to leave. Fifteen minutes later we were on our way to the studios in Barons Court.

"Tica, don't run, we've got time," I said, trying to calm her down. "Let's have a coffee."

"No. I'd rather get there early to warm up."

We walked down the half-lit corridor toward the changing rooms.

"You can change in here with me; it's the men's one, but there's nobody about," I told her.

I put my things down on the floor and went into the toilet; three seconds later I heard a door close, and when I came out, I saw that Tica had already changed and left the room. I stuck my head out the door and found her in the corridor doing little jumps on the spot. We went up to the studio, which was completely dark and empty since there were still forty-five minutes to go before class. I had never arrived so early at a studio in my life.

Before the class started, I approached the teacher, Betty Anderson, to inform her that my girlfriend would be taking the class. The female dancers kept looking at her out of the corner of their eyes, but none of the directors was there yet. It was just as it had been with my audition. Tica retained her composure during the barre exercises and worked as hard as she always did, but as we went into the center, Monica Mason came into the studio and sat down in a chair. The expression on Tica's face showed that her heart was thumping as though her executioner had just arrived. She fell on her pirouettes, was unable to sustain her balance, and slipped on every jump, as if the floor itself were conspiring against her.

At the end of the class the directors said there were no places available in the company and told Tica to try again the following year. We both knew what that meant: they were not interested in hiring her.

On the way back to our flat, Tica did not speak. That night she had a light meal followed by a relaxing bath and fell into bed without saying a word. A week later, she tried with the English National Ballet and received a similar response. That day when I got home from work, I found her staring at the wall.

"Try not to think about it anymore, Tica. It's only when you dwell on it that you feel bad." I tried to encourage her, but nothing could drag her out of her depression. She never complained, though. There was a kind of nobility in the way she bore her pain and in the timid smile with which she greeted my presence when she noticed it.

"I'm worried about Tica," I said to my new friends Othello and Ruswel when we next met. "Leaving Houston has been difficult for both of us, but especially for her."

"The first three years in London are the most difficult," Ruswel said. "If you manage to survive them, then you come to realize this is the best city in the world."

"The best city in the world!" exclaimed Othello. "You mean the most depressing one. London is only good for making money. The quality of life is terrible. That's why everybody owns a cat or a dog, because they feel so lonely. People shut themselves away in their own little worlds and can't even be bothered to get to know their next-door neighbors."

"Why are you still here, then, if you're so critical?" Ruswel asked.

"For the same reason as you are—to make money and to help my family."

"There's something that you're forgetting, Macua," said Ruswel, sipping his coffee. "Life is what you make of it. If you think that life is easy, then it will be; but if you think that it's impossible, it will be impossible. You've made your life one long trail of negativity. London has a cultural scene like no other city in the world: musicals with star casts, the best salsa bands on tour, theater, ballet, exhibitions. You can see van Gogh's *Sunflowers* for free! I mean, how often have you seen a Frida Kahlo exhibition in Havana? And you—"

"Mandrake, forget Ruswel's lyricisms," Othello said, turning toward me and cutting Ruswel off midsentence. "To return to the subject of your girlfriend, living with a woman isn't easy, as Ruswel himself will tell you. He'll even claim that God is an imperfect being because he never passed the most difficult test in life: living with a woman. . . ."

"How many times do I have to tell you that it was the Irish writer James Joyce who said that God was imperfect?" cried Ruswel.

But whatever James Joyce might have said or Othello and Ruswel might have thought, there was no doubt in my head that Tica was the woman for me. And so it was that I decided on a diamond and platinum ring with two sapphires on either side, and waited for the right moment to propose to her. I did not have to wait long because I received a telephone call from the Cuban National Ballet inviting me to dance *Swan Lake* with them on tour in Paris—the most romantic city in the world.

In the taxi from our hotel, Tica stared out the window at all the sights. She had never been to Paris before and everything was new to her, but she had no clue why I was taking her to the Eiffel Tower. We bought two tickets and climbed up to the restaurant on the second floor. The view was already astonishing. You could see the whole city and the bulk of Notre Dame, but the restaurant was full of Japanese tourists with cameras, so we took the lift to the very top of the tower.

I was very nervous because I had absolutely no idea what to do in this situation. My parents had divorced shortly after I was born. In

Cuba, ever since the country had entered the Special Period, people got married for no better reason than to get hold of the crates of beer and extra food that were given out on such occasions. There would be a great party in the neighborhood, and the very next day the happy couple would get divorced so they could remarry and start the process all over again. All I knew about proposing was what I had seen in the movies. I knew you were supposed to get the father's permission, but since I had never had any contact with Tica's family, this was not possible. Nevertheless, I was convinced I could not fail—after all, we were in Paris, the most beautiful and romantic city in the world.

In front of about two hundred other tourists, I knelt down, took her by the hand, and asked, "Tica, will you marry me?"

I had been sure that as soon as I asked the question her eyes would fill with tears of joy, but she remained motionless, staring at me. Then she nodded briefly, slipped the ring I held out to her onto her finger, and that was all. No tears, no nothing.

In all the movies that I had ever seen, when the man proposes to the girl, she breaks down and says, "I do, I do, I do love you! I want to spend the rest of my life with you!"

I had been quite sure that a similarly happy outburst would follow after my giving her the ring. Instead, Tica just hugged me very tight, and we both continued to look out at the city. I found Tica's restrained response a little odd, because I knew she was an emotional person, but by the time we came down from the tower, Tica's face had brightened, and I thought I had probably been imagining that something was not right.

That evening I danced *Swan Lake.* It was the first time I had danced in Paris since winning the competition there in 1990, and so it was a momentous occasion for me. I knew a lot of people who remembered me from the competition would be in the audience, watching to see who that little boy had grown up to become. The show was a triumph. It felt like I was dancing not as a guest, but with my mates. In fact, it almost felt as if I were dancing in Havana. My performance was rewarded with a phenomenal ovation, and when the curtain came down, I was very happy. I hugged my fellow dancers, thanked Alicia Alonso very much for inviting me, then went outside to sign autographs, thinking this had been one of the best days of my life.

In the cab back to the hotel, however, Tica broke down. At first, I thought she was merely overcome, as all the other dancers had been, by the reception the ballet had received.

"What's going on, Tica?" I asked her. "Why are you crying?"

"It's just . . . it's just that, well, you know it's a very important day, and I just didn't imagine it this way." She hiccuped.

I realized at last that she was talking about my proposal. "What do you mean?"

She explained that she had been dreaming of this day for so long, and that she imagined it as more of a big event. In films, the man always took the woman out for a special evening and arranged for the ring to appear in a cake or a drink, so that the woman happened upon it, whereas I had chosen to propose during the daytime, in full view of hundreds of people who had nothing to do with us.

But it was still Paris, I said, and I had proclaimed my love for her. That meant I was saying she was going to be the woman of my life, and we would have kids together—surely that was what counted? But it was not enough.

I looked at her and said, "Okay, why don't we do it this way? You give me back the ring, and I'll find another way to propose to you. Hopefully I'll surprise you next time."

So she gave me back the ring.

When we returned from Paris, I made my debut with the Royal Ballet dancing *In the Middle, Somewhat Elevated* at Sadler's Wells Theatre. This was the first show to be performed in this theater after it had been remodeled, and some of the dressing rooms still did not have hot water. A permanent current of cold air blew down the corridors, and everywhere you looked there were cables hanging from the ceilings and workmen fixing the remaining flaws. Sometimes the corridors would be crammed with dancers, plumbers, electricians, dressers, and floor cleaners, each in their different uniforms, as if we were all part of some strange choreography.

The music was recorded, which meant that there was no tuning of the orchestra, and we did not have to wait for the arrival of the conductor in the pit, which is usually followed by a loud round of applause.

"Tabs going out!" shouted Joanna, the stage manager, from the wings.

"Royal Ballet, here I go!" I said to myself as the music started and we began to move in the abstract way that the choreography demanded. Many of the dancers who were not dancing in the piece sat watching from the downstage wings, which made it feel as if we had two audiences instead of one. I was the only unknown face among the cast, and everybody was waiting to see whether the new kid could dance or not. When my solo arrived, I did my best, even though the role did not allow me to show my full potential. At the end, the director, Anthony Dowell, and his assistant, Monica Mason, congratulated me, and, to my surprise, the dancers who had performed with me did the same. Though I went to my dressing room thinking how much better it would have been to have debuted with the company in a three-act ballet rather than a one-act, the important thing was that I was now officially a principal dancer with the Royal Ballet.

The following week, Tica went to take classes with the Scottish Ballet. She came back from Glasgow extremely animated.

"They picked me, they picked me! The director wants to hire me as a guest artist to dance *Cinderella*!" she said.

"I told you so!" I said, and we hugged and started to jump up and down with excitement.

"When do you start?" I asked.

"Next week."

"I'm going to call Monica Mason and ask her whether you can take classes with the Royal in the meantime so that you don't get out of shape," I said.

"No, no!" replied Tica. "I think it would be better for me to leave for Glasgow tomorrow so I can familiarize myself with the company before starting."

I looked into her serious blue eyes and saw that they were telling me something that had never even entered my head.

"How are we going to see each other?" I asked.

"On weekends, I suppose. Sometimes you can come to Glasgow, and sometimes I'll come to see you."

We looked at each other for a long time. Then she took me by the hand and led me to the sofa, where we made love as though for the last time.

Early the next morning, Tica left for Scotland. I got up with her and helped her carry her suitcase to the tube station. We said good-bye with a kiss.

After my class I had a meeting with Anthony Dowell to discuss my work schedule with the company. He told me that, for the time being, the company was obliged to dance wherever the space could be found: at the Hammersmith Apollo, at the Royal Festival Hall, as well as to do performances in Belfast and in other parts of the U.K. As a result, the company was not able to put on enough shows, and I would be given the chance to dance only about ten shows over five months, many of which would be matinees, or on Monday and Tuesday, nights that rarely attracted large audiences. In Houston, I had danced in an average of twenty shows in November and December alone.

"Oh, and about the tour to Japan and China during the summer," continued Anthony, in his characteristically measured voice, "I was thinking of casting you as Mercutio, as an introduction to *Romeo and Juliet*."

I remembered Othello's words.

"Excuse me, but I don't think that would be a good idea," I said. "It's extremely important that the public see me dance in roles that show me as the principal dancer I am."

"Oh, I totally understand," replied Anthony. "But I think that Mercutio will be a great role for you. In fact, I daresay it's a stronger role than Romeo, one that can really enrich you. When I first started my career and danced *Romeo and Juliet* for the first time, it was as Mercutio."

"But I'm not just starting my career, right?" I said firmly. "I've danced in Japan many times, and it's important for me that the audiences see me as a leading dancer. Otherwise, I'd rather not dance at all."

We looked at each other for a long time.

"Well, we don't have to decide today," said Anthony finally, then ushered me out of his office.

That evening I arrived home in a state of anxiety and instantly phoned Tica to tell her what had happened.

"Don't worry, Carlos, at least you have a permanent job. Things will get better," she said.

I wanted to remain with the telephone pressed against my ear, listening to her voice until I fell asleep, but she needed to rest, and so I hung up feeling a tremendous longing for her. It was still early evening, and the last thing I wanted was to stay at home alone, so I called Ruswel and Othello and went out to meet them at Bar Cuba.

"Told you so!" said Othello, when I explained my conversation with Anthony Dowell.

"Don't take any notice of him," said Ruswel. "You've got one great advantage over everybody else, and in the long term it'll come right for you."

"What advantage is that, might I ask?" said Othello.

"His advantage is all the rice and beans he's had to eat in his life. Seriously, I'm talking about everything he's had to go through to be here," said Ruswel. "For example, that bit in *Romeo and Juliet* when Mercutio is killed—in Carlos's situation it won't be a case of acting rage and pain, he *remembers* the endless buses he took to get to school, all the unhappiness he suffered at being far from home. I very much doubt that any of his colleagues have been through that—which means his interpretation of Mercutio will be the best. It's got nothing to do with whether he's black, white, or yellow."

Two weeks later I danced *La Fille Mal Gardée* for the first time. It is a typically English ballet, choreographed by Frederick Ashton, a rustic idyll, in which the main male, Colas, is a country lad who wears banana yellow tights and a flowery waistcoat. Unusually, the ballet involves numerous props: Colas always carries a stick, which makes getting the elevation on jumps very difficult, and there is complicated choreography involving ribbons. Because we had not rehearsed onstage before the performance, I did not know that the set included a farmhouse, and because I was doing *double tours en l'air,* I was surprised to see a whole bunch of dancers dressed as chickens behind me, as well as a real pony and carriage running around, which was very distracting. After that first performance, I felt like giving up ballet altogether.

I kept looking for the right moment to propose to Tica again. On weekends, when I went to Glasgow and watched her rehearsing *Cinderella,* I would observe the delicate movement of her hands, the sweet way she looked at her partner and then glanced at me. In moments like those, I was more convinced than ever that this was the woman I wanted to have children with. During the performances, she danced like a dream. Nobody communicated the essence of Cinderella the way Tica did. Everybody was delighted with her, and the director showered her with flowers and compliments and offered her a permanent contract with the company. Tica was considering it, and from the way she smiled, it was obvious that she was happy.

At Christmas, we rented a car together and explored the Scottish countryside, visiting the lochs. The sky and snow-capped mountains were reflected in the crystal waters with such clarity that it was hard to know which was the real sky and which was the reflection. It was a beautiful, lonely place, ideal for a romantic proposal. I clasped the ring tightly in my pocket and took a deep breath, but then I thought, What if she refuses me for a second time? Scared, I decided it might be better to wait.

The following week, Othello and Ruswel helped me come up with a suitable plan. On New Year's Eve, I would put on my best suit and take Tica to dine at La Espiga in Soho. Then we would go on to a party Ruswel was organizing with flamenco singers, actors, and artists. When midnight arrived, in the midst of the bohemian swirl and serenaded by a guitar, I would present her with a dozen Black Magic roses and the ring.

"But do you think it will work?" I asked my friends.

"If it doesn't, I don't know what will," said Ruswel.

"Of course it's going to work!" said Othello. "And if it doesn't, I've got karaoke all set up so that you can sing her a romantic ballad. She'll swoon at your feet."

"But I can't sing!" I protested.

"In that case, I'll sing," he promised, and we all laughed.

The night before, I could not sleep for thinking about the following day when Tica would be arriving from Glasgow. I was going to collect her from the airport at about one in the afternoon, and then we would head straight back to the flat, which was looking like new after the cleaning I had given it. Just after midnight, the telephone rang and I jumped out of bed. It was the manager of the Scottish Ballet informing me that Tica had injured her knee during the rehearsal. She had tried to get in touch with me during the afternoon, but nobody had been in.

"Where is she?" I asked, alarmed.

"She took a plane to Houston."

At six the next morning, she called and told me that she had been performing a quite simple step when she had felt something tear in her knee, which had immediately started to swell.

"I'm going to see Dr. Baxter tomorrow. I'm so sorry for leaving like this, but I don't trust anyone except Dr. Baxter. I tried to call you, but you didn't answer."

"No, no, don't worry. You did the right thing. Call me as soon as you know the results of the examination," I said. "I miss you. I love you."

Tica had ruptured the cruciate ligaments in her knee. The operation to repair the injury involved taking two strips from her abductor muscles and pinning them into the knee. The rehabilitation process would be long and painful, and even then there was no guarantee that the recuperation would be complete. Tica was distraught.

"Why me? Why now that I finally have a contract?" she wailed desperately.

There was nothing that I could say to comfort her in a situation like this, so I kept my ear glued to the telephone in silence. All I wanted to do was catch the first plane to Houston, but it was impossible for me to leave my work. I was starting to wonder if someone had put a curse on us.

Without Tica, winter in London weighed even more heavily on me. In the dark evenings, I would stare at the photos of my godson, Robert, and of Tica with my mother, and of Tica with me, but they only made me feel worse. My mood swings were so severe that I hardly recognized myself. One day a man trod on my foot as I walked down the street, and I only just restrained myself from punching him.

At first, Tica and I spoke every day, then the calls went down to three a week. Every time I told her about how I was doing at the Royal, she would get irritable.

"Oh . . . you're performing in the Festival Hall . . . and here I am with a damaged knee and without a career!"

So I stopped mentioning my work.

After a while, she could not continue to pay her share of the rent on our flat in London, and I could not afford it on my own, so I ended up moving into Othello's place.

In May, two weeks before my birthday, I went to visit her in Houston. She came to collect me by car from the airport. Her blond hair was tied back, and she looked healthy and beautiful. We hugged for ages without saying anything and kissed each other lengthily. Afterward we walked in silence toward her car. I asked her about her knee, and she made me feel the pins that were now buried inside it. She told me that her rehabilitation was going well, and she was thinking about starting yoga classes, but she did not ask me how I was or how my life in London was going. As we were driving along, she suddenly said, "What you did last week, don't do it again."

"What did I do?"

"When you say you're going to call me at a certain time, then make sure that you do. If you're not going to, at least give me the consideration that I deserve and let me know. I also have more important things to do."

"What are you talking about?"

"You said that you would call me at eight, and you called me at ten past."

"That doesn't mean anything," I said.

"Perhaps not to you, but to me, it means that I'm not at the top of your list of priorities."

After five months without seeing each other, our bodies had forgotten what they used to feel like together. We needed to retrieve those forgotten sensations. But we always seemed to end up arguing for one reason or another, all inconsequential things. At night, our lovemaking was filled with tears and frustration instead of joy. I told myself that it was only temporary, but as the days passed I could not shake the feeling of love gone cold.

One day we went out with our friends Luis Ortis and Monica to Café Express. We could see in our friends' relationship everything that had gone missing from our own. We had even lost what had brought us together in the first place. Ballet was too painful to talk about. As our friends embraced, kissing each other openly, unafraid to shout their love to the world, we looked at each other guiltily. It was in a Café Express like this one that our own story had started, and now it was slowly coming to an end.

"I'll call you when I get there," I told her at the airport. She looked at me and her tears started to fall thick and fast.

When Othello opened the door to our flat in London, he found me standing there with a pallid face and ashen eyes.

"What's the matter, are you ill?"

"I'm tired," I told him, flopping down onto the sofa.

"It's a long way to go for only a week," he said.

"It's not physical," I told him. "I'm tired of dancing all over the world yet only knowing the route from my hotel to the theater; tired of never seeing a single lousy water tank on any roof in this country; tired of not being allowed to ski, even if I could. Do you know what I'm saying?"

Othello went into the kitchen and came back with a large glass of rum on the rocks. "Sometimes it's good to forget about everything," he said.

I seized the glass and drank the contents down in one gulp.

"Remember one thing," said Othello sagely. "Wisdom comes from getting to know the desert before the palace. The lives of all great men begin that way."

The lives of all great men. My father had said something similar. I did not have strength enough left to think. I started to drift off, floating between Othello's words and the tide of memories that washed over me, until finally I was fast asleep on the sofa.

I remained subdued for the rest of the week, right up to my birthday, when Othello baked me a cake, placed a large candle on top of it, shoved a pointed paper hat on my head, and said, "Now blow, Mandrake; blow and make a wish."

I wished for all that I had ever wanted in life, and I blew the candle out with all the force that I could muster.

"Now we're going to drink a toast to ourselves: to the gentleman from Regla, the intellectual from Cojimar, and the prince from Los Pinos—the Three Musketeers," Othello announced.

"And to Tica's health, too," added Ruswel. "The Lady of Misfortune."

We clinked our glasses in the air and drank them down to the dregs.

A little later I called Houston twice, but there was no reply.

The following day I went into the company fired up with good intentions. The only way that my stay in London made any sense now was if I did my best for me, for Tica, and for my family. I had to let everyone know that I knew I was good, so I carefully studied the behavior of the other stars and I discovered that they did not appear to be too modest but were not too vain either. From then on, I smiled little and spoke only when necessary. Sometimes it is useful being a foreigner, because everyone expects you to behave a little differently.

My acting like a star had not convinced Anthony Dowell to give me the role of Romeo during the Royal Ballet's tour to Japan and China, but I did not mind because I was asked to dance on the opening night in Tokyo in *Swan Lake*. I was supposed to be dancing with Viviana Durante, but she dropped out and I was left without a partner. Anthony Dowell asked me whom I would like to dance with, and I said the Cuban dancer Lorna Feijóo, with whom I had partnered in *Swan Lake* in Paris.

"Okay, we'll bring her for you," said the director.

Two Cuban dancers representing the Royal Ballet is not something that happens every day, and as Anthony gave us free rein to make certain adjustments to the choreography, Lorna and I incorporated some steps from the Cuban version. Lorna did not have time to learn all the choreography, so during the performance some of the dancers had to tell her where her entrances and exits were, while others had to shout out the sequences of the choreography. However, our rapport was such that we were like twin souls in harmony—we had both learned to dance at the same school and had been taught by the same teachers. The applause at the end was overwhelming. Lorna had fulfilled her dream of dancing with the Royal Ballet, and I had fulfilled mine of being seen as a prince. After it was over, Anthony congratulated us both with tears in his eyes.

Shortly after the tour, the company moved into the restored Royal Opera House. It was like a different world. There were five studios, all with white linoleum floors and skylights through which the light poured. There were personal dressing rooms, a physical rehabilitation studio with Pilates machines, a department of physical therapy and massage, as well as a huge rest area with comfortable sofas and a bird's-eye view of the Covent Garden Piazza. There was a canteen with fresh food, and a small alternative theater space. The Royal Opera House is a triumphant refutation of the idea that ballet is an unnecessary art form. Like the French and the Russians before them, the English had finally managed to provide a place that would show off the art at its best.

The theater's opening gala was going to be televised throughout the U.K. The theme was revisiting the most significant moments in the history of the Royal Ballet, from its inception to the present day. When I was asked to represent Rudolf Nureyev in *The Corsair,* I was speechless.

I called Othello at once.

"I'm going to represent Nureyev!" I shouted into the phone.

"You need a Nurofen?"

"Not a Nurofen, you idiot, Nureyev, Rudolf Nureyev, the famous Russian ballet dancer. I'm going to be on television! And I've got an invitation for you and for Ruswel!"

"I'm off to iron my suit immediately so that I can accord you the full honors!"

"The show's not until next week!"

"No matter. I shall plug in my iron right now!"

On the day of the gala, there was a real sense of excitement in the air. My heart had been jumping around in my chest since the morning. To represent a legend like Nureyev on an occasion like this was perhaps the greatest honor I had been given in my entire career. But for me it was also much more than that; it was the culmination of a journey that had started with my father in a cinema and had followed me through a ballet school in the city of Havana. I was doing this for my family, even though they would not be there. Millions of people would be watching the show on television, and what they saw on this historic occasion would remain engraved in their memories.

Dressed in my costume, I walked toward the stage. A huge projection of Nureyev against the backdrop smiled down on me as though saying, "Make me proud."

"I will, Rudy," I said to myself. "Now watch this!"

The soft stage lights enveloped my body and a follow spot projected my image onto the backdrop behind me. This was my moment. In my head there was nobody else in the theater but me, only me, dancing out my sorrows and my woes, singing my loneliness to the night like the owls that had once inhabited Los Pinos. My routine came out just as I had planned it. The applause went on for a long time and continued after I had left the stage. It had not been Carlos Acosta, but Yuli, the mud-eating kid from Los Pinos, who had danced.

As the finale to the gala, everyone connected to the Royal Ballet—

the teachers, the dancers from the school, and the dancers from the company—came out onstage to the music from the last scene of Stravinsky's *The Firebird*. Dozens of photographs suspended by cords dropped slowly from the ceiling—the faces of everyone who had contributed to the glory of the Royal Ballet. From the auditorium, Ninette de Valois looked down on her well-deserved triumph, and I, smiling proudly, looked up at my photo among all those famous faces.

At the stage door, Ruswel and Othello hugged me fervently.

"You made me cry!" said El Macua.

"Othello, you didn't even cry with the two smacks on the bottom they gave you when you were born," said Ruswel. "Excuse my language, Carlos, but you danced fucking brilliantly."

"I'm glad that you both liked it," I said, hanging my head. "It's a pity that—"

"Don't worry," said Ruswel, understanding immediately. "I'm sure that Pedro's saints will be telling him everything that's happened. Right this minute they'll be saying, 'Your boy has just realized your dream,' and your family will be proud."

As I signed programs for members of the public and had my photograph taken, Othello received people as though he had been the one who had danced.

"The only black principal dancer with the Royal Ballet, and he is my friend," he boasted.

That night I rang Tica, and, as always, we ended up arguing, this time about something I should have sent her but had forgotten in all the fuss surrounding the gala. I had to bite back my excitement about the show, and once the phone call was over, I ended up drinking in a nearby bar with Othello and Ruswel.

It could not go on. Tica and I dragged out the misery a little bit longer, until one day I realized that the only beautiful things in our relationship were photographs of happier times, and I could not continue living through them, like a person who tries to regain the past by wrapping himself in a blanket of cobwebs.

The decision was mutual. We agreed that Tica would come to London to collect her suitcases. I would give a set of keys to the apartment I had now bought to one of my neighbors, and Tica would collect her things and leave without seeing me. A meeting would be too painful.

But when I arrived home just after eight in the evening as we had arranged, I found her sitting there waiting. She hurled herself into my arms and her tears fell onto the floor to the rhythm of the rain that was falling outside.

"Where did we go wrong, Carlos?" she asked, with her head leaning against my chest.

"It was nobody's fault. We did the best that we could," I replied, stroking her hair.

Then there was a long silence. We looked at each other one last time, and finally we kissed each other good-bye. Tica got into a taxi and took her body, her injured knee, and those beautiful blue eyes out of my life forever. As she was driven away, I squeezed the engagement ring I still carried in my pocket and hoped that one day Tica would spare me a thought, and remember all the happy years we had spent together.

The very next day, I made my debut in *Manon,* playing Des Grieux, a student who falls in love with a beautiful woman called Manon, who prostitutes herself for money. After forgiving Manon for her betrayal, killing for love, and being sent into exile, Des Grieux is left alone in a swamp with the lifeless body of his lover. I could see only Tica in my arms. I had danced the whole ballet with her.

After the show, my dresser Oliver came into my dressing room to help me off with my costume, then left, after placing a cup of coffee in my still trembling and sweaty hands. Anthony Dowell put his head around the door and, shortly afterward, so did Monica Mason.

"Well done, Carlos, well done!" I heard voices say.

And then I was left alone, remembering what had brought me to this dressing room, staring at my reflection in the mirrored wall, surrounded by flowers, bottles of champagne, all the trappings of glory, and all the same old fears.

Chapter 22

A MOMENT OF HAPPINESS

As if by magic, when the curtain rose, the theater was suffused with the scent of mangos. With my first leap, the stage became a street of wooden houses bustling with carriages and strolling hawkers; the wings turned into trees, where owls hooted; and the ceiling was blue sky with my pigeons flying free. The dancers around me were the inhabitants of the neighborhood: Pedro Julio with his Eat Mud stick, Rene, and Juanito the drunk. Opito and the rest of the gang were break-dancing like we used to when we were children. On the corner of the street, my teachers Nancy, María Dolores, and Chery watched me with smiles on their faces. I was back in my house, in that hovel with cracks in the walls, where humility, innocence, and love found refuge. I could hear my sisters laughing and my mother calling me in to eat. Even the spirit of Aunt Lucia was dancing in the shadows, as if this were one great party shared between the living and the dead, the past and the present, fiction and reality. . . .

Three years had passed since Tica's departure and my bittersweet debut in *Manon*. A short time after she left, I had decided to create a ballet, one that would be completely different from the classical repertoire. I did not believe in fairy tales, but I had reason enough to believe that the fates had protected me along my journey, so I decided to represent my own story through dance.

Now, it was the first night of *Tocororo: A Cuban Tale* at the Sadler's Wells Theatre in London.

Before the curtain went up, I had gathered all the musicians, dancers, and technicians together around me, thirty-five people in all.

"Many of you won't know exactly what the performance today means to me," I said, looking at each one of their faces. "I've been waiting for this moment for many years, and without the help of each of you, I wouldn't have been able to achieve it. Thank you. Thank you for everything. And that's enough speeches, let's give those English a little piece of our Cuba!"

The best thing was that out there in some dark part of the auditorium, applauding me like there was no tomorrow, were my father, my mother, and my sisters.

At the end of the show, my mother dried the tears from her eyes and wouldn't let go of me even for a second, hugging me as if she wanted to keep me all for herself. Marilín and Berta told her she was going to pull my arm off, but she took no notice. My mother was wearing a very elegant dress and looked like a princess. Marilín wore white with her hair dyed black. Her heels were high, she wore little makeup, and she carried her white handbag with studied disdain. Berta was wearing a dark brown dress and low heels, her blond hair loose over her shoulders.

Othello approached us and addressed my mother in an emotional voice. "I am Othello, gentleman from Regla, faithful member of the Three Musketeers. You, madam, are a goddess! Permit me to kiss your hand."

My mother and my sisters were baffled.

"Don't take any notice of him. He's got a screw loose, poor thing," said Ruswel, shoving Othello away. "I'm Ruswel. We're friends of Carlos, so naturally we couldn't miss the chance of meeting you all."

"But I already know you," said Othello. "Mandrake has told me all of your stories, so I feel like I'm part of the family."

My mother looked Othello up and down and smiled nervously.

My father, dressed in a black suit, white shirt, and red tie, had slipped, unnoticed, to one side, where he stood watching me sign autographs for the waiting crowds. Some people wanted to have their photo taken with me; others spoke to me in Spanish about how wonderful the show had been.

"Your family must be so proud of you! Wasn't it your father who got you into ballet?"

When I turned around to introduce my father to the fans who had asked about him, however, I saw that he was walking slowly toward the exit, his gray hair standing out in the crowd. I could see that his head was bowed and his hands were crossed behind his back, but there were so many people around me, I rapidly lost sight of him.

Once the crowds had dispersed, we went to a restaurant in Soho to celebrate. Marilín and Berta sat directly opposite me, with my mother and father on either side. After the food had been ordered, I got up from my seat with a glass in my hand.

"I want to take advantage of this occasion when I have my family here with me, my friends, and everybody connected with the show, to drink a toast to today: the happiest day of my life," I said, smiling from ear to ear.

Everybody remained for a second or two holding their glasses in the air. Berta and Marilín were smiling, and my mother was dabbing at her eyes with a white handkerchief. My father still seemed distant.

"To happiness!" I repeated, as everyone raised their glasses to their lips.

"One moment," said my father, rising abruptly from his seat. "While we're on the subject of that indefinable thing, that fleeting sensation called happiness, I would like to ask the permission of this illustrious company to celebrate my own day of happiness as well."

I looked at my father curiously, as did everybody else.

"I have been happy once, only once in my life, and today I feel inspired to confess that moment. . . ."

Fifty people in the room waited with their glasses of wine and champagne suspended in the air. I could not believe that my father was going to say something to ruin my day. Then my old man, his eyes brimming with tears, leaned toward me and whispered in my ear: "The happiest day of my life was the day when you were born." A fat tear slid down his cheek. "Never forget that, my son!"

ACKNOWLEDGMENTS

Many thanks to the people who have helped to make this book a reality. It has been a dream of mine for many years, and it would not have been possible without Mercy Ruíz, Carlos Melian, Maria del Carmen Mestas, Heriberto Cabezas, Manuel Toledo, Ruswel Piñeiro, George Stanika, Kate Eaton, Angela Taylor, Annabel Wright, and the rest of the team at HarperPress; Whitney Frick, Susan Moldow, and everyone at Scribner; Alexander Agadzhanov, Charlotte Holland, Felicity Bryan, and everyone at the Felicity Bryan Agency; and Rupert Rohan.

This book has been made possible by the tremendous help of Imogen Parker, who worked with me very patiently to bring it to life.